Heidegger, Plato, Philosophy, Death

Heidegger, Plato, Philosophy, Death

An Atmosphere of Mortality

Richard Rojcewicz

LEXINGTON BOOKS
Lanham • Boulder • New York • London

Published by Lexington Books
An imprint of The Rowman & Littlefield Publishing Group, Inc.
4501 Forbes Boulevard, Suite 200, Lanham, Maryland 20706
www.rowman.com

86-90 Paul Street, London EC2A 4NE

British Library Cataloguing in Publication Information Available

Library of Congress Cataloging-in-Publication Data

Names: Rojcewicz, Richard, author.
Title: Heidegger, Plato, philosophy, death : an atmosphere of mortality / Richard
  Rojcewicz.
Description: Lanham : Lexington Books, [2021] | Includes bibliographical references
  and index. | Summary: "Richard Rojcewicz argues that Heidegger and Plato see
  the same connection between philosophy and death: philosophizing is dying in the
  sense of separating oneself from the prison constituted by superficiality and hearsay.
  Rojcewicz relates this understanding of philosophy to signs, anxiety, conscience,
  music, and the COVID-19 pandemic"— Provided by publisher.
Identifiers: LCCN 2021030816 (print) | LCCN 2021030817 (ebook) |
  ISBN 9781793648402 (cloth) | ISBN 9781793648419 (ebook)
  ISBN 9781793648426 (pbk)
Subjects: LCSH: Death. | Philosophy. | Plato. | Heidegger, Martin, 1889-1976.
Classification: LCC BD444 .R64 2021 (print) | LCC BD444 (ebook) |
  DDC 128/.5—dc23
LC record available at https://lccn.loc.gov/2021030816
LC ebook record available at https://lccn.loc.gov/2021030817

Gloucester: O! let me kiss that hand!
Lear: Let me wipe it first; it smells of mortality.

King Lear, IV, vi, 136-37

Contents

Introduction

Weaving its way through this book in the manner of a thread of Ariadne is the connection between philosophy and death. That connection is a theme common to Plato and Martin Heidegger. They both see an intimate bond between philosophizing and dying, but the perspective is different in each case. For Plato, authentic philosophizing is a matter of dying; for Heidegger, authentic dying is a matter of philosophizing. In other words, for Plato, to philosophize authentically is to approach death, whereas, for Heidegger, to approach death authentically is to philosophize. Plato sees dying in authentic philosophy; Heidegger sees philosophy in authentic dying.

Since Heidegger calls authentic comportment toward death "anticipatory resoluteness," as it is usually translated in English, it might seem he is speaking of facing up courageously to death, serenely meeting one's end and in that sense being "philosophical"—that is, unperturbed, resigned—over the inevitable. The authentic person is not afraid of death and has no anxiety about it. The epitome of such authentic dying would be found in the conduct and demeanor of Socrates: having been legally condemned, he steadfastly refuses to break the laws of Athens by escaping from jail, and then he placidly takes his bitter medicine.

From a Heideggerian point of view, Socrates does indeed exemplify authentic dying—but not by being intrepid in the face of death. Such resoluteness is *not* what Heidegger proposes as authentic dying. It is not simply at his last moments that Socrates approaches death authentically; on the contrary, he does so all the other waking moments of his life—that is, inasmuch as he is constantly philosophizing. It is then, even when death is not about to befall him, that Socrates most demonstrates the attitude that is translated in English as "resoluteness."

Heidegger's German term is *Entschlossenheit*. It does indeed ordinarily mean "determination," "fortitude," "gumption." Yet all this is foreign to

Heidegger's use, and he makes it clear, provided the reader reads closely enough, that he is taking the term in the etymological sense: *Ent-schlossenheit*, "dis-closedness." What Heidegger advocates as authentic dying is a matter of *understanding* death. More specifically, it is a matter of understanding the role of death in the life of the beings who are able to comport themselves toward their own death. It is not a matter of preoccupation with death as something outstanding in the future, calculating about this possibility, acting so as to postpone it or perhaps hasten it, reconciling with it in one way or another. Authentic dying is not preoccupation with one's future death at all; it is preoccupation with disclosing the Being of the beings whose death is *not* completely outstanding, the beings who already live in an atmosphere of mortality, the beings whose death is not only constantly imminent but is also to some extent immanent and not entirely in the future, the beings we ourselves are.

The attempt at disclosing the Being of such beings is philosophizing. It is the practice Socrates is constantly engaged in, a striving for self-knowledge. His entire life of self-examination, more than the way he finally passes from this world into Hades, is what marks Socrates' comportment as a prime example of authentic dying in Heidegger's sense. Socrates is philosophical about death—not by maintaining his composure in the face of it, but precisely by seeking to know himself, to know his own Being.

Socrates is constantly practicing the "Socratic method." In his conversations, the matter at issue may ostensibly be some question of ethics or politics, but the intention of the method is always to raise the interlocutor's eyes from examples, beings, up toward the Being of those beings, the heaven of the Ideas. That movement of attending to Being, as differentiated from beings, is the constant concern of Socrates, and it constitutes the "first philosophical step."

Heidegger's magnum opus *Being and Time* attempts the same first step into philosophy. The intention of the treatise is to grasp a being (one that is privileged in relation to the disclosure of what it means to be in general, namely, the being that in each case one of us can call "mine") and to "read off" from this being the meaning of Being in general. This task is intimately tied to an understanding of death.

In order to grasp the privileged being in a way adequate to the task of reading off the meaning of Being, this being must be grasped as a whole. The difficulty is that anyone of us is not a whole until death, when we will cease to be the being we are. Therefore, central to *Being and Time* is the problem of death: How can we grasp ourselves as a whole, in view of the circumstance that we will not be whole until death arrives, at which point we will be unable to grasp anything? How is it that something missing, the end of our life, does not preclude a grasp of wholeness while we live? As for the Platonic dialogues, they portray what philosophy is by way of portraying who

Socrates is. And death looms over this portrayal. Many of the dialogues are tied to Socrates' trial and execution. Furthermore, philosophizing is explicitly called the practice of dying, the separating of the soul to its own autonomous existence. Therefore, *Being and Time* and all the Platonic dialogues could be subtitled: "On philosophy and death." That is what I work out in chapter 1.

Heidegger's magnum opus is not morbid in the sense of maintaining that the prime experience is one of death, negativity, disintegration. On the contrary, Heidegger sees death against a background constituted by a previous experience of integration. This previous experience has to be attested "phenomenally." In other words, what the reflecting philosopher sees as the primary experience has to be attested in ordinary, pre-reflective experience. The basic experience is that of an integrated world, and the primary pre-reflective attestation resides in the experience of signs, any sort of common sign (chapter 2). More than the everyday experience of a breakdown in some item of equipment, and even more than the experience of an item of equipment as missing, signs are disclosive of the world in Heidegger's sense, namely, a *cosmos*, a "well-arranged" whole. Yet a sign, especially a sign such as a barcode, a sign, which approaches perfection and discloses a near-perfect cosmos, is also a *memento mori*.

Socrates does not *fear* death, but that simply means he is not preoccupied with death as a possibility outstanding in the future. Yet, Socrates is not free of anxiety in Heidegger's sense. Anxiety toward death has nothing to do with fear or with outstanding possibilities. According to Heidegger, authentic comportment toward death is essentially anxiety. Inasmuch as this comportment is a matter of *understanding*, so is anxiety; anxiety has disclosive power.

Anxiety (chapter 3) is preoccupation with the Being of the being whose death is not an entirely future possibility. Anxiety motivates the disclosure of the peculiar relation this being has toward possibilities, ones Heidegger calls "most proper" possibilities, possibilities in the most proper sense. The Being of the beings we ourselves are can be differentiated from the Being of things precisely with respect to possibilities. For us, future possibilities are not entirely outstanding but are in a sense already actual, and past actualities are not entirely actual, over and done, but in a sense remain possibilities. Versus things, we are not what we already are and we are already what we are not yet. According to Nietzsche, we are not too old for our victories. That means what we have acquired in the past still remains open for us to appropriate in the way we choose. It could be added that neither are we too young for our defeats: death is already to some extent present.

For Heidegger, the "meaning" of something is that upon which it must be projected in order to be comprehensible. What is the meaning of the Being of the beings we ourselves are? What must be projected in order that our peculiar relation to possibilities could be comprehensible? The answer is time.

Our temporality is a peculiar one inasmuch as past, present, and future are thoroughly intermixed. Our past is not entirely over and done but still remains a future possibility, open in the present for us to appropriate in our own chosen way. And our future is not entirely outstanding; instead, it already colors our present. Accordingly, temporality is the "meaning" of the beings we ourselves are; temporality is what makes comprehensible our peculiar relation to possibilities.

Our complex temporality is especially in play in regard to the one pre-eminent possibility in our lives, the one possibility we will all someday make actual, the one possibility we are all already making actual to some extent, namely, death. Death is a negativity at the very heart of our Being. For Heidegger, conscience (chapter 4) is the experience of this negativity. Conscience, as bad conscience, consciousness of guilt, is disclosive of the Being of the beings we ourselves are. Versus anxiety, however, conscience also discloses positive practical possibilities. Conscience, for Heidegger, is the *Entschlossenheit* mentioned above. Conscience discloses the proper action to take in the given circumstances and is thereby equivalent to *phrónesis*, practical wisdom.

Music (chapter 5) is a prime example of the experience of our peculiar temporality. In order to hear a melody, the notes need to be synthesized with one another in a peculiar way, the complex way characteristic of our temporality. Music then is also disclosive of the meaning of the Being of the beings we ourselves are. In order to hear a melody, the present note must be heard in the context of the past ones and of the ones to come. To a certain extent, the last note is not simply outstanding; it already sounds in our anticipation. Music is then connected to our peculiar comportment toward death; music, at least marginally, is an experience of mortality.

We live in an atmosphere of mortality inasmuch as death is in the air in the figurative sense. But the atmosphere today is also mortal in the literal sense: contaminated with carcinogens and deadly viruses (chapter 6). What would a Heideggerian approach to philosophy and death have to say about the current corona-virus-disease-2019 pandemic? Are there distinct possibilities in our current plight for philosophizing, that is, for disclosing the Being of the beings we ourselves are?

Finally (Conclusion), after many chapters of what might seem morbid preoccupation with mortality, can we find any intimations of immortality in Plato and Heidegger? Or not?

All of the above is, admittedly, abstract and no more than programmatic. Any outline is bound to be so in a book with philosophical aspirations. The reason is that philosophical results make sense only when seen as actually worked out in the course of the investigation. Prior to that, a summary of results is unintelligible and could even be misleading. Hegel expresses this circumstance by maintaining that a philosophical work cannot legitimately begin with a preface, *Vorrede*. Philosophy, for Hegel, strives to disclose the *concrete* universal, that is, the universal as actually ruling over the particulars, or the particulars as actually gathering themselves up into the universal. A summarizing preface, however, could at most provide only an *abstract* universal (a universal by itself and not in relation to the particulars) and so would be partial and consequently false. Nevertheless, Hegel places these derogatory remarks about prefaces *in the preface* to his main philosophical work, *The Phenomenology of Spirit*. Accordingly, an outline of the course of thought, a summary of results, may indeed be useful as a general orientation, provided the reader knows to wait for the pages that follow to bring the summary to life.

Except for chapter 6, the reflection directed to the COVID-19 pandemic, this book is based on graduate lecture courses I presented at Duquesne University in recent years. The courses intentionally consisted in a close reading of primary texts and made only slight reference to the secondary literature. A search through the records of the Library of Congress shows that in the entire history of philosophy, no figure has generated more secondary literature than Plato. In the last 100 years, however, that distinction belongs to Heidegger. Philosophy used to consist in a series of footnotes to Plato; it is becoming a series of footnotes to Heidegger. Accordingly, this book is occupied with themes that have been touched on by many commentators. Yet I claim a certain originality and wish to open up new perspectives on these themes instead of adding another voice to extant debates. In this way, however, I do place myself within the general intention of anyone attracted to the writings of Plato and Heidegger: to take a fresh look with one's own eyes and advance some small measure closer to the matters themselves genuinely at issue in those great philosophies.

All translations in the following pages are my own. The endnotes and bibliography refer to published translations only for the convenience of readers who might wish to place the quoted passage in context or to compare my translation with the published one.

Chapter 1

Being and Time as a Platonic Dialogue (On Philosophy and Death)

PROSE VERSUS POETRY

No one with even the least acquaintance with *Being and Time* would doubt that if a comparison is called for at all the book should be likened not to a Platonic dialogue but much rather to an Aristotelian treatise. Heidegger's magnum opus is not in dialogue form; it is a straightforward treatise. The author himself expressly refers to it as a treatise (*Abhandlung*).[1] Versus the dialogues, *Being and Time* is prose—and not even graceful prose.

Plato was said to have "combed and curled" the dialogues and "neatly braided all the strands."[2] *Being and Time* reads exactly the way the circumstances of its composition would suggest: a text written under the pressure of the need to have a book published in support of an academic appointment. Its diction is in the convoluted style of Aristotle and has nothing of the elegance of Plato. *Being and Time* is unfinished: that is, not only literally incomplete but also unpolished.

Furthermore, the dialogues are dramas, plays; they need to be interpreted in terms of what is enacted in them. They have plots and carry out deeds, and they often put on plays within the plays, such as little comedies and tragedies. The interpretation of the dialogue must also take into account the occasion, historical or imagined, serving as a background to the discussion. Nor are the many mythological references mere decoration. The dialogues are indirect; it is possible to understand all the words and arguments placed in the mouth of the various characters and yet be oblivious to what Plato is saying. *Being and Time*, quite to the contrary, says on the surface all that it is trying to say.

The preceding distinctions between Plato and Heidegger are not in dispute. Yet I wish to show how *Being and Time* is comparable to a Platonic dialogue in the way of beginning, in the central themes, and in the way of ending.

1

Furthermore, they both feature a hero. So Heidegger's treatise is comparable to a Platonic dialogue in beginning, middle, and end and in revolving around a hero. Accordingly, despite the arduous prose, the book is carefully constructed and thoroughly comparable to the dialogues of Plato.

BEGINNING

After Plato's death, a wax tablet in his writing was found inscribed with the opening words of the *Republic* in many subtle variations. This anecdote is among the best-attested ones regarding Plato. Dionysius of Halicarnassus refers to it as if it were common knowledge, familiar "to all who love words," πᾶσι τοῖς φιλολόγοις.[3] Diogenes Laertius also reports the anecdote and appeals to the testimony of two well-known literary figures.[4]

We can therefore assume that Plato wanted the beginning of the *Republic* to read just so. Indeed he is meticulous about the beginning of all the dialogues. The beginning does not merely set the scene extrinsically or provide ornamentation. The beginning almost always is appropriate. If heeded with the same care that went into the writing of it, the beginning can be seen as prefiguring the matter which will be taken up in the discussion. Specifically, the beginning often enacts a certain movement, one which expresses *in nuce* the central theme of the dialogue.

The beginning of the *Republic* is a prime example. The first words consist of Socrates saying he "came down yesterday to the Piraeus" (*Republic*, 327A). I propose here only one of many possible interpretations of this descent.[5] Socrates is descending from Athens, the mother city. The path to the Piraeus is south, by way of the "long walls." These formed a sheltered passageway and were considered part of Athens. A traveler was still in Athens on the journey down. The Piraeus is the port city; it opens out to the wider world. There one left the comfortable confines of Athens and encountered all sorts of odd beings and strange sights. So Socrates' descent is from the mother city, through a narrow sheltered passageway, out to the external world. Accordingly, the *Republic* begins with Socrates' birth. The mystery of birth, that is, the mystery of our presence to the world, is then exactly what will be discussed in the dialogue. The ostensible topics of the conversation may be justice and the founding of cities, but the underlying theme, philosophically expressed, is the relation between Being and beings. How do we descend from the mother (Being) so as to recognize the beings of the world as beings? What does the mother provide us so that we can make our way in the world, confronting beings disclosed precisely as beings?

The *Phaedrus* is another prime example. This dialogue begins with Socrates asking a beautiful youth: "O dear Phaedrus, whither now and whence?" (*Phaedrus*, 227A). The youth replies that he is going from the city to the land beyond the city, from inside the walls to an amble outside the walls. His name *Phaidrós* means "shining," and it will turn out that to shine is exactly what is characteristic of beauty. Socrates' question then is not so much about the individual Phaedrus but about that which shines in a special way, about beauty itself, about Being and the role of Being in allowing us to encounter what lies beyond our natal place in the outer world. So the *Phaedrus* is also about birth, our mysterious coming into the presence of the world, or, more properly expressed, it is about the mysterious presence of the world *to* us, its unconcealment to us.

In philosophical terms, the Platonic dialogues are aimed at opening up the difference between Being and beings. The Socratic method is a refusal to accept a being as a substitute for Being: a courageous instance is not courage itself. The dialogues open up the ontological difference and ask how we move between Being and beings. In other words, how does a prior acquaintance with Being allow beings to be unconcealed to us, and how does empirical acquaintance with beings allow us to gain closer knowledge of Being?

To turn now to *Being and Time*, it begins with these two words, placed in capital letters on a line by themselves exactly in the middle of the page: EDMUND HUSSERL. The next line says the book is dedicated to him as a "revered friend" (*in Verehrung und Freundschaft*). The third and last line on the page provides the date and place: *Todtnauberg i. Bad. Schwarzwald zum 8. April 1926* ("Todtnauberg in Baden, Black Forest, on the 8th of April, 1926"). This is not an indifferent time and place, as if Heidegger just happened to finish writing the book then and there. On the contrary, it refers to the occasion on which Heidegger presented the book to the dedicatee: a gathering in the Black Forest to celebrate Husserl's 67th birthday. Heidegger presented the text in manuscript form to Husserl during the festivities, and the book was published the following year, originally in Husserl's own *Jahrbuch*,[6] and thus bears the publication date of 1927. All in all, the book begins by giving prominence of place to Husserl; he comes first in capital letters. He could not have been made more prominent.

What follows the dedicatory page is the table of contents. There is no half-title or preliminary remark. Instead, what follows immediately in the original German is an untitled page devoted to an epigraph, a quotation from Plato's *Sophist*. The page is not numbered, but the next page is 2, so this quotation constitutes the first page. The words are spoken by the Stranger, the unnamed visitor to Athens who plays a major role in the dialogue. Heidegger himself later said that the quotation was not placed there merely to be decorative.[7] Accordingly, significance is attached to it and to its placement.

In the passage quoted, the Stranger raises perplexity about what it means to be. In accord with Heidegger's way of rendering Greek philosophy, the passage says: "For evidently you have already for a long time been well-acquainted with what you properly mean when you say that something 'is,' but we who once believed we understood have now come into perplexity" (*Sophist*, 244A). The Stranger is speaking to his partner in dialogue, Theaetetus. But the "you" in the quotation is not Theaetetus. It is the plural form of you (ὑμεῖς, rendered in German by Heidegger as *ihr*, second person plural familiar), and the ones addressed are individuals not actually present. They are others, the idealists and realists, who wrangled about Being. They seemed to know what "is" means, what it means for something to be, but we (the Stranger and Theaetetus) are now in perplexity. The Stranger never calls the others "philosophers." On the contrary, they are "story tellers" and are divided into the "muses of Ionia and Sicily" (idealists) and the "more severe muses" (realists) (*Sophist*, 242C-E). The Stranger is using the name "muses" ironically or sarcastically, implying that perplexity over what it means to be is a proper characteristic of the genuine philosopher. The philosopher deserving of the name is someone who finds it necessary to raise the question of Being; such questioning is the first step into philosophy. One who does not question what it means to be is at most a "muse."

Thus *Being and Time* begins as follows: Husserl, contents, Stranger, philosophy. A kind of movement is thereby enacted from Husserl to the issue raised by the Stranger or, in other words, from phenomenology to the question of Being, in order to take the first philosophical step. We learn soon in *Being and Time* that the expression "phenomenology" primarily signifies "a methodological concept" (*SZ*, p. 27). And we learn already from the title of Chapter I of the Introduction that the matter of the book is *die Seinsfrage*, the question of Being (*SZ*, p. 2). That is precisely the issue raised by the Stranger in the passage from the *Sophist*. Thus, the book as a whole will be an application of the method of phenomenology to the question of Being or, in other words, a movement from Husserl to the Stranger.

Therefore, *Being and Time* begins in the manner of a Platonic dialogue; it brings two items together, in this case method and content, such as to prefigure the central theme. The book will attempt to apply phenomenology to the question of Being and so will amount to a phenomenological ontology. That is exactly what the close pairing of Husserl and the Stranger would lead us to expect.

THE HERO

The Platonic dialogues feature a hero. That hero is Socrates. Not only is he the prominent character, the protagonist, the hero in the literary sense, but the dialogues often liken him to an actual hero, Heracles. For example, in the

Republic, Socrates personifies Heracles by founding cities and undertaking labors such as descending to the underworld in order to wrestle with and tame a wild dog (Heracles against Cerberus, Socrates against Thrasymachus).[8] *Being and Time* also has a hero, and that hero, already suggested by prominence of place, is Husserl. This statement holds, provided "hero" is understood in the sense worked out in the book.

Heidegger takes up the theme of the hero in the context of a discussion of historicality. Specifically, the issue is the relation between authenticity and the past. Authenticity would seem to involve a break with history and tradition. Yet we are historical beings through and through. So how is authenticity related to the past?

To be authentic (αὐτο-ἐντης, "self-effectuating") means to be a product of one's own making. Authenticity means not yielding to peer pressure and signifies the exact opposite, namely, autonomy, self-reliance, marching to one's own beat. Authenticity means choosing for oneself and not simply drifting along with the crowd, the "they."

All choices refer to the future and involve a projection upon possibilities. To choose is to commit oneself to some possibilities or other. Which possibilities are seized upon in authenticity? In the strictest sense of authenticity, these are utterly new possibilities, ones not even seen in the past. The authentic person uncovers and chooses possibilities that were concealed to other people. The authentic person thereby opens up a new way of thinking or of art or of practice.

If authenticity involves such a radical break with the past, it would seem to be out of reach for most people. Our imaginations are sluggish, and we cannot envision new ways of thinking and acting. We are tied to the past and are unable to break free of tradition. Nevertheless, Heidegger recognizes a way of authenticity open to anyone. It is accomplished by following a past exemplary authentic existence, that is, by following in the footsteps of a chosen hero (*SZ*, p. 385).

Heidegger intends this "following in the footsteps" in a specific sense. He explains it as an emulation (*Nachfolge*), a repetition (*Wiederholung*), and a rejoinder (*Erwiderung*). With each of these terms, the nuance is the same. Following in the footsteps is at least to some extent a break with the past and is not pure and simple imitation, copycatting. Heidegger is attempting to characterize an *authentic* following, one that adds something new, that does see a new possibility, even if only a variation on the radically new possibility seen by the hero.

Let us take up Heidegger's explanatory terms in order. First, to emulate is not to model oneself after in the sense of mimicking; it is to do *in one's own way* what the hero did in his or her own way. As to repetition, Heidegger means it in distinction to a simple bringing-back (*Wiederbringen*) in the sense of replicating, reiterating. He later clarified it as follows: "The term 'repetition' in *Being and Time* is highly nuanced. It does not mean to roll out again the same old thing just as it was. On the contrary, repetition signifies a seizing, retrieving, gathering up, of what was concealed in the old. . . . It is an *originary* reacquisition of the past."[9] Lastly, Heidegger's word "rejoinder" could mean "reciprocation," the way feelings might be reciprocated. Yet, Heidegger plays on the etymology (*Er*-wider-*ung*) and emphasizes the "counter." To offer a rejoinder is to run counter to some extent; Heidegger even says it is to "disavow" (*Widerruf*, "counter-call"), to respond by rejecting something and adding something new, making one's own contribution.

Thus, in each case, the nuance is the same: to choose and follow a hero as a way to authenticity is not to follow blindly but is instead to vary the direction at least to some extent. It is indeed to remain tethered to the past and not break completely free of it, but it is not to be utterly fettered to the past either.

The sense of following the hero would be very well expressed by borrowing Hegel's term *Aufhebung*. It is what Hegel calls a *dialectical*[10] term, for it has opposed meanings: to preserve and to cancel. *Aufheben* could be translated as "co-opt": to appropriate (and thus to preserve) some possibility already opened up but to do so for one's own purposes (and thus to cancel).

Let us consider two examples: the philosopher and the tyrant. Suppose one's hero is a tyrant. What would following that hero mean in Heidegger's sense? It would at any rate most definitely not mean blindly *obeying* the tyrant. Authenticity is never supine. On the contrary, it would mean striving to be a tyrant oneself, emulating the tyrant, doing in one's own way what the tyrant did in his or her own way. Accordingly, the last thing an actual tyrant would want is to be a hero in Heidegger's sense. An authentic populace would be impossible to tyrannize. If everyone took the tyrant for a hero, if everyone sought to follow authentically in the footsteps of the tyrant, then everyone would try to tyrannize everyone else, including the first tyrant. The result would be a society of all chiefs and no squaws or braves. No one could tyrannize under those conditions, for tyranny demands blind obedience, hero-*worship*, the exact opposite of authenticity.

Suppose one's hero is a philosopher as a thinker who opens up a new path of thought. Specifically, suppose one's hero is the founder of the new philosophical movement known as phenomenology. According to Heidegger, phenomenology is epitomized in its maxim: To the things themselves! (*SZ*, p. 27). The things themselves are things exactly as they show themselves to the one experiencing them, versus what an outside observer such as a scientist might say about experience. Accordingly, the things themselves are phenomena, whence the name "phenomenology." Therefore, to follow in Husserl's footsteps is to practice phenomenology. But to follow authentically is not simply to repeat Husserl or extend his investigations straightforwardly into new domains. For Heidegger, the way to follow Husserl is to be more phenomenological than Husserl, to be more loyal to the maxim, to ask just what does show itself, to search further into exactly what are phenomena. Heidegger might hold Husserl in reverence and friendship, but he reveres the phenomena more.

Any self-showing of something is a phenomenon, but Heidegger distinguishes various senses in which something may show itself (*SZ*, p. 31). Thus, he distinguishes phenomena in the "merely formal" sense, namely, any beings or any properties of any beings, and phenomena in the "ordinary" sense, any beings. But a phenomenon in the preeminent sense is not a being or a property of a being. The directing of the gaze onto this phenomenon is what marks Heidegger's following of Husserl as an authentic one. Within the general framework of Husserl's phenomenology, Heidegger takes phenomenology in a new direction, one that indeed runs counter to the founder's intention.

What then is a phenomenon in the preeminent sense? At first, Heidegger offers only an analogy: this phenomenon is comparable to space and time for Kant (*SZ*, p. 31). Space and time are what Kant calls "pure apriori forms of intuition." They are not empirical intuitions (appearances) but are prior to empirical intuitions and make possible all empirical intuitions by providing the form or order anything needs in order to appear to us. Space and time can be made to show themselves, although we usually overlook them in favor of the *beings* in space and time. So space and time are prior to appearances, make appearances possible, are always somehow in view in any appearance, are ordinarily overlooked in favor of appearances, and yet can be made to show themselves explicitly.

Heidegger draws out the analogy a few pages later. What shows itself in the preeminent sense, the strict phenomenological sense, is Being. Heidegger asks what it is that phenomenology should "let be seen"? What must be called a "phenomenon" in the preeminent sense? What by its very essence is necessarily in view in any self-showing of anything? His answer is that this is something that initially and predominantly does not show itself, something that is instead concealed over and against the things that initially and predominantly show themselves, namely, beings. Yet for Heidegger it is something that essentially belongs to beings, belongs in such a way as to constitute their meaning and ground. A phenomenon in the preeminent sense is not any being but is the Being of beings: accordingly, what demands to be made "the explicit theme of phenomenology is Being" (*SZ*, p. 35).

In the strict phenomenological sense, there is only one phenomenon, Being. Like space and time for Kant, Being is always in view although always overlooked; Being is a prior condition of the possibility of grasping any being, inasmuch as it has to be understood to some extent in order for any empirical grasp of beings to take place, and yet is not any being; Being has no empirical

content but makes possible a grasp of beings with such content; Being constitutes the meaning and ground of beings but is concealed in its meaning and has
no ground; and, finally, Being is difficult to bring to explicit thematic awareness and yet can be wrested out into the open. That bringing into the open is
the task of phenomenology. Being is precisely what phenomenology is to "let
be seen." Thereby phenomenology becomes ontology, a raising of the question
of Being. *Being and Time* is thus the application of Husserl to the Stranger.

This application is a complete *Aufhebung* of the hero, Husserl. For the
founder of phenomenology, Being is exactly what phenomenology prescinds
from. Phenomenology is precisely *not* ontology. For Husserl, the first, indis-
pensable step of phenomenology is the transcendental reduction. That means
to carry out an *epoché* (abstention) with regard to all questions of Being, neither affirming or denying that anything is. In Husserl's other terms, it means
to put Being in brackets, the way a mathematician prescinds from the positive
or negative sign of a number and considers it only as an absolute quantity by
placing the number in brackets: [7] (in American notation, an absolute value
is placed in slashes /7/ rather than brackets).[11] Or, it is to carry out a "neutrality modification" on questions of Being, to put Being in neutral just as an
automobile in neutral gear is not in forward (positive) or reverse (negative).
Or, lastly, it is to be a "disinterested spectator," an onlooker with no stake in
whether the thing observed exists or not.

Thus, Heidegger's explicit focus on Being is a co-opting of Husserl. And
it is not something carried out at the beginning of *Being and Time* and then
set aside in order to take up new themes. On the contrary, Husserl is the hero
of the whole treatise. The entire book is phenomenological ontology, devoted
to letting Being be seen.

This co-opting can be understood in terms of the distinction between the
letter and the spirit. Heidegger attempts to remain faithful to what he claims
is higher, the spirit of phenomenology, to its maxim of returning to the things
themselves, letting show itself what does show itself, rather than remaining faithful merely to the letter, to the way Husserl actually carried out the
program. So the co-opting, the following in the footsteps of the hero, is a
distinction between what phenomenology makes *possible* and the way it has
been *actualized*. Heidegger credits Husserl, beginning with the breakthrough
to phenomenology in the *Logische Untersuchungen*, with providing the
foundation on which *Being and Time* is built (*SZ*, p. 38). Yet Heidegger does
not believe that what is essential to phenomenology resides in the way it has
been actualized as a philosophical movement. On the contrary, higher than
actuality stands possibility, and phenomenology can be appreciated "only by
seizing upon it in terms of possibility" (*SZ*, p. 38).

The Platonic dialogues can all be understood as asking, "What is philosophy?" in the guise of the question, "Who is Socrates?" *Being and Time*

is always asking, "What is Being?" This question takes the guise of asking about Husserl's method as applied to the issue raised by the Stranger. The treatise is always asking the question of Being, *die Seinsfrage*, and is pursuing it phenomenologically. Husserl in *Being and Time* and Socrates in the dialogues might remain in the background, and indeed besides the dedication and a handful of adulatory comments, Husserl is not mentioned in the treatise. Nevertheless, the entire treatise is a co-opting of Husserl, which is exactly what it means to choose and follow a hero.

As for Socrates, he remains the hero of the dialogues although at times he does no more than listen. I will now blend play and seriousness and attempt to show that there are dialogues in which Socrates is present but does not even listen. Instead, he snores right through the discussion carried out by others. Nevertheless, Socrates makes his presence felt.

Consider the *Timaeus*. It occurs the day after Socrates recalls the events recorded in the *Republic*, and those events occurred the day before the recollection. So the three days are: first day, the events of the *Republic*, taking place in the Piraeus; second day, recollection of those events, Socrates having come up from the Piraeus; third day, the events of the *Timaeus* in Athens.[12]

The events recorded in the *Republic* begin on the evening of Socrates' visit to the Piraeus. He is promised a banquet and the treat of watching a torch race of young men on horseback. Instead, however, he becomes involved in a long discussion, so protracted that it goes on all night. In the morning, Socrates ascends to Athens, presumably by himself (since he speaks of the others in the third person), leaving his companions in discussion to get their sleep. On this day he will recollect the entire dialogue. But before he can enter Athens and return home to food and sleep, he encounters a beautiful young man, Phaedrus, at the city gate. This encounter must take place the day after the events of the *Republic*, for in no other way can it be explained what Socrates is doing beyond the gate, since, excepting his visit to the Piraeus, he never leaves Athens.[13] The two friends remain in the countryside and spend the entire afternoon in intimate talk, as recorded in the dialogue *Phaedrus*. In the evening, Socrates says he is going to another of his favorites, Isocrates. It must be in the presence of this Isocrates that Socrates recollects the events of the previous day. Presumably, the recollection takes as much time as the original events, and so Socrates again stays awake all night and again goes without food.

On the following morning, Socrates visits three friends, ones who apparently were present at the house of Isocrates to hear the recollection of the *Republic*. The *Timaeus* begins this way: "One, two, three—but where, O dear Timaeus, is the fourth of those I regaled yesterday and who are supposed to return the favor today?" (*Timaeus*, 17A). Although not mentioned by name, and the source of much speculation, the missing fourth must have been Isocrates. The missing person is said to be suffering from *asthéneia*, "lethargy" (*Timaeus*, 17A). As the one who is closest to Socrates, Isocrates would have learned from the philosopher that it is a comedy to pretend to be pure spirit; the body must be attended to. So Isocrates stays home after being regaled all night by Socrates' recollection and goes to bed.

Socrates himself, however, having been invited to the home of Timaeus, denies himself the comfort of sleep and accepts the invitation. He goes home merely to change his clothes.[14] It is now the third day since Socrates has eaten or slept. In the discussion recorded in the *Timaeus*, Socrates speaks only at the outset. He asks the others if they remember his recollection of the previous day and reviews it for them. But the lacunary review shows that Socrates' mental powers are flagging. Socrates is suffering from his own *asthéneia*. Finally, he gives up altogether and sits back to listen. Timaeus then launches a long-winded and far-fetched disquisition about the creation of the world out of geometrical figures. Socrates' eloquent commentary is to sleep through it all. The commentary amounts to this: it is ridiculous to believe the mystery of the presence of the world can be dispelled by rational thought, not even by that apex of rational thinking, geometry.

The preceding is a perfect example of Plato's artistry: his indirectness and his combing and curling the dialogues and interweaving all the strands, even the apparently insignificant ones. Such a cosmetic character (κόσμησις: "beautiful arrangement of the tresses") is admittedly missing from *Being and Time*, except perhaps for the way of beginning. Nevertheless, Heidegger was indeed capable of Platonic artistry, as I hope to show in chapter 5 by offering a musical interpretation of the book *Gelassenheit*.

MIDDLE

Let us return to the "muses" spoken of derisively by the Stranger. He says they talk to us "as if we were children" (*Sophist*, 242C) by telling us stories. The story is this: beings are ultimately derived from other beings, such as water or air. Thereby these muses are not philosophers; they do not take what Heidegger calls "the first philosophical step" (*der erste philosophische Schritt*) (*SZ*, p. 6). That step consists in recognizing the ontological difference, the fact that at the origination of beings is not some other being but Being itself.

How is Being the origin? Answer: precisely as the phenomenon in the preeminent sense. Just as, for Kant, no objects would be present to us without a prior "pure" (contentless) intuition of space and time, so for Heidegger no beings would be disclosed unless they stepped into the light supplied by a previous self-showing of Being in general. Without a previous understanding of what it means to be, we could not recognize any being as a being.

The recognition could not arise discursively; that is the point of saying that beings cannot be derived from other beings. We cannot run around ("discurs") from one being to another in order to discover what it means to be in general. We cannot make a collection of beings and derive from them—by abstraction to what they have in common—the meaning of Being in general. Being must come first: unless we already knew what it means to be, how would we know what to place in the collection? Any collecting must be guided by some sense of what is to be collected.

That which guides our recognition of any being as a being is Being. It is something we always glimpse but ordinarily overlook. Yet it can be wrested to show itself. There is a method to let it be seen. The method is phenomenology, and what—for Heidegger although not for Husserl—is to be made thematic in the method is Being. So *Being and Time* as a treatise in philosophy is phenomenological ontology. For Heidegger, ontology and phenomenology are not two distinct disciplines within philosophy. On the contrary, these terms characterize philosophy itself: "the first names the object of philosophy and the second the way of dealing with that object" (*SZ*, p. 38).

Socrates is not a storyteller (in the Stranger's sense). Socrates recognizes the ontological difference. He is constantly seeking the Being of beings, but his interlocutors can only offer him examples, beings, which he rejects as not measuring up to Being itself, to what must be seen in order to recognize any being as a being, the Idea (ἰδέα, "that which is *seen* in a preeminent way"). Generals can indeed recognize a brave act, but when Socrates asks what makes the acts brave, what bravery itself is, what is the Being of bravery, the Idea of bravery, those generals can offer only instances. The generals are storytellers.

What Socrates is constantly attempting to open up is the ontological difference. That is the content, the middle, of all the dialogues. It is also the entire content of *Being and Time*. That content amounts to the first philosophical step. Accordingly, all the dialogues as well as *Being and Time* could be subtitled: On philosophy. We are about to see that they could also be subtitled: On death.

For Plato, how do we let Being show itself? How do we come to know what it means to be, if not discursively? That question is what lies behind the "doctrine of recollection." The hero of the Platonic dialogues thereby does become a storyteller, a mythmaker. It is not a story such as those told by the "muses," a story about the derivation of beings from other beings. It is story about Being as the origin. Being shows itself by way of our recollection; to say so is to invoke a myth.

There is a mystery attached to our knowledge of Being, the presence of the light by which we recognize any being as a being. Socrates expresses—and indeed enhances—the mystery by resorting to myth. We gained the knowledge of Being in a previous existence, when the soul in heaven journeyed in procession with all the gods and banqueted by gazing out at the hyper-heavenly place where the Ideas reside (*Phaedrus*, 247C). Upon falling to earth and becoming incarnated, the soul retains a faint recollection of what it once saw, and that recollection provides the light. The light is usually overlooked; the philosopher is the one who attends to it and attempts to make the recollection explicit.

The doctrine of recollection needs to be demythologized, that is to say, taken precisely as a myth and not a literal explanation. The intent of the doctrine is not to provide a rational explanation of how we come to understand what it means to be; the intent of using mythological language is to focus attention on the *inexplicability* of the presence of the world to us. The myth aims to make us wonder, not to remove the sense of wonder through a scientific account.

Socrates maintains that there is a privileged being in the process of recollection. Any being at all could serve to remind us of the Idea which is the Being of that being, but most beings on earth lack luster. They do not shine brightly enough to allow Being to show through. Otherwise put, not all the Ideas are equally lustrous; most do not possess enough radiance to make for easy recollection. Yet, there is one privileged Idea and one class of most lustrous beings. The privileged Idea is beauty, and the privileged beings are beautiful ones, beautiful human bodies in particular. That is why the philosopher is "a lover of beauty and of the arts and is erotic" (*Phaedrus*, 248D).

Let us now turn to Heidegger. For him as well, there is a privileged being in regard to the question of what it means to be in general, a privileged being in regard to gaining access to Being, letting the phenomenon be seen, allowing Being to show itself. That being does not provoke recollection, and so Heidegger does not resort to the myth of the heavenly banquet. Instead, the mode of access is phenomenology; the privileged being is to be investigated phenomenologically. That means to attend first to the way this being shows itself to itself and then secondly to "read off" (*ablesen*) from that self-showing the meaning of Being in general (*SZ*, p. 7).

For Heidegger, the privileged being in the question of Being is the being that actually asks this question, namely, the being we ourselves are. *Being and Time* thematizes this being in a limited respect, only with regard to the question of Being. So Heidegger does not call this being in the traditional way "man" or "human being" but *Dasein* ("existence," literally "thereness"). This being is thematized only as a place, a "there," where a disclosedness of Being resides.

Heidegger emphasizes something apparently obvious, namely: in order to let this being serve as the exemplary being, a condition is actually experiencing it. The problem is that Dasein would seem to elude every grasp, for this being, whether existing authentically (making oneself a product of one's own hand) or inauthentically (sheepishly going along with the crowd, the "they"), is always projecting upon future possibilities. The future is essential to Dasein in the present, but the future is now outstanding. Dasein, at every moment of life until the very end, is futural and so is never whole. Consequently, Dasein cannot be experienced as a determinate being at all. Only death will bring wholeness and determination. But death also brings an end to Dasein as a place of disclosedness. Mortality would then seem to forestall any attempt by someone living to read off from his or her Being the meaning of Being in general. Accordingly, a central theme of *Being and Time* is death: How is death, apparently making impossible an experience of Dasein as a determinate whole, nevertheless not an obstacle in the way of phenomenological ontology?

Close to the middle of both *Being and Time* and a Platonic dialogue is the theme of death. The question of Being and the question of death are closely joined; *the* central question, the question of Being, involves questioning our comportment to death.

Not only is each of the dialogues braided up, but so are these works among themselves.[15] For example, many of the dialogues, if the indications provided by Plato are heeded closely enough, have ties to the trial and death of Socrates. The *Sophist*, the dialogue Heidegger invokes in the epigraph to *Being and Time*, is a case in point.

The *Sophist* begins with Theodorus saying: "According to what was agreed yesterday, O Socrates, we [the partners in dialogue with Socrates on the previous day, namely, Theodorus and Theaetetus] have come ourselves . . ." (*Sophist*, 216A). What was agreed yesterday? Theodorus is apparently referring to the dialogue *Theaetetus*. That conversation breaks off, and Socrates calls for the partners in the dialogue to meet again the next day. His reason for discontinuing the talk is his going to trial. Socrates abruptly brings the dialogue to a close by saying: "But now I must betake myself to the stoa of the King against the indictment Meletus has drawn up and directed toward me. Yet in the morning, O Theodorus, let us betake ourselves here again" (*Theaetetus*, 210D).

A stoa is a roofed colonnade serving as a public meeting place. In this case, it is a court of law. The "King" is the archon (magistrate) who presided over capital cases, and the stoa assigned to him is a large one, capacious enough to accommodate at least 501 dikasts. So Socrates is breaking off the conversation to go to court in order to disclaim the capital offenses he is charged with, and he makes plans to meet Theodorus and Theaetetus in the morning at the place where they are now speaking. Yet, what intervenes between the *Theaetetus* and the *Sophist* is Socrates' trial. Socrates is found guilty and condemned to death. He is remanded to prison until the execution can be carried out. Therefore, the first words of the *Sophist* take on a particular sense: what was "agreed yesterday," the agreement entered into by a majority of the 501 dikasts, was that Socrates is guilty and is to die. So the meeting of Socrates and his friends the day after is not at the same place as their earlier dialogue but in prison.

The beginning of the *Sophist* thereby prefigures a central theme of the dialogue, namely, the possibility of nonbeing: it is Socrates' own nonbeing that hangs over the dialogue. Socrates' death, his possible nonbeing, is what is announced in the beginning, namely, the agreement of yesterday, and thus what is prefigured is the relation between Being and nonbeing which will be put at issue in the discussion.

If the *Sophist* takes place on the morning of Socrates' first day in prison, the prominent role played by the Stranger becomes intelligible. Why is the Stranger the leader of the discussion rather than Socrates? A hint is provided by Socrates' exceedingly curious response when introduced to the Stranger. Theodorus says at the beginning: "we have come ourselves and are bringing this man, a stranger from Elea." Socrates responds: "Perhaps this is no man but a god" (*Sophist*, 216A). Socrates specifies the god as one coming to look into human deeds and judge them (216B).

The dialogue thus reminds us of something Socrates says at the end of his defense speech. Just before his farewell, Socrates announces he will soon be facing "those who are truly dikasts," τοὺς ἀληθῶς δικαστάς (*Socrates' Apology*, 41A), that is, divine judges who will see the truth about him. Socrates may have been referring to his entry into Hades, but he was correct to say "soon," for the very next morning, in prison, the first significant person Socrates encounters is the Eleatic Stranger, and Socrates recognizes him as a god come to judge him. Presumably, this god-like alien from Elea, the land of Parmenides, who is *the* philosopher of Being, will judge him truly, in accord with his Being. Socrates listens throughout the dialogue because the Stranger is looking into his deeds: Is Socrates a charlatan? In other words, the Stranger is determining who truly is a sophist. The dialogue is portraying a sophist in truth and prefiguring how Socrates will fare when he faces judgment in Hades.

Accordingly, the beginning of the *Sophist* is appropriate to the matter of the discussion, the determination of who is the sophist. As usual, the dialogue begins by enacting a certain movement, a certain deed: in this case, the bringing together of Socrates and the god-like Stranger. The beginning thus prefigures what will be carried out in the course of the dialogue, namely, a determination of the sophist in truth and thus an examination of Socrates' claim that he is *not* a sophist. And the *Sophist* is also appropriate to the matter of *Being and Time*. The quotation placed on the first page of the treatise announces the question of Being and also, simply by appealing to the dialogue occurring on the morning after Socrates' condemnation, invokes an atmosphere of death.

Let us then turn to *Being and Time* on the theme of death. As mentioned, death threatens to strangle the project by preventing a grasp of Dasein as a determinate whole. The phenomenological philosopher attempting to disclose the meaning of Being in general by reading it off from his or her own Being will not be a whole until death, and then he or she will no longer be Dasein and so will be unable disclose anything. Accordingly, the project of reading off the meaning of Being by taking Dasein as a privileged being is doomed from the very start. While death is still outstanding, Dasein is not a whole. And when death arrives, Dasein is no longer Dasein.

Heidegger suggests the solution to this problem when he wonders whether this way of thinking about what is outstanding to Dasein does not fall into the error of conceiving Dasein as present-at-hand or ready-to-hand rather than as existence (*SZ*, p. 245). Let us be clear about the distinction between the ready-to-hand and the present-at-hand and then distinguish them both from existence.

The first distinction concerns the degree of closeness of a practical thing to the hand which uses it. Heidegger recognizes three degrees of closeness, expressed by means of prepositions: a thing may be *vor*, *zu*, or *unter* the hand, "on hand," "at hand," or "in hand." If an item of equipment is merely "on hand," then it is extant somewhere in the world but not easily accessible. An example would be an electric drill still in its case and stored away someplace or other. If the equipment is "at hand," then it is ready to be used and within reach. An example would be an electric drill with the battery charged and a bit already inserted, hanging from the workman's tool belt. A thing "in hand" would be a tool actually being wielded by the workman: the drill in the grasp of the carpenter drilling with it. In the customary way of translating Heidegger, the term "present-at-hand" is meant to capture the sense of the merely "on hand." It refers to presence, extantness, somewhere or other. The "ready-to-hand" expresses the sense of the "at hand" and the "in hand." It refers to the practicality of an item of equipment.

The present-at-hand differs from the ready-to-hand corresponding to the distinction between primary and secondary properties, as traditionally understood, and between theory and practice. Primary properties are physical ones such as shape, material, and mass; they are revealed by *studying* the equipment, taking up a theoretical attitude toward it. Secondary properties are those of usefulness, functionality, revealed by *wielding* the equipment in some practical pursuit. For Heidegger, the traditional order of priority is actually a *hysteron proteron*; the practical properties should be called the primary ones, since they are first in the order of experience. Only some subsequent breakdown in usefulness motivates us to focus on physical properties.

According to Heidegger, it would be an error to think of Dasein (understood precisely, not the human being as such, but the "there" of a disclosedness of the meaning of Being) as possessing *any* of the properties of things. So the death of Dasein has to be understood in radically different terms, in the way appropriate to a being that exists. For Heidegger, "existence" (*Existenz*) as a name of the Being of Dasein always has reference to possibilities. "Existence" names Dasein's peculiar relation to possibilities.

Versus things, whether ready-to-hand or present-at-hand, Dasein has a distinctive relation to possibilities. Only Dasein's possibilities are what Heidegger calls "most proper" (*eigenst*, *SZ*, p. 42) ones, possibilities in the most proper sense. They are so because, for Dasein, possibilities, even when actualized, remain possibilities. And possibilities still outstanding are already actualized. Dasein is not yet what he or she[16] already is and is already what he or she is not yet. That expresses a radical difference between Dasein and things.

According to Heidegger, Dasein always is a possibility and also has this possibility, but not in the manner of a "property belonging to a thing" (*SZ*, p. 42). So Dasein actualizes some possibility, and yet the possibility remains a possibility for that Dasein; as existent Dasein, I eat my cake and yet still have it to eat. I possess possibilities in the most proper sense; things do not.

A white door possesses the possibility of being painted red. The red is now utterly absent, and when it becomes present, the door will be utterly red. The redness was at first entirely potential and when actualized will be entirely actual. Accordingly, a thing has properties, pure and simple. But Dasein has no such properties. For Dasein, past actualities remain possible, and future possibilities are already actual. This is so especially with regard to death, but it applies to any of Dasein's possibilities.

Consider the possibility of attaining old age. For someone who has actualized that possibility, oldness is not a property the way redness is a property of a door. An aged person is not purely and simply old, such that that is all there is to it. There are many ways to be old, but there are not many ways for a door to be red. It remains open to the elderly person to take old age as a burden and complain about it, or to fight against age and ridiculously try to recapture one's youth, or to "act one's age" and accept old age gracefully. In other words, old age is still a possibility to someone who has already actualized it. The aged person *is* that possibility, but old age remains a possibility he or she *has*. Every old person is old in his or her own way. As Nietzsche says, cited by Heidegger, "We are not too old for our victories" (*SZ*, p. 264).[17] What we have conquered is still open to being appropriated. It is still open to the elderly to decide how old age, a possibility they have actualized in the past, is *going to be actualized*. What for things constitute properties are for Dasein *existentialia*. Accordingly, Dasein has no "properties." That is a term applicable to things alone; the characteristics of Dasein all have to do with possibility, that is, with existence, and so are rightfully called *existentialia*.

A comparable analysis applies to future possibilities. They are not purely and simply outstanding to Dasein, the way redness is utterly absent from a white door. A young Dasein has the possibility of being old in the future; but oldness is not now utterly absent from a young Dasein. Such a Dasein is already a future old Dasein, in the sense that youth is lived with old age on the horizon. One plans for the future, and even to live entirely in the moment is still to take one's bearings from the future, namely, by purposely turning one's back on it. Old age always looms over youth, but redness does not loom over a white door.

This existential analysis of Dasein's future possibilities applies preeminently to death. That is a possibility every Dasein will make actual, and it is one every Dasein is already making actual. *Every Dasein breathes an atmosphere of mortality.* Death is not utterly outstanding, not something utterly closed off to us while we live, not something purely and simply missing. We all actualize death in a preliminary way and live as future dead persons; we are constantly comporting ourselves to death.

On the other hand, once we do die, we will not be able to comport ourselves to death any longer. There are *no possible ways of being dead*, possible ways of comporting ourselves to death once it arrives *in propria persona*. Death is the one victory (or defeat) for which we will indeed be too old. In Heidegger's terminology, death is "unsurpassable," *unüberholbar* (*SZ*, p. 250); death cannot be "overtaken," *über-holen*. The term applies to automobiles and driving. Death cannot be passed, overtaken, as one car passes another and puts that other car in the rearview mirror. Death cannot be put in our rearview mirror; we cannot overtake it and look back upon it.

Accordingly, being dead is not like being old or being anything else at all. Comportment, even the negative one of flight, requires some understanding of what one is comporting oneself toward, some disclosure of it. But death takes away all disclosedness, all looking, whether forward or back, and so makes impossible any comportment.

Death takes away all possibilities whatsoever, makes them impossible. Death is the possibility of the impossibility of any possibilities. Death is the possibility of the impossibility of possibility and thereby is the possibility of the impossibility of Dasein or of existence (since existence is comportment toward possibilities).

In summary, death is the only possibility that is *always* being made actual (in the existential sense: death is always with us, always menacing, always coloring our lives) and the only possibility that can *never* be made actual (in the ready-to-hand or present-at-hand sense: Dasein cannot be dead, there cannot be a dead Dasein, death makes Dasein impossible).

Being and Time is concerned with death as an *existentialium* and not with death as a thing ready-to-hand or present-at-hand; the treatise is concerned with being-*toward*-death, with the way death enters into our lives as long as we are living. *Being and Time* offers an *existential* analysis, an analysis in terms of most proper possibilities, and shows how Dasein can grasp himself or herself as a whole while still alive. Death is not an obstacle to wholeness, for death is not, even now, something entirely outstanding. The problem of grasping Dasein as a whole therefore seems to be solved. According to Heidegger, even everyday inauthentic Dasein is in constant comportment toward death, although this may be precisely by attempting to flee from death. Death is therefore not something Dasein attains only when deceased. The extreme future possibility of Dasein is always already incorporated into Dasein in being-toward-death. For that reason, Heidegger concludes that it is not justified to infer, based on an ontologically inappropriate understanding of Dasein's death as something outstanding, that Dasein cannot be grasped as a whole. The fact that Dasein is always ahead-of-oneself, by constantly projecting onto possibilities, is not evidence against wholeness in the existential sense; on the contrary, this ahead-of-oneself is what "first makes wholeness possible" (*SZ*, p. 259).

Heidegger goes on to say that the problem of the possible wholeness of this being, the being some particular one of us is in each case, could have been posed in a legitimate way *only* by bringing Dasein's mode of Being as existence into relation with death as the extreme possibility. Yet the issue of wholeness is not resolved so easily, and in the very next sentence Heidegger declares: "Nevertheless, it remains questionable whether the problem has been sufficiently worked out" (*SZ*, p. 259). The theme still to be taken up is authenticity, authentic being-toward-death. As long as authentic being-toward-death has not been exhibited and ontologically determined, an "essential deficiency" adheres to the existential interpretation of being-toward-death (*SZ*, p. 260).

The existential analysis of death shows how future death is incorporated into present Dasein and thus demonstrates the *possibility* of grasping Dasein as a whole. What still needs to be shown is this possibility being carried out, Dasein actually grasping itself as a whole. It is a matter of the transition from theory to practice. In other words, does the theory hold in practice? What has to be exhibited is Dasein in practice understanding itself as a unitary whole, Dasein incorporating death into its way of living. Ordinary, everyday, inauthentic Dasein does not incorporate death but, on the contrary, flees from death and in practice denies that death is always looming. Only authentic being-toward-death faces up to death, even though this "facing up" will prove to be a peculiar one. In any event, the essential deficiency to be repaired has to do with an *exhibition* of Dasein's wholeness, Dasein in his or her wholeness shown to himself or herself as a unitary whole. That exhibition will be supplied by describing authentic being-toward-death.

The distinction between authentic and inauthentic comportment toward death revolves around the character of death as a possibility. Inauthentic comportment does everything to evade this character; authentic comportment enhances it. Authentic comportment is a constant dying. It will turn out that such constant dying is exactly the Socratic comportment toward death.

Inauthentic being-toward-death does everything it can to conceal the fact that death is possible at any moment, and inauthenticity thereby prevents Dasein from taking up his or her own chosen way of being-toward-death. People take concern with death to be morbid. For example, inauthentic (idle) talk about death is meant to be heartening: "they" tell a seriously ill person that there is no need to worry since modern medicine can do wonders. People do recognize there is such a thing as death, but they speak of it as a mere "case" of something that just happens. They pass death off as an ever-recurring actuality and thereby conceal its possibility-character. Accordingly, Dasein is placed in the position of lostness in the "they" with respect to what should be a preeminent possibility for existence, "a most proper possibility to be oneself" (*SZ*, p. 253).

By contrast, authentic being-toward death enhances the possibility-character and discloses this possibility as a most proper one. Heidegger's name for the authentic attitude toward death is "anticipation." It might seem Heidegger is making authenticity a morbid preoccupation, and the German term, *Vorlaufen*, seems even more morbid, since it literally means "forerunning," "running ahead" into death. But of course Heidegger does not mean this "running ahead" as committing suicide, nor does it mean brooding over death, obsession with death. Inauthentic comportment turns death into an object of calculation, an actuality that can be reckoned with either by predicting, avoiding, or hastening. That is what Heidegger means by saying "they" pass death off as an actuality and conceal its possibility-character. Running ahead is precisely *not* such calculation about death.

Anticipation must be understood in the existential sense; it then refers to Dasein's peculiar relation to possibilities. To anticipate death is to live now as a future dead person and to do so in full consciousness of breathing an atmosphere of mortality. To anticipate death is to recognize that death is a most proper possibility, one that is always being made actual and one that leaves a person free to do so in his or her own chosen way. To anticipate death is therefore a way of *understanding* death. Anticipation proves to be a way of "understanding one's extreme possibility as a *most proper* possibility" (*SZ*,

p. 263) and thus proves to be the possibility of *"authentic* existence" (*SZ*, p. 263).

To anticipate is therefore not so much to understand death as such; it is to understand Dasein's relation to possibilities as such. It is to understand that Dasein's possibilities are most proper possibilities, ones which Dasein always runs ahead into and ones which leave Dasein the choice of how to run ahead into them. That choice, the choice to be oneself as a product of one's own making, instead of going along with the crowd, is authenticity. So anticipation is, as Heidegger says, the possibility of *authentic* existence.

Then just how does one anticipate? How does one comport oneself authentically to death? A prime example of authentic being-toward-death is the life of Socrates. Accordingly, the quotation from the *Sophist*, with the death of Socrates in the background, is again appropriate. It again prefigures what the treatise is about. How then did Socrates face death?

The *Sophist* is not the dialogue in which Plato portrays the execution of Socrates, the administering of the poison hemlock. That suggests Socrates' authentic comportment toward death is not his serenity and resoluteness in meeting his end. Such comportment is *not* what Heidegger means by anticipation. Instead, Socrates is the exemplar precisely by his comportment in the *Sophist*.

What does Socrates do in this dialogue? —Almost nothing except listen to a stranger philosophizing about Being, a stranger taking the first philosophical step. For Socrates, taking this step, distinguishing Being from beings, is what it means to die. In other words, Socrates is a prime example inasmuch as he maintains that the philosopher is always dying, that the practice of philosophy *is* dying.

Death is the soul existing by itself, the separation of the soul (*Phaedo*, 64C). Death can even be characterized as the purification of the soul. The philosopher does indeed constantly strive toward this purification and so can be said to practice dying. The crucial question, however, concerns exactly what the philosopher's soul is to be separated from, purified from.

Let us consider three dialogues central to the portrait of philosophy as dying, as separation, purification, of the soul. The *Phaedrus* begins with Socrates in a way purifying himself from his body. Instead of returning home from the Piraeus and satisfying the body's need for food and sleep, Socrates spends the day in philosophical discourse. But what motivates him to reject the body's needs is not the prospect of an afternoon in pure thought. On the contrary, it is something as bodily as can be. Phaedrus entices Socrates into the countryside by offering to read him a speech written on a scroll he is carrying. Phaedrus says the speech is most appropriate for Socrates' ears, and the reason is that the speech deals with erotic matters. Specifically, it is a speech containing trick arguments useful in the seduction of boys. Socrates says he is so eager to learn these arguments that he will follow Phaedrus even as far as Megara, which is a way of saying "all over Attica." Accordingly, the *Phaedrus* does not portray the philosopher as purifying the soul *from the body*. If anything, it portrays the philosopher as preoccupied with the body, with Eros.

In the *Phaedrus*, Socrates not only learns trick arguments for seduction, he also proceeds to employ them. In accord with the trick arguments, Socrates disguises himself as a non-lover and shows Phaedrus the advantage of yielding to him. Phaedrus eventually surrenders (*Phaedrus*, 243E):

Socrates: Where is that lad I was addressing?
Phaedrus: He is always near you, especially close, whenever you want him.
Socrates: So then, O beautiful lad . . .

Socrates in this dialogue shows himself to be exactly in accord with his characterization of the philosopher: a lover of beauty and erotic. If this is death, the separation of the soul, it is most definitely not the separation of the soul from the body.

In the *Symposium*, philosophy is equated with "Platonic love." That is the pinnacle of the "ladder of love" as described by Diotima (*Symposium*, 210A-212A). The ascension up this ladder does amount to a purification of the soul from the body. At the lowest level is the carnal love of one body for another one, a physically beautiful one. During the ascent, the object of love becomes further and further removed from the beautiful body and becomes more and more rarified and ideal. It is no longer the beautiful body that counts, but only the beauty *of* the body, the beauty abstracted from the beautiful body. Indeed the beautiful body eventually becomes optional, and it is bypassed in favor of a beautiful soul. On the subsequent rungs, the bodily is neglected more and more, until, finally, Being, or the Idea of beauty, is not grasped as reflected in anything bodily, or as reflected in anything of our world at all, but is gazed upon directly, without intermediary, and in a way that is adequate to the vision.

If such Platonic love is the practice of philosophy, then this practice is indeed a dying in the sense of a separating of the soul from the body. But is it the sort of love Socrates actually practices? Not at all. In the *Symposium*, Socrates is characterized as a satyr (215B, 216C), that is, a lecher or, in today's parlance, a "dirty old man" and specifically one who proceeds from conquest to conquest (218A–B). Socrates is on the prowl for beautiful bodies and not at all intent on bypassing such bodies in favor of the Idea of beauty. Socrates may well be intent on the Idea, but he grasps it precisely through the intermediary of beautiful beings and not by neglecting them.

Diotima's portrait of Platonic love is a comedy; it is not Socratic love as actually practiced. Yet it is Socrates himself who puts on this comedy, and we are well prepared for it, since he is utterly out of character at the dinner party. He is purified (having taken a bath, most unusual for him), "all fancied up," wearing comedians' socks (versus the buskins of tragedy), and merely repeating things he has heard in a fit of inspiration, the words of a priestess of Apollo. Some sort of buffoonery is in the offing, and we soon learn what it is: Socrates is holding pure, intellectual, non-carnal "Platonic love" up to ridicule.[18] The love actually proper to Socrates is most definitely carnal. Socratic love sees the Ideas *precisely as* reflected in worldly things, as grasped through the intermediary of beautiful bodies, and not as gazed upon directly in the manner of a kind of vision accessible only to the gods. Then how is the practice of philosophy a dying, a separating of the soul? To see that, we need to turn to the *Phaedo*.

The dialogue most explicitly relating philosophy to death is this one occurring on the very day of Socrates' passage into Hades. As his soul is about to take leave of his body, Socrates says he can face the prospect calmly and hopefully, since all his life he has been attempting to free the soul from the fetters of the body. He has done so by practicing philosophy, and in this pursuit the body is a hindrance. Therefore, to philosophize is to die in the specific sense of separating soul from body.

A casual reading of the *Phaedo* does indeed make it seem Socrates despises the body and believes philosophizing is a matter of simulating death. Yet, a Platonic dialogue never yields up its treasures to a casual reading. Attending to the dialogue with the same care[19] that went into the composing of it, we find indications enough that, as surprising as it may be, throughout his final day on earth Socrates is again putting on a comedy. As with all Socratic comedies, this one expresses a deliberately exaggerated position, one designed to be so extreme that its untenability will be manifest to everyone (excepting those with no sense of humor).

The comedy is suggested at the very outset of the discussion of philosophy and death, when Socrates, sitting on the side of his prison bed and placing his feet on the ground, says he himself has no knowledge of the matters to be discussed and will merely repeat things he has heard. Throughout the dialogue, Socrates does not speak in his own name. We know that when Socrates speaks for another, as when he speaks in the name of Diotima, he will say something ridiculous. That his feet are on the ground only makes it more obvious by contrast: he is about to say something groundless.

The comedy begins with the very first topic, the prohibition against suicide. Socrates relates what he has heard: "Are we not the property of the gods, and just as the gods will be displeased if we take our own life, so likewise if some animal that was our property killed itself on its own initiative, would we not be angry with that animal and punish it?" (*Phaedo*, 62C).

The comedy continues as Socrates turns to death itself, not merely suicide, and offers an absurd definition. "Death is the releasing of the body from the soul, such that the body by itself then comes into its own, and is likewise the releasing of the soul from the body, such that soul by itself then also comes into its own. Is not death precisely this?" (*Phaedo*, 64C). Accordingly, the soul is the prison of the body, just as the body is of the soul. At death, both these prisoners are released and come to their full potential. The soul is bad for the body, and vice versa. I scarcely need to make the absurdity explicit: if the two cases are indeed analogous, as Socrates has heard, then the soul after death is as corrupted as a corpse. If that is the full potential of the body, namely, decay and corruption, and if the full potential of the soul is an analogous one, then it is absurd to suppose such a soul could attain the heights of philosophy.

Socrates goes on repeating the hearsay. But he never actually makes any assertions, and that might be his way of distancing himself from the things he has heard. He speaks about philosophy as the practice of death, but he only poses questions: Is it not then the case . . .? Does it not then seem . . .? Would we not then say . . .? The entire discourse is a hypothetical one. Inasmuch as it is all based on the hypothesis of an absurd definition of death, it is equally absurd.

The absurdity is evident in the long catalog of experiences the philosopher would supposedly repudiate. It is most evident in regard to sex. Socrates asks: "It does not then seem, does it, that the philosophic person would pursue aphrodisial pleasures?" (*Phaedo*, 64D). He receives a sharp negative reply: In no way! But Socrates, as we have just seen, was famous for his amorous encounters, and earlier in this very dialogue that would repudiate sex, Xanthippe is said to be visiting Socrates with a babe in her arms (*Phaedo*, 60A). Therefore, Socrates married a woman much younger than himself and was begetting children even when he was sixty-nine years old. So much for the repudiating of Aphrodite!

The same sort of performative contradiction occurs again (*Phaedo*, 63D-E). Socrates is proposing the view that the philosopher should not postpone death but instead should embrace it as soon as lawfully possible (that is, not by suicide). Philosophy is the practice of dying, so it would be irrational of the philosopher to delay death for even one moment. In the midst of this discourse, Socrates is interrupted. The executioner warns him that by speaking so much, Socrates will warm his body and will impair the chilling action of the poison. Socrates might then need to take another dose and if that is not effective, even a third. By speaking with so much heat, Socrates is delaying death. Socrates' response is to tell the executioner to prepare all three doses, for the talking will go on. In the very midst of claiming that the philosopher would do nothing to delay death and will be speaking with better people in the other world, Socrates delays death, precisely to go on speaking with the people of this world. The exquisite irony is not lost on Crito, who says he was certain Socrates would not take the executioner's advice.

Shall we then simply dismiss the notion that for Plato philosophizing is dying, the separating of the soul? No; to philosophize is indeed to seek such a separation, but it is not the separation of the soul *from the body*. Instead, it is separation from exactly what makes the Socratic discussion of philosophy and death comical, namely, hearsay. That is the lesson of the *Phaedo*: the struggle of the soul to come into its own autonomous existence is a struggle against unexamined presuppositions, the unexamined life, taking things for granted. The body is not the prison of the soul; on the contrary, the prison is constituted by secondhand knowledge, idle talk, average everydayness, mediocrity. The prison is inauthenticity.

The soul of the philosopher needs to be dead to what "they" say, needs to release itself from thralldom to the way things are bandied about in everyday chatter. The soul comes into its own by separating itself from everyday life. That, if we read Plato carefully, is how philosophizing is dying. In other words, the Socratic method, refusal to accept the usual substitution of beings for Being, coincides with philosophizing, with separating the soul from its prison, with authentic anticipation of death. In other terms, it is exactly the practice of Socratic love: intimate, *personal* contact with a being in order to grasp the Idea reflected in that being.

For *Being and Time*, what most concretely is authentic comportment toward death? What is it to be constantly dying by choosing one's own comportment toward death? What is it to "face up" to death? As I read Heidegger, it is not at all a matter of thinking about death as such but instead is a way of understanding Dasein's existence, Dasein's relation to possibilities as most proper possibilities. It is thus a matter of intimate contact with a particular being, Dasein, and attempting to read off from it the meaning of Being in general. For Heidegger, authentic being-toward-death, anticipation, is, most concretely, a matter of pursuing phenomenological ontology.

Authentic being-toward-death is thus nothing other than what Socrates is constantly striving for, the disclosure of Being by penetrating into beings. Authentic being-toward-death is not preoccupied with death; it is preoccupied with the Being of the being who is always comporting himself or herself toward death. That is how the middle of *Being and Time* is comparable to the middle of the Platonic dialogues: the central concern is the first philosophical step, carried out in the context of death. The pursuit of philosophy, phenomenological ontology, is exactly what constitutes authentic being-toward-death.

Both Plato and Heidegger see an intrinsic bond between philosophizing and dying, but the perspective is different in each case. For Plato, to philosophize is to approach death, to release the soul from the prison constituted by everyday understanding. For Heidegger, authentic dying is philosophizing, understanding one's own death as a most proper possibility. For both Plato and Heidegger, philosophizing and authentic dying have the same opposite, namely, reliance on hearsay, and amount to the same practice, namely, wondering about the meaning of Being.

To return to the question of the wholeness, the unity, that was to be supplied by authentic being-toward-death, it follows from Heidegger's analysis that the life of philosophical thought is the most unified one. For Socrates, in order to institute wholeness in oneself, a person requires a paradigm, a prime example of something unified, something preeminently one and self-same. These paradigms are the Ideas, since, in contrast to the things that partake of them, the Ideas cannot possibly deflect from their self-sameness. Beautiful things may change and may come and go, but the Idea of beauty always is and is always the same, even if we possess only a more or less adequate grasp of that Idea. The philosopher, constantly lifting his or her gaze to the Ideas, thereby acquires something of the paradigm of unity needed to make himself or herself a unified whole. For Heidegger, everyday Dasein is dispersed into moments: past, present, and future. Everyday Dasein does not understand possibilities as most proper ones and instead takes death as outstanding and the past as over and done. Only authentic being-toward-death, philosophy, grasps these as intertwined, as unified, and thereby provides the paradigm of unity. Thus, the pursuit of philosophy attests to the possibility of grasping oneself as a whole and accordingly exhibits the possibility of interpreting the Being of the being we ourselves are and of reading off from it the meaning of Being in general. Thereby the earlier solution to the problem of grasping Dasein as a whole is shown to hold; it is not merely a theoretical solution. The transition from theory to practice is carried out in authentic being-toward-death, and the "essential deficiency" is thereby repaired.

ENDING

The Platonic dialogues and *Being and Time* end the exact same way: they reach an impasse and break off. They take the first philosophical step but stop short of the second. They distinguish Being from beings but do not proceed to the second step, the actual determination of the meaning of Being.

Some of the dialogues are altogether negative, in the sense that they merely say what Being is not, namely, not any of the beings, any of the examples offered to Socrates when he is seeking the Idea. These dialogues thereby precisely take the first step and then simply give up the search for Being. Most of the other dialogues, instead of taking the second step, end with a myth or an invocation of the gods. It would not be wholly unjustified to say that the trajectory of the Platonic dialogues in general is from the first philosophical step to myth.

The *Phaedrus*, for instance, begins with the first step and ends with Socrates offering a prayer to Pan. The *Republic* begins with the first step and ends with the myth of Er. The *Sophist* begins with the first step inasmuch as it invokes Parmenides of Elea, *the* philosopher of the difference between Being and beings, and ends by distinguishing the divine and the human workman. Many other dialogues invoke the gods at the very end or near the end. Let us look more closely at the trajectory of the *Republic*.

The *Republic* begins with Socrates' birth, his descent from Being to beings, and it ends with a myth about birth, the embodiment of the soul of Er. This myth is Socrates' own fabrication, and we can suppose he is purposely tying the end of the *Republic* to the beginning. Indeed, the name Er (Ἡρός, from ἀρόω) means "begotten," "born." Furthermore, Er is said to belong to the "tribe of Pamphylos" (γένος Παμφύλου, literally "the genus of all-phyla," the "tribe of all-nations") (*Republic*, 614B). Accordingly, the myth, just like the story of Socrates' descent to the Piraeus, is meant to have universal applicability. Er is even told that he is to be a "messenger to all mankind" (*Republic*, 614D).

The myth of Er is a demonic one, devoted mostly to the strange sights grasped by the soul of Er in the other world, prior to embodiment. The myth reaches its conclusion with the embodiment of that soul, and the crucial point is this: Er does not know how he came to be embodied, how he entered into the world (*Republic*, 621B). He merely finds himself there, in the presence of things, unable to account for how this presence came about.

Accordingly, the trajectory of the *Republic* is from a coming into the presence of the world to a myth about that coming into presence. What the myth expresses is an inability to account for the unconcealment of the world to us. We cannot say how we come into the world, how we recognize beings as beings, how we know what it means to be in general. The myth turns back to the first step and declares it to be inexplicable. Therefore, the reason the dialogues do not take the second philosophical step is that they cannot account for the first step and thus cannot move beyond it.

The presence of beings is a mystery to us; it depends on something that has to be expressed in myth, such as the myth of the prenatal grasp of the Ideas at a heavenly banquet or the myth of Er. The unconcealment of beings to us depends on something demonic, divine, something beyond our power.

The same trajectory, from the first philosophical step to myth, is also that of Heidegger's general course of thought, his path from *Being and Time* to his later philosophy. In what follows, I offer at least a guideline to the complexities of that development beyond *Being and Time*.

Heidegger's magnum opus was supposed to "work out" the question of Being. The book itself specifies the tripartite structure of any questioning, namely, an interrogation (1) of something (2) about something (3) in order to find out something (*SZ*, p. 5). *Being and Time* was to work out the question of Being by interrogating some being about its Being in order to find out the meaning of Being in general. The three parts of the structure of questioning correspond to the three divisions of Part One of the treatise. The first division chooses the proper being to interrogate, Dasein. The second division interprets the Being of Dasein, and the third division was to read off the meaning of Being in general. The treatise stops with the completion of the second division.

The successive editions of *Being and Time* for twenty-five years announced on the title page: "First half." That designation was then abandoned, since what the missing part would offer could no longer be attached to the treatise as it stood. It would not be the second half of that particular first half. Yet, for Heidegger, the path of *Being and Time* remains necessary in order to stir up in us the question of Being. Thus, *Being and Time* raises the proper question but leads in the wrong direction. The question of Being remains; the projected answer is untenable. *Being and Time* is valid in taking the first philosophical step but not in the projected second step. Twenty-five years of thinking made it more and more evident that the second step, the determination of the meaning of Being in general, would not be what it was projected to be.

The Being of Dasein, existence, has to do with possibilities: Dasein's possibilities are most proper ones. It could be said that existence refers to Dasein's peculiar way of aging. We are not too old for our past actualities nor too young for our future possibilities. Past actualities are still present possibilities, and future possibilities are already present actualities. Our aging, our existence, is such that our past, our future, and our present are thoroughly tangled together; these are not outside one another but, quite to the contrary, are unified, preeminently in authenticity.

What then is the *meaning* of existence, the meaning of the Being of Dasein? In other words, how does *Being and Time*, in its second division, interpret the Being of Dasein? For Heidegger, to ask about the meaning of something is to ask for that upon which it must be projected in order to be comprehensible (*SZ*, p. 151). Existence, the peculiar relation of Dasein to possibilities, Dasein's peculiar present relation to past possibilities and to future possibilities, is made comprehensible by projecting Dasein onto time. Dasein's existence is comprehensible only if Dasein has a peculiar tangled relation to past, present, and future. This peculiar relation is what Heidegger calls Dasein's "temporality," *Zeitlichkeit*. So temporality is the meaning of the being who asks the question of Being.

The third division of *Being and Time* would read off from temporality the meaning of Being in general. Heidegger proposes that that meaning would also have to do with time. But it would be a distinct sort of time, given a

distinct time-name, not *Zeitlichkeit*, but *Temporalität*.[20] The task of fundamental ontology, namely, the interpretation of Being as such, consists in
"working out the *Temporalität* of Being" (*SZ*, p. 19) Only an exposition of the
problematic of *Temporalität* will provide the "concrete answer" (*SZ*, p. 19) to
the question of the meaning of Being. The transition from the second to the
third division of Part One was to have been a transition from *Zeitlichkeit* (the
time of Dasein) to *Temporalität* (the time of Being).

The transition was never carried out. The book was left unfinished, and
nothing in Heidegger's later philosophy corresponds to the projected third
division, an interpretation of Being as fundamentally time. Heidegger does
not say explicitly why the meaning of Being cannot be understood as time,
not even as the peculiar time called *Temporalität*. Could it be because such an
interpretation of Being would amount to storytelling? It would be doing what
the "muses" mentioned by the Stranger in the *Sophist* proposed: reducing
Being to some particular being. Instead of water or air, this being would be a
most peculiar one, time. But such a reduction would still be treating us like
children and would amount to an undoing of the first philosophical step. It
would disrespect the ontological difference by using a being, time, to explain
Being. It would indeed provide a "concrete" answer to the question of the
meaning of Being. But any concrete answer to this question is storytelling.

A concrete answer would dispel the perplexity regarding the meaning of
Being. Heidegger's philosophical progression from *Being and Time* onward
is the opposite, an enhancing of the perplexity. He makes Being more enigmatic, not more concrete. Heidegger's later philosophy is aimed precisely
at calling attention to the mysteriousness of Being, the inexplicability of the
presence to us of the light by which we recognize beings as beings. That is
why he employs what has to be called mythological language. Such language
is an *asylum ignorantiae*; it is resorting to fable out of exasperation. Being
is so uncanny that it is wiser to call attention to our ignorance by resorting to myth than to suppose we could offer a rational explanation. Thus,
Heidegger's later philosophy corresponds to the myth involved in the theory
of recollection or to the myth of Er: an attempt to explain the disclosure of the
world to us, our recognition of beings as beings, but an attempt so outlandish
as to call attention to the fact that this disclosure cannot be explained. All we
can do is wonder at it.

Heidegger's mythological talk amounts to his committing the pathetic fallacy. The overriding misplaced pathos is the central enigma of Heidegger's
later philosophy, the so-called "history of Being." Heidegger speaks of
Being itself as having a history; *on its own initiative*, Being shows itself to
us more clearly or withdraws more and more. That is the history of Being,
and for Heidegger it is history properly so called. The self-showing and self-
withdrawing of Being are *the* events, and they motivate the corresponding

human epochs: the relatively clear self-showing of Being sends on its way the ancient epoch, and the relative withdrawal of Being, whereby we are granted a less and less adequate understanding of what it means to be, destines the current technological epoch. Or Heidegger will say that truth is a goddess, one who unveils herself to us more or less. Truth itself is given a new name: "unconcealment." Heidegger emphasizes the negativity and passivity in this name; unconcealment is not something we humans accomplish but instead is something granted *to* us. Accordingly, for the later Heidegger, the beings we ourselves are, Dasein, should not be understood, in the manner of *Being and Time*, as *disclosers* of the meaning of Being but as ones to whom that meaning *is* disclosed. Thereby Dasein is most properly understood as shepherd, steward, preserver.[21] Or again, Heidegger comes to agree with Parmenides that Being and thinking are the same. Heidegger, however, understands this identity in his own way as appropriation: Being appropriates our thinking. We understand what it means to be because we think in accord with the way Being shows itself, the way Being appropriates our outlook on what it means to be in general. Our thinking is a *response* to something that claims us. The philosopher does not take up the topic of Being; on the contrary, Being takes up the philosopher, just as the goddess Aletheia took Parmenides by the right hand. Or, to choose a final example, Heidegger calls Being a clearing, the lighted space we step into which allows us to see beings. But the clearing is not something we accomplish; it *grants itself* to us, and the degree of clarity is primarily in the hands of that which does the granting.

All of these instances of the pathetic fallacy, misplaced attributions of intentions and actions, are versions of the first, the attribution of a history to Being. Furthermore, the pathetic fallacy is a version of myth, and all myths draw our attention to something inexplicable, something demonic and beyond our power. Accordingly, the trajectory of Heidegger's philosophy is the same as that of the dialogues: they end the same way by progressing from the first philosophical step to myth, from the first step to an explanation of that step which is not an explanation at all but an enhancing of its mystery.

Heidegger's trajectory is not from the first step to the second but to myth as an expression of perplexity, an expression of wonder about the first step. It is the trajectory of the Platonic dialogues and also the trajectory of Socrates' personal itinerary as a philosopher.

In the *Phaedo*, a few moments before he calmly drains the bitter cup, Socrates looks back on his philosophical itinerary. He says it began when he tried to learn the causes of things and was dissatisfied with the extant answers. These were the answers proposed by "muses," as the Stranger calls them. The causes were said to be "air, the ether, water, and many other such ἄτοπα" (*Phaedo*, 98C). Socrates recognizes these as *átopa*, "things badly placed." These causes place a being on the level of Being, reduce Being to a being.

Socrates' recognition of these as *átopa* means he began with the ontological difference, the first philosophical step. But the ending is not the second step. Earlier in the *Phaedo*, Socrates tells his friends what has been occupying him in prison while awaiting his delayed execution (delayed because of an Athenian religious observance). What he finds most fitting for him to pursue at the end of an itinerary that began with the first philosophical step is not to venture the second step but to mythologize, μυθολογεῖν (*Phaedo*, 61E).

CONCLUSION: *BEING AND TIME*
AND PLATO'S *SOPHIST*

If *Being and Time*, in its beginning, middle, and end, can be likened to a Platonic dialogue, then it can be likened especially to the one invoked by the epigraph, namely, the *Sophist*. Just as, for Heidegger, the asking of the question of Being leads inexorably to the problematic of death and to philosophy itself as authentic being-toward-death, so everything in the *Sophist* turns on the relation between the question of Being and the determination of the genuine philosopher:

> In the *Sophist*, Plato considers existence in one of its most extreme possibilities, namely, philosophical life. Specifically, Plato shows indirectly who the authentic philosopher is by displaying who the sophist is. And he does not show this by setting up an empty program, that is, by saying what one would have to do to be a philosopher; on the contrary, he shows it by actually philosophizing. For one can say who the sophist is as the true non-philosopher only by actually living in philosophy. Thus it happens that this dialogue manifests a peculiar intertwining of Being and philosophy. Precisely on the path of a reflection on the Being of beings, Plato interprets the sophist, and thus the philosopher, in their existence.[22]

If we recall that in this case the genuine philosopher to be differentiated from the sophist is one who is listening in his jail cell with a sentence of death over his head, then the likening of *Being and Time* to the *Sophist* is complete.

Chapter 2

Signs and Mortality

PHENOMENAL ATTESTATION THAT
THE WORLD IS A COSMOS

As does Hegel at every step of the dialectic, Heidegger stresses the necessity for the assertions of the reflecting philosopher to find attestation in pre-reflective experience. In the terms Heidegger employs in *Being and Time*, the distinction at issue is that between the phenomenological (*phänomenologisch*) and the phenomenal (*phänomenal*).[1] Any self-showing is a phenomenon, but things as they show themselves phenomenologically, to the phenomenological philosopher, may be mere semblance—unless they are also disclosed in the same way phenomenally, that is, disclosed to everyday experience, to practical engagement with things and not simply to the reflective gaze. Everyday Dasein—right in midst of his or her practical preoccupation with things—must sense, at least to some extent, the structures made explicit in phenomenological philosophizing. What the reflecting philosopher sees while taking distance from practical experience must also be seen by pre-reflective Dasein while immersed in practical experience.

Consider the structure of the world.[2] For the philosophical reflections of *Being and Time*, the world is a cosmos in the Greek sense. The κόσμος is indeed the whole, everything taken together, but the focus of the Greek term is not the whole but the togetherness. The cosmos is a *well-ordered* whole. Thus, the opposite of the cosmos is not nothingness; the opposite is chaos. The cosmetician is for the Greeks the hairdresser, the one who arranges hair beautifully. And the opposite of ordered hair is not baldness but is dishevelment, messy hair. The general is also called a cosmetician: the one who arranges troops in well-ordered battle formation. By extension, the world as a whole is a cosmos, not simply everything that in some way or other avoids nonbeing and not simply what is all-encompassing, the context for everything; instead, the cosmos is the *beautiful arrangement* of everything.

The Latin term for world, *mundus*, corresponds exactly to cosmos. The basic meaning of *mundus* is "neatness," "elegance," and only by extension is it applied to the world, in virtue of the splendid order of everything in the universe.

In *Being and Time*, Heidegger expresses an understanding of the world as an ordered whole not by using the terms κόσμος and *mundus* but by devising synonyms for them: relational totality, equipmental totality, referential structure, involvement, significance. All of these designate the world as an ordered whole, a totality wherein the parts are well arranged, are assigned to one another and fitted together.

Despite what might seem a morbid cloud hovering over *Being and Time*, in virtue of the prominence of the themes of death, guilt, and anxiety, the primary experience according to Heidegger is a positive one: an understanding that the things of the world hang together, that the world is in joint. The world is of course not in perfect order, not a perfect cosmos. But for Heidegger the disorder stands out from a more general background of order, not vice versa.

Indeed Heidegger does emphasize the negative. He appreciates the negative even more than did Hegel, appreciates it for its disclosive power. For example, as was mentioned earlier, Heidegger's word for truth in the primordial sense, the sense of the Greek *alētheia*, is "unconcealment." Heidegger is constantly calling our attention to the negative, the concealment. For something to appear, it must overcome a prior concealment, must step out of a previous darkness. Yet, what is most important for Heidegger is not the negative as such but the fact that we humans are not the ones who overcome this prior concealment and darkness. We have no capacity to do so; on the contrary, that overcoming is a gift to us. We can deal with things in the light, but the fact that things are illuminated at all is not in our power. We have some control over present things, but their presence as such is not in our control. So the emphasis on the negative is meant to inculcate a sense of piety toward something that has gifted us with the presence of things.

In regard to the world in general, for Heidegger our first experience is one of an ordered whole, although it might initially be a weak whole, vague as to details and indeterminate in content. Yet again what is most important is that we humans did not bring this order out of chaos. The ordering has already been done for us; it is a gift to us. Heidegger is calling on us to respect what has given us this gift, although he does not say who or what this giver is. Nevertheless, Heidegger's philosophy is basically a positive, optimistic philosophy, not a morbid one.

Accordingly, Heidegger's emphasis on being-toward-death must be placed in context. For Heidegger the primary experience is not death, disintegration, negativity; on the contrary, the disintegration stands out against a previous background of integration. The first experience is not that of fragments, which are then built up into a whole; instead, what comes first in experience is the wholeness from which the fragments are broken off. In Heidegger's terms, the "worldhood of the world," the vague, global sense that things fit together, is prior to any experience of particular things fitting together. If death is the experience of disintegration, of our world falling apart and falling out of our grasp, then that is possible only because of a prior experience of the world as integrated, as holding together, as in our grasp. But what is the phenomenal evidence that the world is experienced as a cosmos? And how does the negative experience of death arise in contrast? Those are the questions I address in this chapter.

Phenomenal evidence means disclosure to everyday practical Dasein. How then is the world as cosmos supposed to be brought home to such Dasein? Practical Dasein concerns himself or herself with the task at hand and does not stop to reflect on the structure of the world in which he or she is immersed. So how is the world as an integrated whole brought to light for everyday Dasein? How does this Dasein, precisely in the midst of his or her preoccupation with practical affairs, sense that the world is a cosmos, that all things hang together? Heidegger finds the phenomenal evidence in two everyday situations: the ordered totality is lit up to everyday Dasein through the breakdown of the usual relations among use-objects and also through the experience of signs.

I wish to take a fresh look at Heidegger's analyses. Despite almost 100 years of commentary on them, I do not believe they have been exhausted, and I hope to bring out something still latent in them. I will also expand the analyses by adding new phenomenal evidence, tied to price tags. Finally, I will ask whether the experience of an integrated world does not in fact make the atmosphere of mortality more stifling—indeed all the more stifling as that integration approaches perfection.

TOOLS AS CONSPICUOUS, OBTRUSIVE, OBSTINATE

Let us begin with the first way of disclosure mentioned by Heidegger. It is a lighting up of the cosmos, the ordered totality, through a disturbance in the relations among use-objects (tools, gear, equipment). To repeat, Heidegger, the reflecting philosopher, is looking for a motive in the midst of practical dealings that would make the world as a whole stand out to the very one who is dealing with things practically. Heidegger wants to appeal to practical experience, and so he proceeds by way of examples. They all have to do with hammers and nails, either those wielded by the shoemaker or the carpenter.

The crux of the problem is that the cobbler (or carpenter) is submerged in his or her work and does not even attend to the tools he or she wields, let alone to the totality of references in which the tools are involved. What then could motivate the cobbler to step back from practical preoccupation and come to the verge of theory, that is, to look directly upon the relations between hammers and nails instead of taking those relations for granted?

Heidegger discovers the motive in unusual, although by no means rare, occurrences, namely, negative ones: things do not always run smoothly. The well-ordered totality breaks down at times, the relations among things become disrupted, the assignments of one part of the world to another get thrown out of joint. These negative experiences harbor the disclosure of something positive; the breakdown of the assignments constitutive of the world calls attention to those very assignments. The order that is now missing becomes palpable by its absence.

Heidegger discusses three sorts of cases (*SZ*, pp. 72–76). First, the worker may encounter something unusable: a damaged tool or some unsuitable material. The immediate consequence, in Heidegger's terms, is that the equipment becomes "conspicuous," which is to say that it calls itself to our attention and we are forced to gaze on it in a radically new way.

The term "conspicuous" designates very well the new way of gazing, for ordinarily tools are just the opposite: they are transparent. The skilled worker attends to the work and not to the tool. The tool is as transparent as the hand. Just as a normal person does not attend to the hands while working or to the tongue while talking or to the feet while dancing, so do tools become incorporated into the body and share its transparency.

From an objectivistic perspective, such as that of Aristotle (*De Anima*, 432a1–2), the hand is a tool, admittedly the innermost tool, the first tool, the tool that uses other tools, but nevertheless is on the side of external objects. The subject, the user of the tool, is further inward, the soul. From a phenomenological perspective, the hand is not innermost tool; on the contrary, the tool is the outermost hand. The tool, as well as the hand, is on the side of the subject. No normal person wields his or her own hand as a tool, one that could be misplaced, for instance, and skilled workers even wield very complex tools as hands. Tools and hands are transparent; they are overlooked in favor of the work to be done.

What happens when hands are injured or tools break? We then gaze on them as foreign objects. That is, they lose their transparency and we look on them in terms of their physical properties. We look on them not as use-objects but as sheer physical things with physical properties or, in Heidegger's terminology, not as ready-to-hand but instead as present-at-hand.

Heidegger brings up two other sorts of disturbances to the usual order in the equipmental totality. An item of equipment may be missing or may be in the way. If the hammer is missing, then its counterparts, the nails, become *obtrusive*. They force themselves on our attention under the guise of inert matter simply lying there. If the hammer is in the way, blocking access to some other item of equipment, then the hammer becomes *obstinate*. It loses its transparency and forces us to deal with it in a new way; it looks unruly and instead of wielding it we must transport it as dead weight to some other location in objective space.

What is the point? What is disclosed to everyday Dasein in these common negative experiences? According to Heidegger, what is brought home to Dasein is not simply the fact that tools are *also* present-at-hand objects and thus are usually ready-to-hand. That would not be the disclosure of a cosmos. What is disclosed rather is that tools are interconnected with other items of equipment. What is most important in the negative experiences is the disruption of the *relations* among the items of equipment.

Consequently, from a Heideggerian perspective the most disclosive negative experience is not, as is commonly thought, the encounter with the *broken* hammer. For the most part, this experience brings home to Dasein only the circumstance that the hammer is usually transparent rather than conspicuous. Heidegger stresses that the broken hammer is not fully displaced into the realm of the present-at-hand. The broken hammer remains ready-to-hand; as a result, Heidegger sees this experience as announcing only a *tension* in the relations between the hammer and the nails and not a full disruption. The more radical negative experiences, and thus the more disclosive ones, are the other two, those of obtrusiveness and obstinacy.

In these latter experiences of a full displacement of the ready-to-hand into the present-at-hand, what is disturbed, and thereby illuminated, is the *relation* between the hammer and the other items of equipment. Indeed the purest case is the one of the *missing* hammer, for then it is expressly the nails that obtrude on our attention and not simply some item of equipment or other, as in the case of the hammer that is obstinate. The hammer in the way could not be experienced as blocking access to nails, for the hammer has to be picked up in order to use the nails. A hammer resting on top of nails would not be experienced as obstinate but precisely as ready-to-hand. The obstinate hammer must be blocking access to something else, such as nuts and bolts.

It is the *missing* hammer, not the obstinate one and certainly not the conspicuous one, that highlights the relation between the hammer and its proper counterpart, the nails. The obtrusive nails then disclose not simply that items of equipment belong together, that they form a whole; on the contrary, what is now lit up is the fact that this is a *well-ordered* whole. At least marginally intruding upon the gaze of everyday Dasein on account of the absence of the needed hammer is now something previously taken for granted, the beautiful arrangement of the whole, the way all the parts of the world fit together: hammers with nails, nails with leather, leather with ranching, ranching with barbed wire, barbed wire with blast furnaces to convert iron ore into steel, and so forth.

Accordingly, Heidegger has found the evidence he was seeking. What is disclosed by the negative experiences (especially by the missing hammer), called to the attention of everyday Dasein in the very course of his or her practical dealings, that is to say, disclosed phenomenally and not merely phenomenologically, seen close up by everyday pre-reflective Dasein and not merely at a distance by the reflecting philosopher, is that the world is a cosmos.

TOOLS AS OSTENTATIOUS

Heidegger does not claim the three sorts of disturbances he mentions are the only ones throwing out of joint the ordered relations among use-objects. Indeed there are no doubt many other motives in everyday experience to look on equipment and tools wrenched from their normal context and to focus on their present-at-hand properties. I wish to bring up one other such motive, whereby use-objects are disclosed not as conspicuous, obtrusive, or obstinate, but as ostentatious.

It is by no means a rare experience for a worker to need to shop for a new tool. Nevertheless, shopping is a disruption of the relations constitutive of the work world, for the tools on display in a store are removed from the totality of their involvements with other items of equipment. We do not reach for a hammer on display in order to drive nails with it. On the contrary, we focus on the physical properties of the hammer. We consider the shape, size, mass, and material of the hammer, all of which we overlook when actually wielding the hammer in the course of work. So the hammer on display is something present-at-hand.

Yet we do evaluate that hammer in terms of our specific needs. In other words, what sort of nails will the hammer be assigned to? The nail used in cobbling shoes is different from the one used by a carpenter in framing a house. The respective hammer will need to have its own distinctive size and heft. The nail also dictates the shape of the hammer: cross peen for the cobbler, claw peen for the carpenter. The nail dictates the material of the hammer as well. The tiny nail of the cobbler requires a hammer made such as to maximize precision, the large nail of carpenter calls for a hammer that maximizes force. Therefore, the cobbler's hammer will have a bare handle in order to transmit feeling to the user's fingers, and the handle of the framing hammer will be wrapped in order to dampen shock. The nail may even dictate the magnetic properties of the hammer. The cobbler's nail is of brass, the carpenter's of steel. Accordingly, carpenters may at times profit from a hammer with a magnetized head, whereas such a hammer would be of no use to the cobbler.

A comparable analysis could be carried out in regard to shopping for nails. The choice of nails is dictated by the material to be nailed, which in turn is dictated by the thing to be built, which is ultimately dictated by that for the sake of which the hammering is done in the first place, namely, the satisfying of some interest of Dasein, such as the desire to live in a house sheltered from the elements or to walk on rough ground without injuring the feet. Thus, nails in a store are present-at-hand things evaluated in terms of the role they will play in a practical context.

The point of mentioning all these relations between hammers and nails and other equipment is that they are relations taken for granted in the workplace but made the focus of concern in the store. Shopping for tools thus lights up the referential structure as a whole. Shopping is a motive, within everyday practical experience, to come to the verge of theory and look directly upon the ordered references of one part of the world to another. The common experience of shopping, therefore, provides phenomenal evidence to everyday practical Dasein that the world is a cosmos.

The hammers on sale in a store also announce a vastly different context of tools, beyond their references to other tools. It is a context indeed always present in the workplace but only remotely sensed there as a far horizon. It is the context of financial commerce. The hammers on display in a store do not simply hang there as unembellished tools. On the contrary, they are attractively packaged and pretentiously advertised.

The tools all bear a brand name, and the various brands compete for sales. Therefore, tools in a store are not simply displayed; they are touted. Each manufacturer sings the praises of its own tools and even gives the tools grandiloquent names. What is to all appearances an electric drill as sold by Milwaukee Tools is not actually a drill; it is a "Magnum hole shooter."

Everything about an item of equipment on display in a store is meant to catch the eye and to persuade. A worker may want a tool in a workshop to stand out prominently, so he or she does not need to fumble for it. But in a store a tool is made prominent not for the sake of ease of use but only in order to be more readily sold.

The tool grasped in order to wield it is not the same as the tool picked up in order to buy it. The first is something ready-to-hand, transparent, overlooked in favor of the task. The latter is something present-at-hand, focused on for itself as a physical object. Comparable to the case of the broken, missing, or obstructing tool, the one in the store is a present-at-hand object; the difference is that there is nothing wrong with this present-at-hand object. On the contrary, it is—or at least is touted as—an ideal example of what the tool should be. As does a broken tool, the tool on display forces itself on our attention, but it does so as something attractive rather than disagreeable, something that will make the work fly rather than disturb it. A tool in the store, dressed to the nines and praised to the skies, is—as I would call it—ostentatious.

The ostentatious tool announces not only the referential totality of other tools but also a more encompassing economic world. The reason is that tools in a store always bear a peculiar sign, the price tag. The price of something is colloquially called the "bad news." But in a store, even the price is attractive and ostentatious. For the price tag is not simply a ready-to-hand thing carrying useful information about the cost. In a store, the price tag is placed in a context of persuasive salesmanship. That is why prices on a tag in a store are invariably preceded by the word "only" and succeeded by at least two exclamation points.

The price tag does not merely supply information about the number of dollars that will be accepted by the store in exchange. The tag, situated within all the advertising, also attempts to persuade the prospective buyer that he or she will in fact be saving money by purchasing this tool rather than another. No matter what its price, the tool will lead to increased profits. The price tag thus places the tool in a context wider than that of the relation of one item of equipment to another. It places the tool within that art which, according to Socrates, all artisans practice in addition to their own proper art. This additional art is the one Socrates calls the "money-making art" (*Republic*, 346C).

The price tag is therefore not merely one thing pointing to another thing, the wallet; on the contrary, it also invokes a whole context that surrounds all work, the encompassing economic world. Therefore, the theme of price tags leads to the other way—besides the breakdown of the usual functioning of tools—in which, according to Heidegger, the cosmos is illuminated phenomenally, that is, lit up for everyday practical Dasein, namely: through the experience of signs.

SIGNS

The section on signs in *Being and Time* (Part One, First Division, Chapter III, §17) is one of the most tortuous discussions in the entire treatise. Let us try to make our way through the tangle.

Heidegger notes that there is a twofold referential structure involved in signs. Like any other item of equipment, signs are referred to some useful task. Signs possess an in-order-to, a usefulness, a serviceability. In this way, signs merely fulfill the ontological structure of any tool or item of gear. The complication is that the useful task of signs is itself to refer. Signs fulfill the task they are referred to by referring in turn. But these two referrings are not the same. This constitutes a first complication. The second is that signs, more than other tools, refer not merely to some other item of equipment but instead point to the referential structure as a whole. The title of this section 17 of *Being and Time* is "Reference and Signs," and the most problematic word in the title is "and." Just how are references intertwined with signs?

Let us begin by taking up the first complication, the distinction between the two ways of referring. The sign is referred to its task differently than the way the sign itself refers to something. The sign refers in the specific mode of "indicating." Thus, Heidegger says in a typically abstruse passage from this section: "Every reference is a relation, but not every relation is a reference. Every 'indication' is a reference, but not every referring is an indicating. It follows then that every 'indication' is a relation, but not every relating is an indicating" (*SZ*, p. 77).

To make sense of this, we need to gather from Heidegger's text the exact meaning he is giving to the terms "relation," "reference," and "indication." "Relation" (*Beziehung*) is the general term and applies to the "going together" (*Zusammenhängen*) of two things in any way at all, no matter how intrinsically or extrinsically. The cause is in a relation to the effect, but so is the tangent to the circle. "Reference" (*Verweisung*) is the peculiar going together characteristic of tools or equipment. A synonym Heidegger introduces in this section is "serviceability." All tools are serviceable for something; that is how tools refer. "Indicating" (*Anzeigen*) is the peculiar serviceability of signs (*Zeichen*); signs refer by indicating. Thus, in paraphrase, the quoted passage runs as follows. "Every way an item of equipment is serviceable for something constitutes an instance of a relation, but not every way two things go together is a matter of one being serviceable to the other. Every indicating is a way an item of equipment is serviceable for something, namely, by referring to it, but not all serviceability is by way of the indicating performed by signs. It follows then that every indication through signs is a way two things are related, but not every relating of two things is a matter of one indicating the other by a sign."

So Heidegger is saying that a sign, as an item of equipment, is referred to some task, is put in service to some task. That task is to refer, by way of indication, to something else. But this latter referring, the indicating, is not a serviceability; it is merely a pointing out. A tool such as a hammer refers to nails by way of serviceability; the hammer serves to drive the nails. But a sign pointing to nails is not in service to the nails. The sign is in service to whoever wants to have the nails pointed out, and the sign performs this service merely by showing the way to the nails. Indeed this may be a necessary function, since no one can hammer nails if he or she cannot find them. But the showing of the way is a different sort of referring than is the hammering. Thus, there are two referrings at play in signs: the referring done *to* the sign (its assigned serviceability), and referring done *by* the sign (its pointing something out). These referrings are not the same; the first is characteristic of all equipment, signs included, the second is peculiar to signs.

Heidegger's example has to do with driving a car. Specifically, the example is the "red pivoting arrow" which indicates, for instance at an intersection, the path the car will take. The position of the arrow is controlled by the driver, but Heidegger notes that it is ready-to-hand equipment not only for the driver, the one concerned with steering the car, but also for the other drivers sharing the road. These others make use of the equipment they see deployed and either move to the other side or stop. As an item of equipment, the directional arrow is constituted through reference. It has the character of an in-order-to, a particular serviceability; it is in order to indicate. The indicating of the sign can be understood as a "referring." But then it must be stipulated that this referring as indicating is not the one of the "ontological structure of the sign as equipment" (*SZ*, p. 78).

The ontological structure of the sign as equipment is a matter of being referred to some task. The referring as the indicating performed by the sign is not to refer something else to some task but merely to point to that something.

Let us extend Heidegger's example and consider the directional arrow and also the steering wheel. Both the wheel and the arrow are related to the heading of the car. And they also both *refer* to the heading. But they refer to it in two different ways. The steering wheel refers in the way of all equipment, namely, by being in service to the heading; the steering wheel is there in order to change the heading. The arrow refers only in the way peculiar to signs, namely, by indicating the heading. The task of the steering wheel is to change the heading, the task of the arrow to indicate the heading. If this indicating can also be understood as a "referring," then two distinct referrings are operative in signs.

The distinction can be seen in the fact that the referring constitutive of equipment assigns a task to something; the steering wheel assigns a task to the steering mechanism. But the referring constitutive of indication is not the assignment of a task; the arrow does not assign any task to the steering mechanism. Yet, even here, a complication sets in, implicit in Heidegger's statement that the indication performed by the arrow is especially useful to the *other* drivers. Those drivers either get out of the way or stop. In other words, the arrow does assign a task to the other drivers. They do not merely look on the arrow as providing neutral information. They need to act on this information. Consequently, even the sign engages further tasks and therefore does also refer in the way constitutive of all equipment.

This complication leads to the second one mentioned above, namely: the sign is not simply one thing referring to another, one item of equipment pointing to another, but instead is an item of equipment pointing to the equipmental structure as a whole. The experience of signs, of any sign, illuminates the hanging together of all things and is therefore phenomenal evidence that the world is a cosmos.

Heidegger's statement is as follows. He maintains that a sign is not merely a thing that stands to another thing in an indicational relation. Instead, a sign is an item of equipment that "explicitly" raises to circumspection the equipmental totality, whereby *"the ready-to-hand world announces itself as an integrated whole"* (*SZ*, p. 80). Although Heidegger here uses the term "explicitly," he does not mean this circumspection of the equipmental totality is clear and full. In other passages on the same pages as the quotation, he says the view of the whole offered by signs is merely a survey, is not an actual grasping, and may be altogether indefinite. Therefore, signs offer only a *glimpse* of the cosmos, as do unusable tools, but the question is how signs offer any view of the whole at all.

Let us take an example correlated to Heidegger's, an example from the domain of driving a car. Consider a stop sign. A Heideggerian analysis would proceed along the following lines. The sign at the intersection and the brake pedal at the disposal of the driver are both related to the stopping of the car. They both refer to the stopping but do so in different ways. The pedal is assigned the task of bringing the car to a stop, whereas the sign has the task of telling the driver it is time to press on the pedal and engage the braking mechanism so as to make the car stop. Bringing a massive car to a halt is not like stopping a child's wagon or a sled. One cannot simply extend a foot and scrape it along the ground. The driver is aware, at least in the back of his or her mind, that a great deal of force is required to stop a car. Yet, the driver will merely apply a small amount of pressure to the pedal. Nor is this pressing down on the pedal in a natural relation to the stopping, since pressing on the adjacent pedal has the opposite effect of accelerating the car. Accordingly, the driver has some sense that a very complicated artificial connection has been instituted between the pedal and the stopping. The driver might be totally ignorant of master cylinders and of the hydraulic system involved in the braking mechanism, but he or she is aware that some complicated mechanism or other is in play multiplying the force exerted on the pedal and distributing it to the wheels. The driver is aware that the brake pedal is assigned a task and that the pedal will in turn assign other items of equipment other tasks until the desired result is achieved. The driver thereby glimpses that things in the car hang together and form an ordered totality.

Furthermore, the order continues on beyond the car and its braking mechanism. The stop sign tells the driver not only that it is time to press on the brake pedal but also that vehicular traffic as a whole is a regulated system and that this system occurs within a larger system comprising all possible travel destinations and all the reasons for traveling to them. And travel exists within a more comprehensive system that constitutes modern life as such. Consequently, the organization of the entire world looms on the horizon of the stop sign. In other words, that is, in Heidegger's words, the sign is not merely one thing pointing to another thing, the brake pedal, but instead is an item of equipment that announces the entire ready-to-hand world as an integrated whole.

Could not reflection on any tool make the same announcement? Does not any item of equipment offer circumspection of the equipmental nexus? No doubt; yet, Heidegger claims, "A need for signs is pregiven" (*SZ*, p. 108). Although he does not spell out the reason, it is plain. Whereas there is no motive to reflect on the equipmental nexus in the ordinary course of work, the sign, even when practical affairs are proceeding smoothly, as usual, does offer such a motive. Quite apart from any malfunction in the braking system, the stop sign brings to explicit circumspection the linkage between the brake pedal and the stopping mechanism. Phenomenal evidence is supposed to be disclosure to everyday Dasein right in the midst of his or her practical preoccupations. Malfunctioning equipment motivates a change in attitude: from the everyday practical attitude to a reflective theoretical one. So the referential totality is thereby disclosed, strictly speaking, *outside* of the practical attitude. On the other hand, signs offer a disclosure of the totality without disturbing the practical preoccupation of every Dasein. The broken hammer suspends Dasein's activity of cobbling; traffic signs do not take Dasein's attention away from driving. The disclosure of the referential nexus by way of signs occurs *within* the practical attitude, on the margin of it, but still within it. Therefore, it is rather in signs, more than, as is commonly thought, in unusable equipment, that is to be found what Heidegger seeks, phenomenal attestation to the world as a cosmos.

Does any sign at all have power to illuminate a ready-to-hand structural whole? The question of whether the Heideggerian analysis can be applied to any sign whatever is an empirical one. It could be answered affirmatively only by way of induction, that is, by considering all the signs that ever existed. Wincing from this impossible task, let us consider instead only a few examples, taken from a neutral source.

Husserl considers indicational signs in the first investigation of the *Logical Investigations*.[3] His examples are meant to be as varied as possible and include the brand of a slave, the flag of a nation, the canals on Mars as signs of intelligent Martians, memory aids such as the knot in a handkerchief, fossils as signs of antediluvian life, public memorials, and characteristic marks. Surely not even one of these signs is an instance of a thing merely pointing to another thing. The brand draws attention to the entire institution of slavery; the flag recalls the complex whole which is the nation; the canals on Mars, if taken as signs of intelligence, make us envision the intelligent construction of the canals by the Martians; the knot in the handkerchief, said to be "popular" (*beliebt*) by Husserl and also mentioned by Heidegger (*SZ*, p. 81), is a sign not simply of some thing but of the need to go to the store and buy that thing on the way home; fossils light up the complexity in the propagation of life; public memorials memorialize not merely some person but the accomplishments or heroic deeds of that person; and characteristic marks such as scars or birthmarks do not simply point to the person bearing the mark but also bring to mind the complex circumstances which produced the mark. Just as any thing is complicated and involved in a wide range of relationships, so the sign pointing to the thing will also allow a glimpse, even if only by survey and altogether indefinitely, of all those relationships. On the horizon of every sign is the cosmos.

In summary, a sign for Heidegger is not merely one thing pointing to another. Every sign opens out onto the entire equipmental context which is the cosmos, the world as such. Another name for this integrated whole, as was mentioned above, is the "worldhood of the world." This worldhood is not something external to Dasein. Dasein is not an isolated subject requiring some sort of bridge in order to escape from interiority and make contact with outer things. For Heidegger, the worldhood of the world is an essential moment of the Being of Dasein. Heidegger makes the intrinsic connection between Dasein and world explicit in his discussion of anxiety. Anxiety also opens up the worldhood of the world and so is disclosive of the Being of Dasein (see below, p. 65). But the same connection is in play already here in regard to signs. Accordingly, for Heidegger it is insufficient to say that a sign is not merely one thing pointing to another or even to the world as a whole; more than that, the experience of signs is an encounter with the Being of Dasein.

BARCODES

In our electronic age, things are more interconnected than ever. Let us then consider a typically modern sign and the modern way of responding to it. The sign is the modern price tag, namely, the barcode affixed to an article for sale, and the corresponding response is to pay by credit card.

The numbers on an old price tag are not merely signs pointing to a certain amount of cash. As was mentioned, those numbers open out onto the whole world of financial dealings, even if the medium of exchange is currency and coins. Afortiori, today's barcode is not simply one thing pointing to another. Even to an external gaze, without knowing what the barcode means, this sign looks like something artificially produced and deriving from unknown but complicated devices. A handwritten or typed price tag, viewed simply as a sign, already points to the ink and pen or the printer that produced it. In turn, ink and pen and printer have their wider horizons, expanding out to the cosmos as a whole. The barcode has the same horizons; due to its unintelligible provenance, however, the barcode raises those horizons to explicit circumspection. The circumspection remains altogether indefinite, and everyday Dasein has only some vague sense of how the barcode is produced and how it can mean anything. But this vague sense includes amazement. The price tag with a barcode is much more amazing than a tag with handwriting. The amazement leads to explicit circumspection of the whole electronic world to which the barcode points. No one is amazed that a handwritten price tag points to ink and paper and to the outer horizons of ink and paper, and so there is no motive to pay those horizons any heed. But the unintelligible interrelations of the electronic world make them all the more striking.

Clerks in stores nowadays no longer ask, "cash or plastic?" Almost everyone pays with a credit card, except for those who pay by smartphone. To swipe a credit card or to scan a smartphone is to engage a most mysterious chain of events. Very few persons, if any, could say exactly what connects the swiping of one's card and the balance in one's bank account. Yet, everyone knows that this indirect connection is highly efficient and free of error. The clerk is much more likely to make a mistake giving change for cash than the electronic processes are prone to error. The ready-to-hand world today is an electronic world rather than a mechanical one and is much more of an integrated whole. The concatenation of assignments from one part of the electronic world to the other has become flawless. A typewriter platen would at times move two spaces when the typist struck the space bar once; a word processing keyboard never disobeys the operator's commands.

Consider again the brake pedal and the stopping of the car. In older cars, the linkage between these, although completely mechanical, was already complex. Today the complexity has increased exponentially, because computers have intervened. The average new car today is equipped with fifty microprocessors, including those that distribute braking to the wheels in such a precise way that skids and swerves are things of the past. In other words, the linkage between pedal and wheels has become amazingly sure and precise. The braking system of a car, now more than ever, is a ready-to-hand integrated whole.

To return to price tags in the form of barcodes, the point is that these signs open out not only to the financial horizon surrounding everyday practical Dasein but also to the electronic horizon incorporating more and more of everyday life and doing so more and more efficiently. Circumspective glimpsing of the electronic horizon, motivated by signs such a barcodes, thus provides phenomenal evidence that now more than ever—although perhaps not entirely to the good—the world is a cosmos.

GENETIC PHENOMENOLOGY

Before concluding his discussion of signs with a summary, Heidegger devotes the long penultimate paragraph to "primitive Dasein" (*SZ*, pp. 81–2). Heidegger is referring to prescientific Dasein, and such Dasein no doubt exists nowhere else in today's world than in childhood and exists even there less and less. Very early on, today's child is deprived of innocence, the innocence of protection from exposure to the objective attitude of natural science.

Heidegger's discussion of primitive Dasein is a "genetic" one in Husserl's sense. Such an analysis seeks to describe experience in its temporally earliest stages, that is, in childhood.[4] Heidegger had already said, in a previous section of *Being and Time*, that familiarity with the primitive mentality can be helpful in phenomenology (*SZ*, p. 51). The reason is that phenomenology measures the distance between things as experienced and things as science conceives of them. For adults who have grown up in the scientific age, however, it is difficult to know what is actual experience and what is only the scientific theory of experience. There is a gap between, for instance, what we do perceive (such as depth) and what the science of the eyes tells us we perceive (flat images).[5] Science covers experience over with debris, and it is difficult for us modern adults, imbued with the scientific spirit, to recognize the debris as debris. Hence the importance of a genetic phenomenology, a consideration of the experience of prescientific Dasein. How do children experience tools and signs: as things ready-to-hand or as present-at-hand? Or as something else altogether?

A fundamental phenomenological thesis maintained by Heidegger asserts the priority of the ready-to-hand over the present-at-hand. What we come across "initially and predominantly" (*zunächst und zumeist*) are practical things understood precisely in terms of their practical properties. It is a later attitude that discloses these things as present-at-hand, as physical objects with mere physical properties. For Heidegger, the present-at-hand is *subtracted out of* the ready-to-hand. The ready-to-hand properties are not *added on* to a previous experience of things as mere physical things constituted by the so-called primary properties of size, shape, and mass. Only in the scientific outlook are these properties primary; in the order of experience, they come second.

Yet Heidegger does not offer evidence. He asserts the priority of the ready-to-hand as if anyone who considers it will recognize immediately that this priority holds good. He even makes fun of the opposite position: "It is not the case that things are at first present as bare realities, as things in some sort of natural state, and that they then in the course of our experience receive the garb of a value-character, so they do not have to run around naked."[6] Bare nature, nature as bereft of values, nature as conceived in science, is not the foundation of the ready-to-hand world; it is just the reverse. The discussion of the primitive mentality in the context of tools and signs is meant to be helpful to phenomenology by providing phenomenal evidence for these phenomenological assertions.

Heidegger's analysis begins with what might seem to be a denial of the priority of the ready-to-hand. Heidegger says the primitive mentality does not know tools and does not use signs. But the reason is that children *merge* the sign and the thing signified. For example, the shadow is not a *sign* of the person; it *is* the person. That is why children are careful when walking not to have their shadow stepped on and not to step on someone else's shadow.

For the primitive mentality, the sign coincides with the signified; thus, children have no experience of signs as ready-to-hand items of equipment, as things referring by indication to other things. But this coinciding of sign and signified does *not* amount, Heidegger stresses, to an identification of two present-at-hand things. The "remarkable coincidence" of the sign with the signified is not a matter of the sign-thing undergoing some sort of "objectification," as if it were experienced as a pure thing and placed, along with the signified, in the ontological region of the present-at-hand. The "coincidence" is not an identification of previously isolated things but instead is the sign as not yet liberated from what it designates. The coincidence is not founded in a prior objectification but in an "utter lack of objectification" (*SZ*, p. 82).

To objectify is to look upon something from an outside perspective. To objectify the eyes, for example, is to take them as characterized in science. If children do not objectify, they could have only a rudimentary sense of their own body as a physical thing. Children shut their *eyes* tight in order to block out an unpleasant *smell*. Children do not understand the sensory modalities as objective systems. Children are caught up in the world and have only a rudimentary sense of the body's modes of access to the world. That is why, for Heidegger, the primitive mentality does not view a sign as one present-at-hand thing identified with another: there are no present-at-hand things in the child's world. But it also explains Heidegger's claim that signs in the primitive mentality are not ready-to-hand either. There are no tools or ready-to-hand things in primitive experience. Tools are means to an end; there are no means in the child's world, only the end, the world. For the child, there are no organs of vision or olfaction, only undifferentiated access to the world; no sights and smells, only things to see and smell not differentiated from one another.

There are no tools in primitive experience—not because primitives do not use implements but because primitives do not *detach* the implement from the work to be done. In Heidegger's words, the use of tools in primitive Dasein is completely engrossed in its directedness toward what is to be accomplished by the tool, so that the tool "cannot in the least detach itself" (*SZ*, p. 82).

Accordingly, what is first in primitive experience is neither the present-at-hand *nor* the ready-to-hand. Then how *are* things experienced by prescientific Dasein? What makes up the world of children? Are so-called primary properties first, or are secondary properties first? Heidegger answers in a negative way: the ontology of the ready-to-hand provides no clue for interpreting the primitive world, and, to be sure, even less does the "ontology of pure things [= the present-at-hand]" (*SZ*, p. 82). So we are told only what the primitive world is *not*. But this negativity might be disclosive.

The world of prescientific Dasein is composed neither of things ready-to-hand and even less of things present-at-hand. This world is then removed from the secondary qualities and is even more removed from the primary qualities. On this basis, the basis of what it is *not*, the conclusion would follow that the primitive world is composed not of things at all but only of the tertiary properties of things, their emotional values. Furthermore, this conclusion has positive phenomenal meaning; it discloses pre-reflective experience.

Heidegger does at least hint at the priority of the tertiary qualities by twice relating the primitive mentality to magic (*Zauber*) (*SZ*, p. 81). The world of primitive Dasein, the world of children, is a world populated not by things but by enchantments. That means things in the child's world are first perceived only in terms of their emotional values. Accordingly, to take a prime genetic example, the child first perceives the *warmth* on the parent's face, a warmth stemming from the-child-knows-not-what. As a later acquisition, the child perceives the smiling face as such, as a thing, and then finally the child might (or might never) attend to the shape of the parent's mouth in forming the smile and the color of the parent's eyes. In the course of development out of childhood, perception proceeds from tertiary properties (emotional values) to secondary properties (useful things) to primary properties (physical shapes and sizes). So the temporal progression is from enchantments without things to ready-to-hand things to present-at-hand things.

In the end, the genetic phenomenology ventured by Heidegger does offer phenomenal evidence for the priority of the ready-to-hand over the present-at-hand. Such a priority does hold, except that something has been disclosed of even greater priority. What are first perceived, what are first in the order of experience, are not bare things, nor tools, but emotional values: not present-at-hand things with physical properties, nor ready-to-hand things with useful properties, but enchantments, magical properties *without any things*. That is why in *Being and Time* the primary disclosure of the world is not through reason or perception but rather through moods. The first experience is not that of *things* hanging together; the first experience is not of definite things at all, any sort of things, even tools, but is a vague sense of hanging-togetherness, a mood attuned to the holding together of I-know-not-what, a mood of enchantment. The worldhood of the world, from which individual worldly things stand out, is the correlate of a mood. That mood is the primary modality of Dasein's disclosedness, and it is a mood of integration, not disintegration. Therefore, the primary experience for Heidegger is a positive one: the world holds together.

BARCODES AND THE ATMOSPHERE OF MORTALITY

One difference between barcodes and the equipment familiar to Heidegger is that such price tags have attained perfection or at least have come within negligible distance of perfection. They are perfect items of equipment and also perfect signs opening out onto a more perfect cosmos than the referential totality envisioned by Heidegger.

Price tags in the form of barcodes are, as *tools*, perfect items of equipment compared to hammers and nails. Barcodes cannot break down, be missing, or get it the way; thus, they cannot be conspicuous, obtrusive, or obstinate. They cannot break, and even if torn or scratched such that only an invisible trace of them remains, they can most likely still be read by electronic scanning equipment. Barcodes cannot get in the way of anything, because they are immoveable and are purposely placed so as not to cover over any useful information. And barcodes cannot even go missing. Barcodes nowadays are not stickers glued onto the item for sale. They are imprinted directly on the packaging and so cannot be lost. For items sold without packaging, such as books, the barcode is imprinted directly on the item. If this disquisition on Heidegger and price tags makes its way into some volume or other, a barcode will be imprinted on the back cover. It may be a painful reminder to the reader that he or she has greatly overpaid to learn of my humble ideas, but she or he will not be able to peel the barcode off. And it will make no sense to rub it out, cover it over, or snip it off. That will merely call attention to the price even more. Inconspicuous, unobtrusive, and nonobstinate barcodes are perfect tools.

As *signs*, barcodes are perfect not merely insofar as they never make mistakes in carrying out their pointing function and always ring up the correct price on the electronic cash register. As do all signs, barcodes also announce the all-encompassing horizon of what they point to. In the case of barcodes, the horizon announced is the integrated system held together by microprocessors and incorporating all aspects of reality. More than ever before, the world is a cosmos, an ordered whole that at least in comparison to the braking mechanism of an automobile or the referential totality of the cobbler's equipment, is perfectly arranged.

Price tags as barcodes are perfect tools, perfect signs, and provide phenomenal evidence of a ready-to-hand world integrated more perfectly than ever before. Yet, they do not keep us from breathing an atmosphere of mortality. On the contrary, they make that atmosphere all the more close and stifling.

In the first place, we are so very dependent today on the smooth functioning of the electronic world that the unlikely but still possible breakdown of a microprocessor can cause much more widespread damage than a breakage of some mechanical device. The more the things in our lives are dependent on electronic devices, the greater is the threat of chaos from a malfunction. That is the lesson of the sorcerer's apprentice. The "apprentice in magic" (the *Zauberlehrling* of Goethe's poem) inundated the house because he did not know the incantation which would *restrict* the forces he had set in motion. The indiscriminate unleashing of magical powers, though they promise integration, also harbors the danger of unprecedented disintegration and havoc.

Electronics make our world fragile as no other world ever was. Not only may the magical powers malfunction or be misused accidently, they may also be exploited for well-nigh-universal mayhem by persons of ill will. We are banqueting with a sword suspended by a thin thread above our heads.

Most fundamentally, however, the electronic world reminds us of our mortality simply by way of contrast to what is not electronic, namely, our own bodies. Of course, electronics can keep us alive as never before. But high-tech medical devices are among the worst offenders; they remind us most forcefully that our bodies are not perfectly integrated, which is why we require the devices in the first place. Modern medical devices have increased our life expectancy. But the more these devices are publicized and the more the increase in life expectancy is called to our attention, then the more we are aware of what cannot be postponed indefinitely, our death. To feel assured that modern medicine can do wonders and allow us to turn our back on death is to make prominent exactly what we are turning from and thus is to increase the sense of our own mortality.

Any high-tech device, medical or not, has the same effect of bringing to at least implicit awareness our own bodily imperfection and fragility. The phenomenal evidence derives from the fact that we, embodied persons, are always part of the world opened up by a sign, any sign, even a barcode. In paying for some item, I am reminded of the labor of my body which allowed me to earn the money to make the purchase. The microprocessor that controls the brakes reminds me of the foot that still has to press on the pedal. And even if the brakes themselves are totally controlled by an on-board microprocessor, such that I merely have to sit back and watch the car drive itself, this system still reminds me of the body which these efficient brakes are meant to protect. The perfect world of computers is always connected to my body, a body which shows its imperfection and mortality all the more by contrast.

To eschew all high-tech things and attempt to return to a simpler life, closer to nature, would of course be counterproductive, for a person would need to be constantly conscious of where the high-tech things are—precisely in order to avoid them. To be preoccupied with turning one's back on something is a sure way to let that thing enter into one's life and indeed would mean being ruled by that thing.

For Heidegger, disintegration, being-toward-death, is not the first experience; it stands out against a previous experience of integration, a whole in which everything hangs together. But if the integration nearly attains perfection, then any imperfection stands out all the more prominently. Barcodes, electronics, the perfect integration of the world—these bring home all the more impressively the contrast to our own imperfect bodies, where disintegration is seriously possible at any moment. Accordingly, with the advent of barcodes and the cardiac pacemaker, all the heavier became the atmosphere of mortality.

ACKNOWLEDGMENT: POETIC MOTIVATION

I was motivated to take up Heidegger's analysis of signs and think it in the direction of price tags and barcodes by a poem, "Sans soleil," by Rita Malikonytė Mockus.[7] According to this poem, the "utter light of diurnal logic" "accounts adjectives price tags," whereas, in the "sunless place," "compliance is a priceless noun."

This poem is taking the first philosophical step. It is distinguishing the diurnal domain of beings from what is sunless and nocturnal, Being. The poem, perhaps unintentionally, is a commentary on one of the first distinctions Heidegger's magnum opus draws between beings and Being. Heidegger expresses the distinction in his own Latin and leaves it untranslated: *enti non additur aliqua natura* (*SZ*, p. 4).[8] In terms of the poem, the translation would run: "To Being, there cannot be tied any price tag."

In the day, adjectives can be assigned to beings. Things have a determinateness and are distinguished from one another. Diurnal things possess sharp contours and stand out against one another. That is how everyday logic "accounts" things, puts a price tag on them, allowing them to be traded. That is to say, price tags allow beings to be taken up in everyday "commerce."

In the night, however, in the sunless place, contours merge and show no sharp distinctions. Things blend into total compliance[9] with one another; nothing steps out as unique. Night is the great melting pot, the uncanny domain where no commerce is possible. This is the domain of Being, the nebulous domain into which all things fall and from which they will emerge in daylight. In order to show themselves as individuals, beings will need to demonstrate noncompliance, that is, take on definite contours and thereby stand out from one another and from the nebulous background which engulfs them.

Being is without a price tag, without a denomination in the linguistic sense. Nothing can determine Being. Therefore, after he speaks Latin, Heidegger also says: Being cannot come to the "determinateness which would allow it to be addressed as a being" (*SZ*, p. 4). To recognize this indeterminateness is to take the first philosophical step.

If the realm of beings is the everyday, earthly, most common one, then the realm of Being is the most uncanny, unearthly, demonic one, Hades. What the poem motivated was a grasp of the connection between signs, especially price tags and barcodes, and death. What price tags disclose—at least implicitly—is that which has no price tag, no denomination, namely, Being, Hades, death. Accordingly, a sign, any sign, perhaps especially a modern electronic sign such as a barcode, is not merely one thing pointing to another thing; it discloses our mortality.

This poem trades in images: light, day, darkness, night. These are of course only images and must not be taken literally. To see in the light of day means to grasp beings (whether by vision or in any other way) with an understanding of what it means to be in general, not with the illumination measurable by a photometer. But the images (beings/light/day, Being/Hades/night) are appropriate. We see beings in the light, but that light is provided by something which itself is dark. The self-showing of Being is the light, but all light recedes in favor of that which it allows to be seen. Without an understanding of what it means to be, we could not grasp any being as a being. But that understanding itself is most obscure: we cannot say how we came by it or what it amounts to. It is uncanny, demonic. From sunless Hades comes the light which illuminates the upper region. Persephone is the goddess of the dark, the underworld. Yet, she is intimately related to the upper region and spends time there every year; perhaps that is why Hölderlin translates her name as *Licht*, "Light."[10]

Chapter 3

Anxiety and Mortality

ANXIETY AND WONDER

The understanding of authentic dying as philosophizing, such as I have proposed and attempted to work out in the first chapter, might seem irreconcilable with Heidegger's explicit statement that "Being-toward-death is essentially anxiety" (*SZ*, p. 266). This seems so especially because the statement occurs precisely in the section of *Being and Time* (§53) devoted to an existential projection of authentic being-toward-death. It would then seem that the authentic approach to death is a matter of the dread of dying, a preoccupation with death, rather than, as I maintain, a matter of taking the first philosophical step, preoccupation with Being.

Yet Heidegger does not say anxiety is primarily, or even at all, *directed* at death. It is certainly not *fear* of death, and Heidegger even calls such fear a "perversion" (*SZ*, p. 266) of anxiety. Indeed in his own copy of *Being and Time*, Heidegger later attached a qualifying remark to the statement about being-toward-death as essentially anxiety. The remark reads: "but not merely anxiety, and afortiori not anxiety as mere emotion," *aber nicht nur Angst und erst recht nicht: Angst als bloße Emotion* (*SZ*, Gesamtausgabe edition, p. 353n).

If not mere emotion, then anxiety is precisely what it is said to be in the title of the section of *Being and Time* devoted to it, "a preeminent mode of Dasein's disclosedness" (*SZ*, §40). Therefore, I wish to look closely at what anxiety discloses and to show that my understanding of authentic dying is confirmed and not contradicted by Heidegger's characterization of being-toward-death as essentially anxiety.

To be anxious, in Heidegger's sense, indeed has an emotional aspect. Anxiety is an unsettling experience, an upheaval, but it is not a negative experience in the sense of apprehension or fright. Anxiety, as I read Heidegger, is wonder, the wonder which motivates a distinguishing of beings from Being, a taking of the first philosophical step.

Anxiety for Heidegger is basically the experience of affective detachment from the beings of the world. Beings no longer provide orientation for an understanding of what it means to be, and thus the way is paved for distinguishing beings from Being. Anxiety is finding the presence of beings inexplicable. Anxiety thereby motivates a wondering about this presence, and wonder, as Aristotle says, is and always was the beginning of philosophy.[1]

ANXIETY AND THE "FOR-THE-SAKE-OF-WHICH"

Anxiety in *Being and Time* is the experience of the beings of the world, including things and people, as deprived of significance. It is not a matter of the disappearance, absence, of the beings of the world, as if Dasein took no notice of them. Beings are not insignificant in the sense of remaining in the background, attracting no attention. On the contrary, for anxious Dasein beings obtrude all the more—but as foreign, as there without rhyme or reason. The world goes on as before, unbroken, intact, but leaves the anxious person untouched. The melancholic Hamlet expresses this experience exactly:

> How weary, stale, flat, and unprofitable
> Seem to me all the uses of this world. (*Hamlet*, I, ii, 133–34).

The uses of Hamlet's world are not broken in themselves, they remain in good order, and he does not disregard them; on the contrary, they jut out, but they do so as barren: "This goodly frame, the earth, seems to me a sterile promontory" (*Hamlet*, II, ii, 317–18).

Heidegger distinguishes two kinds of relations in regard to the world. In the previous chapter, I focused on the first kind: the things in the world are interrelated inasmuch as one of them is taken up "in order to" accomplish something else. Hammering is undertaken in order to fasten boards, which is in order to build a wall, which is in order to frame a house. These relations are "the uses of this world." But such in-order-to relations are themselves undertaken "for the sake of" something, namely, Dasein, some possibility of Dasein. All the relations involved in building a house are for the sake of providing shelter to Dasein.

There can be breakdowns in both kinds of relations. As discussed above, hammers may become unusable, or go missing, or get in the way. These are everyday disruptions in the functional relations among things and are indeed disconcerting, but they do not occasion anxiety. They may provoke frustration, worry, even misery, but not anxiety in Heidegger's sense. Anxiety is a breakdown in the order of the other kind of relations, the "for the sake of which," the "seems to me." Anxiety is a fracture in the connection between the beings of the world and some particular Dasein. It is the experience of the world as no longer for the sake of any possibility of this Dasein, as foreign to any possible project of this Dasein, as seeming to be weary, stale, flat, and unprofitable.

Thus, anxiety has nothing to do with apprehension about health, wealth, popularity, or any other worldly affair. Concern over these matters implies a connectedness to the world (Or else why be apprehensive about them?), and it is precisely such a connection that is sundered in anxiety. Anxiety is the experience that health, wealth, and the rest do not matter. For the most part, anxiety in Heidegger's sense arises precisely when worldly affairs, the in-order-to relations, are proceeding smoothly and are *not* troubling.

Accordingly, when Heidegger declares that being-toward-death is essentially anxiety, he cannot be referring to the dread of dying. A person dreads death only if he or she is still attached to the world, wants to maintain contact with the world. If such contact is of no matter, then dying cannot be a source of apprehension.

Is it possible that authentic being-toward-death, anxiety, is the dread of something that comes after death? Hamlet asks:

> Who would fardels bear,
> To grunt and sweat under a weary life,
> But that the dread of something after death,
> The undiscover'd country, from whose bourn
> No traveller returns, puzzles the will,
> And makes us rather bear those ills we have
> Than fly to others we know not of? (*Hamlet*, III, i, 76–82)

In other words, can being-toward-death be anxiety in the sense of dreading the fires of hell? Can a person feel detached from this world while nevertheless feeling attached to the next? Perhaps. Such dread of hell, however, would surely be a prime instance of the fear which Heidegger calls a perversion of anxiety. Heidegger characterizes it as "cowardly fear" (*SZ*, p. 266), and indeed it would be cowardice to concern oneself with escaping hell without feeling the necessity of actually doing something in this world to deserve heaven. Furthermore, the dread of the undiscover'd country cannot, as a matter of principle, be what Heidegger means by being-toward-death as essentially anxiety. The reason is that *Being and Time* deliberately remains on this side of death: it is "purely 'this-sided,'" *rein "diesseitig"* (*SZ*, p. 248). The book makes no decision on an afterlife or on whether or not it is even possible to ask what lies on the other side of death (*SZ*, p. 248).

THE BEFORE-WHICH OF ANXIETY

Heidegger distinguishes two moments in the full structure of anxiety: the *Wovor* and the *Worum*, the "before which" and the "about which." The same moments occur in fear, but in the case of fear the *Wovor* and the *Worum* are particular beings in the world. That is to say, these beings are particular and are worldly. In the case of anxiety, no such beings are involved. I might be fearful as I stand before the raging storm and about the possibility of my property being flooded. Or I might be fearful before the current economy and about losing money on my investments. In fear, the menace arises from a definite place in the world and concerns a particular possibility of Dasein's worldly existence.

On the other hand, the *Wovor* of anxiety, that before which anxiety is anxious, is completely indefinite. The *Wovor* cannot be specified; the anxious person says, "It is nothing," that is, no identifiable particular object or event. Something is definitely menacing in anxiety, but the source of the menace is completely indefinite. It comes from nowhere. Yet, according to Heidegger, this "nowhere" is not without meaning; what is illuminated in anxiety is a locality in general before which anxiety is anxious. This space is occupied by beings as a whole.

According to Heidegger, anxiety does not see a definite "here" or "there" out of which the menace is approaching. What characterizes the "before which" of anxiety is the circumstance that what is menacing resides *nowhere*. Anxiety does not know what it is anxious before. This "nowhere," however, is not meaningless. On the contrary, for Heidegger, therein lies a locality in general, the disclosedness of the world in general for "essentially spatial being-in-the-world" (*SZ*, p. 186). What menaces in anxiety can therefore not approach from a determinate directionality within what is round about; it is already there. Although it is indeed nowhere, it is so close as to be oppressive.

Heidegger concludes[2] that the "before which" of anxiety is the world as such. But in anxiety this world is disclosed in a peculiar way. It remains a world of things in good order, in joint, but appears as "irrelevant," "insignificant," "inconsequential" (*SZ*, p. 186). In anxiety, one does not encounter anything with which one could be "involved" (*SZ*, p. 186). "Involvement" is another way of expressing the "for the sake of which." Anxiety is the experience of a broken relation—not between one worldly thing and another, but between beings as a whole and Dasein. The world is not now disregarded, but just as in the case of broken tools, the world takes on a specific character, indeed comparable to the change of a ready-to-hand thing into something present-at-hand. Now, however, it is the entire world that undergoes this transformation.

Heidegger applies to the world as a whole the same analysis he carried out with regard to ready-to-hand beings within the world. Just as in the case of a breakdown in the assignments of one tool to another, the tool becomes conspicuous (broken tool), obtrusive (missing tool), and obstinate (tool in the way), so in the case of anxiety, that is, with a breakdown in the order of the for-the-sake-of-which, the entire world in a similar way becomes a sterile promontory.

OBTRUSIVENESS

In the first place, according to Heidegger, for anxious Dasein, innerworldly beings are in themselves so completely unimportant that on the basis of this *insignificance* of what is within the world, the "world in its worldhood" alone still obtrudes (*SZ*, p. 187). Recall that the "worldhood of the world" is Heidegger's name for the vague global sense that things fit together, prior to an experience of particular things fitting together. So Heidegger is saying that in anxiety this global sense of the system of in-order-to relations obtrudes.

According to the earlier analysis of tools, when a hammer is missing, the nails become obtrusive: they force themselves on our attention transformed into inert matter simply lying there, bearing no message to us. The nails appear as present-at-hand things, looking alien to any use we could make of them. In the case of anxiety, the entire ready-to-hand system, the worldhood of the world, undergoes the same transformation. The world obtrudes as something inexplicable. What obtrudes is not this or that, and also not all present-at-hand things taken together as a sum; what obtrudes instead is the possibility of the ready-to-hand in general, that is, "the world itself" (*SZ*, p. 187).

The hand of the ready-to-hand is always the actual hand of some Dasein. If the ready-to-hand in general seems impossible, that could be only because the link to the hand has been severed. If a disruption occurs *within* the realm of the ready-to-hand, that realm appears as needing to be repaired, but not as impossible. For the entire realm to seem impossible, it must be cut off from Dasein. In other words, the world must show itself as unprofitable *to me*, as inexplicably there, cut off from any project of mine. In anxiety, the world *obtrusively* shows itself as inexplicable; beings as a whole force themselves on my attention, but they do so in a way that makes me wonder what they are doing there.

OBSTINACY

In anxiety, the world also appears as *obstinate*. Within the realm of innerworldly things, the obstinate tool is the one in the way, blocking access to some other item of equipment. A hammer in the way loses its usual transparency (transparency in favor of the work to be done) and forces us to deal with it a novel way. Instead of wielding the tool as it is intended to be wielded, we must transport it as dead weight to some other place in order to gain access to what it is blocking. Heidegger's word, translated as "obstinate," is *aufsässig*. The usual translation would be "rebellious," "defiant," or "refractory" (in the manner of an unruly child). But "obstinate" captures Heidegger's sense very well. "Obstinate" (from Latin *sto*, "stand") and *aufsässig* (from Latin *sedeo*, "sit") share the same basic meaning: to occupy a place defiantly, insolently, unwilling to be displaced.

Heidegger applies the term in the context of anxiety as follows. In the before-which of anxiety, the "It is nothing and nowhere" becomes manifest. The obstinacy of the innerworldly nothing and nowhere thus signifies phenomenally: the before-which of anxiety is "the world as such" (*SZ*, p. 187). Heidegger is saying that what presents itself as obstinate in the experience of anxiety is the character of the before-which as nothing and nowhere. This obstinacy is comparable to that of a tool in the way, but it operates in reverse. What is obstinate resides in the circumstance that the menace in anxiety *refuses* to occupy a definite place and be a definite thing. The menace is unwilling to be placed at all. It will not stand or sit anywhere.

This obstinacy is exactly what is uncomfortable in anxiety. A definite thing at a definite place in the world can be confronted. To confront is to turn the menace into an object of fear. That is what Heidegger expresses by noting that the way to dispel anxiety is to absorb oneself in worldly things (*SZ*, p. 186). Even if these are broken and troublesome, they offer the comfort of certainty: a definite something at a definite someplace. As Hamlet recognizes, we would rather bear the ills we have than venture those we know not of.

It is in this context of distinguishing anxiety and fear, the indefinite menace and the definite one, that Heidegger claims, without explanation, that anxiety makes fear possible. Or is he saying that fear makes anxiety possible? His German phrase is ambiguous: *Angst, die ihrerseits Furcht erst möglich macht* (*SZ*, p. 186). That could mean: "anxiety, which for its part first makes fear possible" or "anxiety, which fear for its part first makes possible." Since both readings are justified grammatically, we need to look to the sense in order to decide.

The question reduces to this: do we progress from the definite menace to the indefinite one, or vice versa? Do we first find individual things menacing, and then by some sort of process of induction conclude that the world as a whole is menacing? Or is a vague global sense of menace prior? Heidegger's answer is intimated by the conclusion he draws regarding the obstinacy of the nothing and nowhere. He says, as just quoted: this obstinacy "signifies phenomenally: the before-which of anxiety is the world as such." Heidegger said the same earlier: the "nowhere" is not meaningless; on the contrary, therein lies a locality in general, the disclosedness of the world in general for essentially spatial being-in-the-world. How does this conclusion follow, and what does it say about the priority of fear or anxiety?

In play here regarding obstinacy is basically the same account of anxiety as in the case of obtrusiveness, but now the analysis is couched in terms of place and the disclosedness of the world for essentially *spatial* Dasein. Accordingly, I will appeal here to one of the arguments propounded by Kant in the "Metaphysical exposition of space" of the *Critique of Pure Reason*. Kant argues: "We could never represent to ourselves the absence of space, although we can quite well think it as empty of objects" (A24/B38).

The intention of a "metaphysical exposition" is to show that a certain concept is apriori. So this argument is meant to show that space is apriori, that is, prior to acquaintance with the individual things and relations actually found in space. Space is prior to these relations and not abstracted out from them. The representation of space as such, the realm of spatiality, must precede any empirical acquaintance with what is in space. In the argument just quoted, Kant is presumably reasoning as follows: there would be a contradiction involved in representing the absence of space, for space is the realm that makes possible any presence or absence.[3] In order to think absence, we would need to represent space already, and so it is impossible to think the absence of space; it would be thinking the absence of what makes possible the thinking of absence. But there would be no contradiction involved in thinking of space as absent of objects, since space is not abstracted out from spatial objects. Accordingly, space has been metaphysically exposed as apriori.

Applied to *Being and Time*, the same sort of argument would run: it is impossible to disclose spatial objects without representing the worldhood of the world, but we can represent worldhood without any objects in it. In other terms, unless the spatial "locality" is open to us, we could not have disclosed to us any definite spatial objects; but the locality is not necessarily populated by any definite things. This means the indefinite locality, the nowhere, that is, the no particular where, must precede any definite somewhere.

Therefore, inasmuch as anxiety for Heidegger is the disclosedness of the locality in general, it is prior to fear, which is the confrontation with individual worldly beings. Accordingly, the proper translation of the ambiguous passage above is: "anxiety, which for its part first makes fear possible." Only because we are anxious can we be fearful. Only because we have a sense of the worldhood of the world can an individual item in the world stand out. Only because we find something in general menacing, something we know not what, do we find individual items emerging in their particular menace.

Heidegger maintains that anxiety is an original and direct disclosure of the world as world (world as world = worldhood of the world). It is not the case that this disclosure emerges by "deliberate abstraction" (*SZ*, p. 187) out of innerworldly beings, which would be first experienced, leaving only the thought of the world, before which anxiety might subsequently arise. On the contrary, anxiety, as a mode of affectivity, is the "very first" (*SZ*, p. 187) disclosure of the world as world.

Anxiety makes fear possible—provided anxiety is not understood as mere emotion. Anxiety, as Heidegger has described it, is primarily a disclosedness, although indeed one accompanied by discomfort. Anxiety is the disclosure not of individual present beings but of the realm that allows beings to be present, namely, the worldhood of the world (= Being). But anxiety is not the same as any other disclosure of the world, such as the one through perception or through practical immersion in things. Anxiety is the disclosure that there is something remarkable about the presence of beings. They stand out from a vague background, one which we glimpse but cannot directly face. Anxiety is the sense that there is something inexplicable, uncomfortable, perplexing, about the presence of things, something we cannot confront. The disclosure, in anxiety, of the obstinacy of the nothing and nowhere is thus equivalent to a sense of wonder. Anxiety is the disclosure, at least implicitly, that the background from which beings emerge is not a being on the level of other beings; the presence of individual beings cannot be accounted for by appealing to some other beings. The way is thus paved for the perplexity which motivates the first philosophical step, the recognition of the difference between Being and beings.

CONSPICUOUSNESS

The conspicuous item of equipment is the defective one. As discussed in the previous chapter, for Heidegger defective equipment falls on our gaze (is *auffällig*, "striking," "prominent," "conspicuous") such as to call attention to itself. But the attention received by the broken tool is negative; we look upon the broken tool as sheer matter, not a tool but a present-at-hand thing with physical properties. Yet, for Heidegger, as we know, the broken tool is not fully displaced from the ready-to-hand into the present-at-hand. The broken hammer remains, in some measure, ready-to-hand. Presumably Heidegger is thinking that a hammer with a broken handle can still be wielded by the peen and used for hammering. Defective equipment is still viewed as equipment, usable but exhibiting, as we discussed earlier, a *tension* drawing it toward the present-at-hand.

With regard to the disclosure of the world in anxiety, Heidegger does not use the word "conspicuous." I suggest it is because nothing compares here to the *imperfect* displacement of ready-to-hand things into the domain of the present-at-hand. The transformation of the world in anxiety is complete. We are detached completely from the world and do not merely feel a tension drawing us away. Furthermore, in anxiety we are detached from the entire world and not merely from some part of it. In anxiety, we do not find some areas of the world flat and unprofitable and other areas engaging. Nor can we make some idiosyncratic use of the world, the way a broken hammer, with a little improvisation, might still be employed in hammering. Finally, for anxious Dasein the flatness of the world has an aura of constancy. The conspicuous tool does not present itself as *never* being able to serve a practical purpose, as *never* able to be repaired. But in anxiety, as Heidegger describes it, the unprofitability of the world is experienced as constant. Therefore, instead of speaking of the conspicuousness of the world as disclosed in anxiety, Heidegger thematizes its constancy, *Ständigkeit*.

Heidegger refers to the constancy of anxiety in the course of discussing authentic comportment toward death. A difference between authentic and inauthentic being-toward-death resides in the circumstance, as was discussed above in the first chapter, that authentic comportment enhances the possibility-character of death. Death is possible at every moment, something inauthentic comportment attempts to cover over. Yet, death is *always* menacing, and authentic anticipation of death must live in recognition of this constant menace. For Heidegger, it is anxiety that discloses the constancy of the menace and allows the menace to remain open.

Heidegger asks about constancy and answers his own question in a very brief passage. How does anticipation disclose the *indefiniteness* of the preeminent possibility of Dasein such that the "when" remains constantly indefinite? In the anticipation of indefinitely certain death, Dasein is open to a constant menace. Authentic being-toward-the-end must maintain itself in this menace and can so little play down the menace that it must rather accentuate the indefiniteness. How is the genuine disclosure of this constant menace possible? For Heidegger, all understanding bears an affective tone. He then says that the affect capable of holding open the "constant menace to Dasein is anxiety" (*SZ*, 265–66).

Heidegger is connecting the indefiniteness of the certainty of death with the indefiniteness of the before-which of anxiety. Anxiety is the experience of the nothing and the nowhere, of no thing which can be confronted, and so anxiety in its disclosedness bears an affective tone of uncomfortableness. Such an affect could indeed correspond to the menace of indefinitely certain death. Anxiety would allow authentic being-toward-the-end to sustain the indefiniteness of the menace of death. On the other hand, *Being and Time* often declares that authenticity, including, presumably, authentic being-toward-the-end, is *not* constant. Authenticity is the exceptional state, a departure from inauthenticity, and will always return back to inauthenticity. How then does anxiety hold open a *constant* menace?

Attached to the last word of the quotation above is a footnote referring the reader to "§40, pp. 184ff." That is the earlier section we had been discussing, about anxiety as a preeminent mode of disclosedness. The section includes a single allusion to constancy. Heidegger first characterizes the before-which of anxiety as the uncanny, and then he says, "This uncanniness pursues [*nachsetzt*, "sets out after"] Dasein constantly" (*SZ*, p. 189). Heidegger offers no explicit explanation, so we need to look for ourselves in order to grasp the sense of such constant pursuit.

Heidegger introduces the concept of uncanniness by distinguishing anxiety from Dasein's everyday familiarity with the world. The publicness of the they introduces into the average everydayness of Dasein a comfortable self-assurance, a self-evident feeling at home. Anxiety, on the other hand, hales Dasein back out of falling absorption in the world. Everyday familiarity collapses. Dasein is individualized, but is so nevertheless precisely *as* being-in-the-world. Being-in attains the existential mode of *not being at home*. According to Heidegger, nothing else than this not being at home is meant by the talk of "uncanniness" (*SZ*, p. 189).

It might seem that the sense of uncanniness, of not being at home in the world, arises in opposition to the already established, average everyday sense of comfortable familiarity. Anxiety would disrupt the familiarity and introduce a novel way of looking at the things of the world. Anxious Dasein, instead of supinely taking orientation from the they, would be individualized, would find its individuality for the first time by breaking with the they. But this apparent order, authenticity following upon everydayness, is incorrect, as Heidegger intimates by saying that anxiety hales Dasein *back* from absorption in the world. Anxiety does not introduce anything new; it is a return to the old. The everyday absorption in the beings of the world is not original; on the contrary, it is a matter of "falling." And falling, for Heidegger, is a falling *from* somewhere, a fleeing *from* something, something more original.

Accordingly, what now becomes phenomenally visible is the before-which of falling, that from which it, as flight, actually flees. It does not flee *from* innerworldly beings but rather flees precisely *toward* them, as things with which Dasein, lost in the they, can dwell in comfortable familiarity. The falling flight into the being-at-home of publicness is flight from the not-at-home, from the uncanniness, which lies in Dasein as thrown being-in-the-world. According to Heidegger, this uncanniness pursues Dasein constantly and menaces, even if not explicitly, one's "everyday lostness in the they" (*SZ*, p. 189).

It is an axiom of *Being and Time* that the experience of flight, of turning one's back on something, is disclosive. We must know what it is we are turning from, must take orientation from it, in order to avoid it. We must have some understanding of what is pursuing us in order to flee from it. Flight takes direction from that which it is fleeing, which must therefore be already disclosed, at least implicitly. So Heidegger is saying in the passage just quoted that the absorption in beings, along with the comfortable familiarity involved in such absorption, is made possible in its orientation (toward beings) by a prior experience of not feeling at home. That experience is uncomfortable, and we flee from it. Inasmuch as Dasein's normal, average everyday mode of comportment is inauthenticity, then Dasein is *always* fleeing from authenticity. That is what it means to say that uncanniness constantly pursues Dasein. To flee from uncanniness, to turn one's back on authenticity, the authentic and the uncanny must already be disclosed. Dasein must know, at least implicitly, what it is falling from.

Inasmuch as the before-which of anxiety is the uncanny, Heidegger's claim that anxiety holds open the constant menace is intelligible. *The world disclosed in anxiety has an aura of constancy precisely as that from which average everyday Dasein is constantly fleeing.* We are constantly pursued by uncanniness, that is, by what we find uncomfortable in anxiety, namely, the indefiniteness of the certainty of death. Inauthenticity is nothing other than the flight from this pursuit, nothing other than flight from anxiety. That is how, as quoted at the beginning of this chapter, being-toward-death is essentially anxiety. At least it is so as regards inauthentic dying. Such being-toward-the-end is essentially anxiety not as brooding on death, or dreading it, but as taking orientation from what is disclosed in anxiety, namely, the indefinite certainty of death. Such being-toward-the-end takes the negative path, the shunning of anxiety. In doing so, however, it is determined by anxiety and merely takes the opposite course. It is anti-anxiety, but, as Heidegger says, everything anti- thinks essentially in the spirit of that which it is anti-.[4] Accordingly, inauthentic being-toward-death is essentially anxiety but is not merely anxiety and afortiori not anxiety as mere mood.

Inauthenticity covers over the indefiniteness of the certain possibility of death and thereby turns anxiety into fear. It attempts to make death an actuality which can be confronted. But that comportment is precisely a fleeing from death as possibility. So inauthentic being-toward-death, the dread of dying, is a *fear of anxiety*, cowardice toward anxiety. When Heidegger asserted that being-toward-death is essentially anxiety, he added that incontrovertible although only indirect proof of this assertion is provided by being-toward-death as characterized earlier, when it perverts anxiety into cowardly fear and, with the overcoming of this fear, manifests "cowardice toward anxiety" (*SZ*, p. 266). How does the one prove the other?

Heidegger is referring to the earlier characterization of inauthentic being-toward-death, where even thinking about death counts publicly as cowardly fear, as insecurity in one's existence, and as morbid flight from the world. The "they" does not recognize the courage required for anxiety toward death.

The infallible though indirect proof then amounts to this: when inauthenticity, the dominance of the they, overcomes the fear of death, which presumably happens by turning death into an actuality that can be calculated and thereby confronted and disposed of in some way or other, then inauthentic Dasein is displaying cowardice toward anxiety, toward the indefinitely certain possibility of death. And such cowardice demonstrates, by way of contrast (by way of "indirectness"), that authentic being-toward-death is essentially anxiety in the opposite sense of courage toward anxiety. Inauthenticity overcomes the fear of death out of fear of anxiety, out of fear of the uncomfortableness of the indefinitely certain possibility disclosed in anxiety. What inauthenticity turns its back on is what authenticity embraces, namely, anxiety. Thus, authentic being-toward-death is essentially anxiety, a living in full awareness of the indefinite. Accordingly, both authentic and inauthentic being-toward-the-end take their orientation from what is disclosed in anxiety. One attitude flees, the other embraces. But both are essentially anxiety.

Anxiety makes fear possible. That is the conclusion Heidegger again draws from his discussion of uncanniness. Heidegger first repeats that the disclosure of the world as uncanny has priority, and then he calls fear a fallen mode of anxiety. The comfortable-familiar way of being-in-the-world is a modal variant of the uncanniness of Dasein, not the reverse. Existentially-ontologically, the experience of not being at home must be considered the more original phenomenon. For Heidegger, only because anxiety always already determines being-in-the-world, can Dasein, in concernful and affective involvement with the world, ever be afraid. Fear is anxiety which has fallen into the world, is inauthentic and therefore "self-concealed anxiety" (*SZ*, p. 189).

Heidegger says uncanniness is more original—provided "originality" is taken in the existential-ontological sense. Authenticity is more original than inauthenticity in that sense. In that sense, inauthenticity is a modal variant of authenticity, and not the reverse. But there is another sense in which the reverse does hold, and that is the sense in which *Being and Time* declares so often that *authenticity* is the modal variant, the exceptional phenomenon that endures only for a moment; inauthenticity is the rule. It is so in what would have to be called the existentiell-ontical sense in contrast to the existential-ontological one. Ontically, that is, factually, experientially, inauthenticity is prior; it is where we first find ourselves. But ontologically, that is, in terms of conditions of possibility, authenticity is first, since inauthenticity must know, as implicit as this knowledge may be, what it is turning its back on. Factually speaking, fear is more original than anxiety; it is predominant and anxiety is latent. Ontologically, the order is reversed. Accordingly, *Being and Time* is not inconsistent in claiming here that not being at home is the more original phenomenon.

A question remains with regard to authentic being-toward-death. Such authenticity is an embracing of anxiety rather than a fleeing from it. It is possible to shun anxiety constantly, but could Dasein actually live constantly in anxiety? Can the affect characteristic of anxiety, the uncomfortable sense of the indefinite, the not-at-home, the uncanny, be sustained? Can one live constantly in perplexity and wonder? Can one live a life of constant dying, constant openness to the indefinite menace? Is it possible to enhance constantly the uncertain possibility in its possibility-character? If shunning anxiety is cowardice, then fully embracing it and never falling away from it would be not only courageous but even heroic. Is such heroism possible? Have there ever been such exceptional instances of Dasein, such heroes? I wish to leave these questions open for now and reserve the answer for the end of this chapter on death and anxiety.

THE BEFORE-WHICH OF ANXIETY
AS THE BEING OF DASEIN

Despite all the previous analyses in which Heidegger determined the before-which of anxiety as the world, the locality in general, the worldhood of the world, the entire system of ready-to-hand relations, the nowhere and the nothing, he concludes by identifying the before-which in an apparently unrelated way. The identification offers support for my understanding of anxiety and authentic dying as preoccupation with disclosing Being, philosophizing, rather than preoccupation with death. But the conclusion, the final identification of the before-which of anxiety, will seem surprising, and Heidegger offers it in a few brief sentences without explanation. Therefore, it will require some effort to make sense of it. What Heidegger concludes is that the before-which of anxiety is the Being of Dasein. The before-which of anxiety is nothing ready-to-hand within the world. Yet this nothing is not a total nothingness. The nothing of the ready-to-hand is grounded in the "most original something" (*SZ*, p. 187), namely, the *world*. Ontologically, however, the world belongs essentially to the Being of Dasein as being-in-the-world. Accordingly, if the nothing, that is, the world as such, manifests itself as the before-which of anxiety, then that signifies: the before-which of anxiety is "being-in-the-world itself" (*SZ*, p. 187).

Heidegger's motive in taking up the topic of anxiety was to find phenomenal evidence for the unity of what he asserted to be an utterly unitary condition, namely, being-in-the-world. In *Being and Time*, that is the name for the Being of Dasein (along with other names, such as existence, *Existenz*, and care, *Sorge*). Although unitary, being-in-the-world can be considered in terms of its three constitutive moments: the world, the disclosive activity of being-in, and the self, the who of being-in-the-world. Being-in-the-world cannot be separated out into discrete pieces, but that does not preclude its having a multiplicity of structural moments.[5]

Heidegger proceeds to phenomenological reflection on the three moments, discussing them separately but never losing sight of their unity, and then he seeks the phenomenal evidence. Such evidence, as we know, means disclosure to everyday Dasein and not merely to the reflecting philosopher. Anxiety is the everyday experience to which Heidegger appeals for the requisite evidence. In anxiety, the three moments of being-in-the-world are revealed in their unity, while the distinctiveness of the individual moments is respected as well. The before-which of anxiety corresponds to the world, the about-which is the who, and anxiety precisely as affect is an exemplary phenomenon of being-in. In the experience of anxiety, the structural moments of being-in-the-world are gathered together and shown in their unity to everyday Dasein, the one undergoing the experience, and not merely to the reflecting philosopher. At least that is Heidegger's claim and is his motive for making anxiety so prominent in *Being and Time*.

For Heidegger, Dasein is not an isolated subject, one needing some sort of bridge to connect to the world. Dasein is not a subject in the usual sense, a consciousness aloof from the object. That is one of the reasons Heidegger chooses the name "*Da*sein" for the beings we ourselves are. We are already out *there*, in the world. I believe this immediate connection to the world cannot be proved; phenomenology can only point it out and offer it for our acceptance or rejection. An opposing philosophy, such as idealism or empiricism, can always deny this immediate connection and supply its own equivalent of it.

Accordingly, Heidegger is not attempting to *prove* that Dasein is already out in the world and that there could be no worldless Dasein. He is not trying to convince anyone that the world belongs essentially to the Being of Dasein. And I do not wish to argue for or against. What I question is how the world as revealed in anxiety can be the sort of world Dasein is intrinsically related to.

Heidegger maintains there is no such thing as a worldless Dasein, yet that is precisely how he has described anxious Dasein. The world as revealed in anxiety is entirely severed from Dasein, whereby indeed some artificial bridge or shock might be required in order to arouse interest. In anxiety the world is disclosed, quoting again Heidegger's own words, as irrelevant, insignificant, and inconsequential, as a world in which Dasein has no involvement. Anxiety is the experience of affective severance from the world. Then how is this world one that essentially belongs to the Being of Dasein as being-in-the-world? And how is the experience of anxiety supposed to supply phenomenal evidence, that is, evidence to anxious Dasein himself or herself, that he or she is intrinsically connected to the world?

Heidegger does not address these problems directly, but he seems at least implicitly aware of them when he writes about the solipsism of anxiety. Anxiety individuates and so discloses Dasein as *solus ipse*, "self-alone." Yet, for Heidegger, this existential "solipsism" so little places an isolated subject-thing worldlessly suspended in a "harmless void" that it instead brings Dasein exactly before its world as world and thereby before itself as being-in-the-world (*SZ*, p. 188).

The most significant word above is "harmless" (*harmlos*). Heidegger maintains that the world disclosed in anxiety, even if seemingly remote from Dasein, is not a harmless one. Indeed no harm can come to a subject-thing suspended in empty space. Nothing could assault this subject, touch it with the intention of doing harm. But the specter of such an isolated Dasein is by no means comforting. Such a Dasein would not have unbounded freedom, on the grounds that nothing is hemming in that freedom. On the contrary, there would be no freedom at all, since there would be nothing on which to exercise the freedom. A void would do extreme harm to freedom.

The classic analogy is drawn by Kant.[6] It is a central tenet of the critical philosophy that the higher faculty must remain tethered to the lower on pain of falling into illusion. Reason must retain a bond to sensibility; otherwise, what follows is not unbounded knowledge but no knowledge at all. So the situation is comparable to that of a dove flying through the sky. The dove feels the resistance of the air against its wings and thinks to itself that if only that resistance were removed it could really soar. The bird is not disclosive Dasein and does not realize that what resists is also what makes possible.

Anxiety, by holding up the specter of an utterly distant world, calls Dasein back to his or her senses. Anxiety provides the shock motivating the recognition that Dasein *is* being-in-the-world. Anxiety then does bring Dasein in an extreme way before its world as world, as the place where it can exercise its powers. A worldless Dasein is a contradiction in terms; without a world Dasein would have nothing on which to exercise its disclosiveness. A worldless Dasein would not be *da*, would not be *there* for any disclosedness. Anxiety discloses this connection to the world by holding up the specter of the opposite: Dasein without a world. Anxiety grants the wish of Kant's dove: it removes the resisting air. Presumably, the bird quickly learns the lesson: a void does extreme harm.

Heidegger indicated in the section title that anxiety is a preeminent mode of Dasein's disclosedness. It is preeminent inasmuch as it discloses the very Being of Dasein as being-in-the-world. Therefore, Heidegger's conclusion holds good: the before-which of anxiety is the Being of Dasein in the sense of being-in-the-world, in the sense of intrinsically belonging to the world. Anxiety is not a brooding over death; it is a motive to philosophize about the Being of Dasein.

THE ABOUT-WHICH OF ANXIETY
AS THE BEING OF DASEIN

What is anxiety anxious about? What is menaced? As in the case of the before-which, the about-which of anxiety is nothing definite. It is not any particular possibility of Dasein, not anything which could be a for-the-sake-of-which. Versus the case of fear, what is menaced cannot be identified with any particular thing or event, not even death. Accordingly, death can be feared, but it cannot be that about which anxiety is anxious. Dying is neither the before-which nor the about-which of anxiety. Yet, we will see again that being-toward-death is essentially anxiety.

The about-which of anxiety is not any definite thing which would be of concern to Dasein, for the obvious reason that the world is meaningless for anxious Dasein. The about-which is not a definite possibility of Dasein with regard to some particular thing in the world. Just as the before-which is the world as such, the worldhood of the world, and not any particular worldly thing, so the about-which is Dasein's relation to the world as such, to world-hood, and not to any worldly thing. The general relation of Dasein to the world is a matter of authenticity or inauthenticity, Dasein understanding itself in terms of the world, including things and other Daseins, or in its own freely chosen terms. Since, in anxiety, beings become meaningless, they can no longer provide orientation for one's self-understanding. Dasein is thrown back on his or her own resources for self-understanding. That being thrown back on oneself is the about-which of anxiety. In anxiety, beings ready-to-hand within the world sink away, as do all worldly beings whatsoever. The world has nothing more to offer, and just as little does one's fellow Dasein. Anxiety thereby takes from Dasein the possibility of self-understanding in the manner of fallingness, that is, in terms of the world and the way things have been publicly interpreted.

Anxiety individuates; since it deprives worldly things of significance, it motivates taking oneself in one's own hands, making oneself a product of one's own devising. Anxiety is thus a motive to authenticity. That means anxiety reveals to Dasein its freedom to choose its own way of being-in-the-world. Freedom concerns Dasein's peculiar relation to possibilities as most proper ones. The about-which of anxiety is the Being of Dasein as being-in-the-world with respect to the *who* of being-in-the-world. The about-which of anxiety is the authentic self rather than the they-self. Anxiety is the disclosure of the freedom of Dasein with respect to the possibility of authenticity.

The preceding paragraph is a skeleton outline of Heidegger's analysis of the about-which, a very dense, almost cryptic, analysis. I will attempt to explicate it as follows.

Anxiety throws Dasein back on that about which it is anxious, its authentic possibility to be in the world. By depriving the public world of significance, anxiety deprives Dasein of its inauthentic way of self-understanding, its taking the easy way out, namely, supinely going along with the crowd. Instead, anxiety discloses to Dasein the path to authenticity, and that path is exactly what Dasein is anxious about in anxiety. Anxiety opens up a daunting prospect, namely, the possibility of rejecting peer pressure and choosing for oneself one's own way to be in the world. This is a throwing *back*, because in falling into inauthenticity, Dasein is turning away, at least to some extent deliberately, from authenticity. Dasein knows, at least implicitly, where its authenticity lies, and that is how Dasein is able to turn away from it. Anxiety is the making explicit of what Dasein has been turning from, and that is the about-which of anxiety, the prospect of relying on oneself. This making explicit is a *throwing*, because it is not simply a neutral disclosure of the path to authenticity but rather contains an element of reprimand; in anxiety, Dasein is *urged* toward authenticity.

Anxiety individuates Dasein toward its most proper being-in-the-world, which, as partaking in understanding, essentially projects upon possibilities. Anxiety individuates Dasein from the they and toward its own freely chosen way of being-in-the-world. Every way of being-in-the-world includes some disclosure of what is involved in such a way; in other words, every way of being-in-the-world includes an element of understanding. Moreover, understanding is always projective; to understand is to grasp something in terms of some context or horizon, and this context or horizon is not given, but is instead projected by the one who understands. Understanding has in itself the "existential structure we call *projection*" (*SZ*, p. 145). There are two directionalities of the projection involved in self-understanding, directionality toward two sorts of possibilities, which means toward two modes of existence (since existence always has to do with possibilities, which is why the structure of projecting upon possibilities is called an *existential* structure). Dasein can understand itself in terms of possibilities it devises from its own resources, whereby the understanding and the existence are authentic, or Dasein can understand itself in terms of the possibilities derived from the world and other Daseins, whereby the understanding and the existence are inauthentic. This latter way is easy and makes no great demands on Dasein; the authentic way is what anxiety is anxious about.

In the about-which of anxiety, therefore, anxiety discloses Dasein as possibility and indeed as that which it alone can be on its own basis as something individuated. In anxiety, there is a disclosure to Dasein of the fact that it faces a choice of possibilities, and so anxiety discloses to Dasein where its authenticity lies, namely, by making of itself something unique, something it alone, as an individual, can be, an individual entirely individuated, totally taking its orientation from itself and not from the world or other Daseins.

Anxiety manifests in Dasein a *being-toward* a most proper capacity to be, which means a *being-free for* the freedom of seizing upon oneself and choosing oneself. Anxiety discloses to Dasein its own individual possibility to be, which means it discloses to Dasein its freedom to seize itself by its own hands and choose for itself its own mode of being-in-the-world.

Anxiety brings Dasein before its *being-free for* the authenticity of its Being as possibility, a possibility it always already is. Anxiety does not disclose merely negative freedom, freedom from constraint, but instead shows Dasein what it is free for. What Dasein is most properly free for is the possibility of authentic Being. But Dasein always already *is* this possibility inasmuch as it has chosen some form of existence, and yet Dasein always also *has* this possibility in the manner of Dasein's distinctive relation to possibilities, which are for Dasein, but not for things, most proper ones, ones that remain open even after being chosen.

Yet, this Being is at the same time that to which Dasein as being-in-the-world is delivered over. Dasein has been delivered over to authenticity, which is not purely and simply outstanding, something entirely futural. Dasein has *already* been delivered over to this way of being-in-the-world; even the most inauthentic existence is lived with at least a vague sense that there is more to human potential than merely going along with the crowd. Every Dasein senses a call toward authenticity, a deliverance over to authenticity, and anxiety is the forceful experience of this call. The about-which of anxiety is not something new but is instead something Dasein has already been consigned to, the possibility of authentic existence.

In summary, the about-which of anxiety is the Being of Dasein. Anxiety is the disclosure of the authentic mode of Being. Anxiety holds open to Dasein the prospect of choosing one's own way to be in the world. It is a daunting prospect versus the ease of falling into inauthenticity. In any case, the about-which of anxiety is not death; anxious Dasein is not anxious at the prospect of dying. Nevertheless, authentic being-toward-death is essentially anxiety—provided such being-toward-death means philosophizing, preoccupation with Being. Anxiety brings home to Dasein not its end but its relation to possibilities. Anxiety is a coming to understand the Being of Dasein as essentially possibility. Anxiety brings Dasein before the authenticity of its Being as possibility.

The before-which and the about-which of anxiety are therefore the same, not death, but the Being of Dasein. Both the before-which and the about-which are being-in-the-world, but are so in two different perspectives. The before-which is being-in-the-world with the moment of world brought into relief. Anxiety is disclosure of the world as essentially belonging to Dasein, as an intrinsic moment of the Being of Dasein as being-in-the-world. The about-which of anxiety is the Being of Dasein with the moment of the who brought into relief.

This who is disclosed in its possibilities of the authentic self and the inauthentic, the individuated self and the they-self. In both the before-which and the about-which, what anxiety discloses is the structure of the Being of Dasein. That is what anxiety is preoccupied with, not death. If preoccupation with disclosing the Being of Dasein is, as I claim, what Heidegger means by authentic dying, then being-toward-death is essentially anxiety.

ANXIETY AS BEING-IN

For the sake of completeness, let us discuss the third moment of being-in-the-world, the moment of being-in. It too is made prominent in anxiety, whereby anxiety discloses the unity of all three moments of being-in-the-world. The about-which of anxiety reveals itself to be also the before-which: being-in-the-world. The sameness of the before-which of anxiety and its about-which extends even to anxiousness itself. For anxiousness, as affect, is a basic mode of being-in.

Heidegger's term "being-in" does not refer to spatial relations. Water is not in a bucket in Heidegger's sense of being-in. Being-in requires disclosedness. To be in the world means to abide there disclosively, to have some understanding of what one is doing in the world. In Heidegger's sense, only Dasein is *in* the world.

Heidegger recognizes three modes of disclosiveness, three modes of being-in: understanding, discourse, and affect, or: reasoning, talking things through in words (discourse is not simply an expression to the outside of things already disclosed but is itself a disclosing to the one who is talking; we learn our own thoughts by attempting to express them), and having moods. For Heidegger it is the latter that is most disclosive. The other, higher modes for the most part only bring to conceptuality what has been more primarily disclosed by bodily attunement. This is a common phenomenological theme, echoed for example by Merleau-Ponty when he maintains that perception is most basically not a grasp of colors or shapes but a grasp of the emotional essence of the thing perceived.[7]

Among all the affects, anxiety is in *Being and Time* the preeminent one, the preeminent mode of Dasein's disclosedness. That is exactly what is expressed in the title of the section on anxiety. Accordingly, anxiety is a preeminent modality of being-in (since being-in = disclosedness). And what anxiety discloses, as we have seen, is the Being of Dasein, being-in-the-world. Included in the understanding of its own Being is an understanding of its own disclosedness. Included in the self-understanding of anxious Dasein is at least an implicit grasp that the world is revealed *by* the experience of anxiety. That is the reason the sameness of the before-which and the about-which extends to anxiety as affect; it too discloses being-in-the-world, and in this case the moment of being-in is set in relief.

It follows, then, that anxiety is phenomenal evidence for the unity of being-in-the-world. The three moments are unified in anxiety: they all are disclosive of being-in-the-world, and each makes prominent a particular moment. Yet we might doubt: is this actually phenomenal evidence? Does the person experiencing anxiety sense a disclosure of this unity? Would it not require reflection to see the unity rather than merely undergoing the experience? Does anxious Dasein, while undergoing the experience, sense this unity of the before-which, the about-which, and the affect? Or is this revealed only after the fact, that is, revealed to the reflecting phenomenologist? Heidegger does not address this problem directly, but he offers a clue to it in speaking of the rarity of anxiety: with the predominance of fallingness and publicness, "authentic anxiety is rare" (*SZ*, p. 190). Heidegger goes on to observe that even rarer than the existentiell fact of authentic anxiety are the attempts to interpret this phenomenon in its basic existential-ontological constitution and function. The reasons, according to Heidegger, reside partly in the general neglect of the existential analytic of Dasein but more especially in an obliviousness to the phenomenon of the disclosiveness of affect, the phenomenon that affect is itself disclosive. The factual rarity of the phenomenon of anxiety, however, does not deprive it of its suitability for assuming in principle a methodological function for Heidegger's existential analytic. On the contrary, the rarity of the phenomenon is an indication of the fact that Dasein (for the most part concealed to itself on account of the way things have been interpreted publicly by the they) becomes disclosable in an original sense in this basic affect.

The first, most obvious question concerns *authentic* anxiety. What is it? Heidegger does not say more than that it is rare. Presumably it is the opposite of inauthentic anxiety, which Heidegger does not characterize either, but which could very well be the anxiety of someone who experiences the insignificance of worldly things and feels the motivation toward individuation and authenticity but does not act on that motive. Such a person would shrug off the anxiety and return to his or her obsession with daily tasks. Such a person, after the fact, would indeed say, as Heidegger claims, "It was nothing." Heidegger believes that that means "nothing definite," but it could also mean "nothing important," nothing that touches me personally, nothing that requires a response on my part. If authentic anxiety is taken as the opposite, the positive response to the urge toward authenticity, then its rarity would certainly be intelligible. Many people experience anxiety, yet inauthenticity predominates, that is, "fallingness and publicness" are the rule.

There is another possible way of understanding authentic anxiety. Heidegger hints at this way when he immediately goes on to complain about the neglect of his philosophy. Following up this hint, I wish to show that authentic anxiety could be the anxiety of someone who is already existing in authenticity, the anxiety to which only an already authentic person is impelled. Indeed a multitude of problems immediately arises in regard to this view, for anxiety is the precondition of authenticity, not vice versa. Anxiety includes the discomfort of being urged out of inauthenticity into authenticity. An already authentic person would not feel that discomfort.

Yet authenticity could be a condition of anxiety, and the rarity of the phenomenon could also be explained thereby. The issue is the motivation of anxiety. Heidegger hints at only two motives, darkness and physiology, and I will pursue those hints in the next section of this chapter. Yet besides those hints, Heidegger, in the context of discussing the motives to anxiety, inserts this complaint of the neglect of the analytic of Dasein, the obliviousness to the phenomenon of disclosive affect, and the extreme rarity of attempts to interpret anxiety in its existential-ontological constitution. What is rare, in other words, is any philosopher thinking along with Heidegger, any philosopher attempting an analytic of Dasein. If authentic anxiety is rare *because* of this neglect of the analytic of Dasein, then Heidegger's philosophy is itself a motive to such anxiety.

A philosopher following in the footsteps of Heidegger is not necessarily authentic. It is possible to be a Heideggerian simply because it is the *in* thing to do. Heidegger is not suggesting that only Heideggerians are authentic. In fact, he later mostly complained that he has no authentic followers, that is, no one who genuinely engaged with his philosophy, even by opposing it. He complained that his so-called followers were not thinking for themselves but were occupied with Heidegger-scholarship. They were concentrating on his words instead of thinking for themselves about the matters at issue in his philosophy so as to make their own original contribution. I believe Heidegger is exaggerating. No one attracted to his philosophy has ever been, or would be, content to be an epigone and merely spout Heideggerian jargon without even attempting to clarify it.

The prime matter at issue in Heidegger's philosophy is the question of the meaning of Being. It is the neglect of this question that he laments. Authentic anxiety does not require reading *Being and Time*. But it does require openness to what that book is attempting to provoke, namely, perplexity in regard to what it means to be. And such perplexity does include an element of authenticity, for it requires, as the Stranger says, dissatisfaction with what the previous "muses" believe about the meaning of Being. In Heidegger's terms, it requires individuating oneself from the usual sanction of the neglect of the question of Being on the grounds that we are all already well-acquainted with what it means to be.

To someone sharing the Stranger's perplexity, the experience of anxiety might indeed provide phenomenal evidence of the unity of being-in-the-world.

Wondering about the Being of Dasein could "occasion" authentic anxiety, just as, we will see, a particular physiological makeup could. It is not a matter of causality; perplexity is only a nudge in a certain direction. But it might make one alert to what anxiety could disclose about Being. Thus, anxiety might be phenomenal evidence to a philosopher—but not in his or her later reflection on the experience; it would be evidence while the experience is transpiring. Thereby, anxiety is *in principle* phenomenal evidence. But it is not evidence to inauthentic Dasein, to the they. It is phenomenal evidence only to authentic anxiety, that is, to someone provoked into perplexity by Heidegger's philosophy. That is how authenticity could be a condition of authentic anxiety and not just a result of anxiety. It would also explain Heidegger's assertion about the rarity of authentic anxiety. Indeed, in view of his complaints, we might conclude that Heidegger is of the opinion that he himself is the only one who experiences in anxiety phenomenal evidence for the unity of being-in-the-world.

MOTIVES OF ANXIETY

What motivates anxiety? Heidegger is maddeningly noncommittal about the motives. He offers only two, very ambiguous hints. The first concerns darkness. In the discussion of uncanniness, he says that anxiety does not need darkness: anxiety can arise in the most innocuous situations, nor is there need for darkness, which does commonly foster a sense of uncanniness. In the dark, we are offered, very emphatically, nothing to see, although the world is precisely and indeed "*more obtrusively*, there" (*SZ*, p. 189).

In the dark, I cannot take my bearings from things, and so I am thrown back on my own resources to find my way. Since I must negotiate unseen obstacles, the world obtrudes all the more—as a foreign place. Thus, darkness is similar to the situation of anxiety: things offering no orientation, the world itself obtruding as unfamiliar, myself thrown back on my own resources.

Yet, the differences between anxiety and being in the dark are so great as to make the similarities insignificant. First of all, in darkness the orientation I am deprived of is purely spatial, whereas in anxiety what is at stake is self-understanding. Furthermore, in darkness the obtrusiveness of the world is purely a jutting out of individual things which I may collide against; this is incomparable to a disclosure of the worldhood of the world, an obtruding of the entire system of ready-to-hand relations. Finally, darkness does not call on me to individuate myself; on the contrary, the task is precisely to insert myself seamlessly into the everyday world. Therefore, Heidegger is not wrong to say anxiety has no of need darkness, but his statement falls far short. In fact, anxiety is *impossible* in the dark.[8] I might fear for my safety in the dark, have an eerie feeling, and find the things of the world obtrusive. But I am too preoccupied with these matters to have the leisure for anxiety in Heidegger's sense.

According to Heidegger, anxiety can arise in the most innocuous situations. Here we do have a motive or at least a condition of anxiety. If things are going badly, then I have to focus on fixing them. If there is a breakdown in the realm of the in-order-to, then I have to occupy myself with repairing it. If I am worried about death, I am focused on my physical well-being. If I am preoccupied with any worldly concern, if something is not innocuous, then I have no leisure for anxiety. So anxiety even *requires* the most innocuous situations.

Accordingly, leisure is a necessary condition for anxiety. A counter-proof is that the way to dispel anxiety, as Heidegger says, is to throw oneself into practical tasks. Preoccupation with worldly concerns is the way to flee anxiety. To be anxious is not, despite what *they* say, insecurity in one's existence (see above, p. 63); on the contrary, insecurity is what motivates the flight *from* anxiety.

If, as I maintain, anxiety is a matter of disclosedness, preoccupation with the Being of Dasein, philosophizing, then leisure will all the more appear as a necessary condition. According to Aristotle, philosophy begins in wonder, but he also recognizes leisure as what makes wonder possible. The sciences concerned with wisdom arose only when people had leisure from the necessity of *producing* things, whether those things catered to necessity or luxury (*Metaphysics*, 981b).

The other motive mentioned by Heidegger is physiology. "Anxiety is often 'physiologically' conditioned" (*SZ*, p. 190). Yet, for Heidegger, this fact is an *ontological* problem, not merely a problem in regard to its ontical occasioning and progression. Physiological inducement of anxiety is possible only because Dasein is anxious "in the ground of its Being" (*SZ*, p. 190).

Despite this naturalistic way of speaking, Heidegger could not possibly mean that anxiety can be *caused* by physiology. That would fly in the face of a basic phenomenological tenet: in the realm of experience, there can be no causes, only motives. Causality is restricted to inanimate nature. Phenomenology is not empiricism. Therefore, the conditioning, occasioning, and inducing mentioned by Heidegger must be taken in the sense of motivating; one's physiological makeup may make one more or less prone to anxiety, but physiology never by itself causes anxiety.

According to Heidegger, physiology can induce anxiety only because Dasein is anxious in the ground of its Being. What is the ground of the Being of Dasein? We know (chapter 1) that for Heidegger temporality is the *meaning* of the Being of Dasein, that on which the structure of being-in-the-world must be projected in order to make it comprehensible. Temporality could also be considered the *ground* of the Being of Dasein. I believe, however, that it will be more fruitful to take ground here in a somewhat different sense, not as meaning, as condition of possibility, but as what is most basic to Dasein, what is most proper, what makes Dasein be Dasein, most fully Dasein. The ground is Dasein at its deepest level, the level attained only in perfection: in other words, ground not as *arche* but as *telos*.

What then is the *telos* of Dasein, what would make Dasein most properly Dasein? The answer is authenticity. Let us first ask how authenticity is anxious, intrinsically anxious, and then ask how the anxiety of authentic Dasein could be physiologically induced.

Authentic Dasein is always anxious if anxiety means not mere emotion but affective disclosure. What authentic Dasein most discloses is itself, being-in-the-world, with the three moments shown in their unity as well as their particularity. This disclosure is disclosed preeminently in anxiety, and so authentic Dasein is intrinsically anxious.

The physiological conditioning Heidegger is invoking here cannot be a sheer matter of brain functioning. Heidegger's philosophy is as far from today's neuroscience as can be imagined. Heidegger is not envisioning something as ridiculous as an anxiety-neuron. So Heidegger must mean physiology in a loose sense, equivalent to temperament. We at times do refer to the temperaments in physiological terms: rich blooded versus poor blooded, gutsy versus gutless, lion-hearted versus chicken-livered. There are bold temperaments and timid ones. Macbeth upbraids a pusillanimous servant: "Go, prick thy face and over-red thy fear. Thou lily-liver'd boy" (*Macbeth*, V, iii, 14–15).

From the manner in which Heidegger distinguishes fear and anxiety, we could say that the timid temperament tends toward fear and the strong one toward anxiety. Authenticity and anxiety require courage. So the physiological condition that makes a person open to anxiety is that of a stout-hearted temperament, not a weak-kneed one. That is how anxiety could be induced physiologically, that is, fostered, but only because Dasein is basically anxious, anxious in its *telos*, authenticity. A strong temperament may make a person more open to anxiety in Heidegger's sense, but of course, as Heidegger says of darkness, anxiety does not *require* such a physiology.

What then does motivate anxiety? Anxiety is basically wonder. There are conditions attached to the possibility of the feeling of wonder: leisure and an openness to perplexity. Anxiety as wonder also requires courage. All these are *conditions* of anxiety but not causes. Dasein cannot of its own resources place itself in anxiety or provoke a feeling of wonder. Dasein can resist the feeling of wonder and can flee from anxiety into cowardly fear. The most Dasein can do positively is to prepare for anxiety, perhaps by attempting to come to self-knowledge. Nevertheless, anxiety is unmotivated, and that would explain why Heidegger is so vague about the motives. In the end, anxiety has to be understood as a sheer undeserved gift. Anxiety, like philosophy, is not something Dasein takes up; on the contrary, anxiety and philosophy take up Dasein. Anxious Dasein should feel privileged.

CONSTANT ANXIETY

Let us return now to a question raised earlier: Is a life of constant anxiety possible? According to Heidegger, anxiety in the guise of uncanniness always pursues Dasein. It is certainly possible to live entirely in accord with this pursuit—in the negative sense of constantly fleeing from it. That is the life of inauthenticity. The question is whether it is possible to live an entire life embracing anxiety. The avoidance of anxiety is a cowardly life; it turns anxiety into fear. The life that embraces anxiety would then be one of extreme courage and heroism. Is such heroism possible?

This heroism would be a matter of constantly dying, constantly being-toward-death, constantly open to the indefiniteness in the certain menace of death, constantly separating oneself from hearsay, constantly purifying the soul of everydayness. Has anyone ever lived such a life? I wish to propose two examples of such heroes, ones we have already met as heroes in a different context: Socrates and Husserl. The philosophical life is already an extreme form of Dasein, and Socrates and Husserl are extreme examples of that life. They never cease philosophizing all their waking hours, which I take to mean that they are constantly preoccupied with wonder, with perplexity, with distinguishing Being from beings. Such preoccupation is precisely what it means to approach death authentically, and it also means to live constantly in anxiety, not as emotion but as disclosedness of the Being of the beings we ourselves are.

With regard to Socrates, I will follow three lines of evidence: his never leaving the city, his alternative penalty at his trial, namely, meals for the remainder of his life at public expense, and his portrayal in Aristophanes' *Clouds*. All three cases are instances of Socratic irony; Socrates shows who he is by giving the appearance of who he is not.

Socrates is famous for never leaving the city, and I exploited this fame in chapter 1 so as to place the *Phaedrus* between the *Republic* and the *Timaeus*. By never leaving the city, Socrates seems preoccupied with worldly affairs. That is how he was understood by Cicero; instead of pursuing things that transcend the human sphere, Socrates "called philosophy down from the heavens and relegated it to the cities of men and women."[9] Thus Socrates' questions were ethical and political: What is courage? What is piety? What is the ideal polity? But this is sheer irony; as mentioned earlier, even when the ostensible topic of his conversation is some moral issue, Socrates' aim is always to open up the divine realm, the realm of the Ideas. In other words, he is concerned with bringing philosophy, or the human gaze, up to heaven. Only in the superficial, physical, spatial sense does Socrates remain in the city; his attention is constantly on what lies beyond, in the realm of the Ideas. Indeed, Socrates is famed for his aphrodisial encounters. He does not practice Platonic love in the sense of bypassing the carnal so as to gaze at the Ideas "by themselves, in the clear, unmingled, uninfected with the slightest tinge of anything bodily or human" (*Symposium*, 211E). Nevertheless, Socrates is not *mired* in carnality. Socrates is intent always on recollecting the Ideas, especially that most lustrous idea, beauty, but he approaches the divine realm *through* intimate contact with the beautiful bodies of this world, not apart from them. In that sense, it could be said that Socrates is most in the city and also most beyond, most immersed in beings and also most intent only on what can be attained by passing right through them.

Socrates was found guilty on charges that basically amounted to hubris, and the prosecuting citizens proposed the penalty of death. Socrates offered an alternative: a lifetime of free food (a reward reserved for heroes of Athens such as champions in the Olympic games). This proposal struck the dikasts as so hubristic that eighty of those who had found him innocent then voted to execute him.[10] Socrates' alternative presents the appearance of hubris, but it may be Socrates' way of acknowledging he is a man as are other men—he needs bodily nourishment and does not feed on Ideas alone. But this appearance of humility is itself ironic: Socrates is famous for needing very little food, sleep, and clothing. He does live more than would seem humanly possible in the world of the Ideas and does not eat as do other men.

Aristophanes presents Socrates as living up in the clouds. The Socrates of the play does not merely ascend to the clouds at times, he resides there. An ancient anecdote reports that Socrates was in attendance at the first performance of the *Clouds*, and when the actor portraying him entered (though he did of course not *walk* on stage), Socrates stood up and turned around so the other audience members could see how the mask of the actor faithfully matched the original. The irony is that by this gesture Socrates was showing that he took no offense at this portrayal; it is all a joke. But in fact Socrates did live up in the clouds, not in the pejorative sense of Aristophanes, whereby Socrates is a charlatan teaching trick arguments, but by constantly practicing recollection of the Ideas. Socrates is closer to heaven than is anyone else.

Husserl was the proverbial absent-minded professor. But that too is an ironic characterization, because from a philosophical point of view, absent-mindedness is precisely attention to practical affairs. Present-mindedness is to be preoccupied with Being in distinction from beings. And Husserl was apparently as distant from the practical, material world as could be imagined.

Husserl's powers of concentration and sustained study were legendary. He wrote every day, amassing 35,000 closely written pages, found after his death. His assistant provided him a stack of newly sharpened pencils every morning, and they all had to be sharpened the next day. Husserl took distance from the real world, as if he was constantly carrying out his transcendental reduction.

This reduction, as mentioned in chapter 1, is an abstaining of judgment regarding the existence of the world. It is entirely comparable to the experience of anxiety as described by Heidegger. Under the reduction, the things of the world are looked upon from a distance; they do not touch the philosopher, who becomes, in Husserl's terms, a "disinterested spectator." Husserl's entire phenomenology is carried out in this attitude, which seems to have been Husserl's way of being-in-the-world in general. The transcendental reduction does not arise from denial or doubt concerning the things of the world. They are held at arm's length for the sole purpose of contemplating them. Therefore, as Merleau-Ponty says, the best way to characterize the reduction is to call it wonder.[11] It seems to have been Husserl's constant state.

SUMMARY OF HEIDEGGER ON DEATH AND ANXIETY

The understanding of being-toward-death as preoccupation with disclosing Being, with reading off the meaning of Being in general from the Being of Dasein, is confirmed and not contradicted by Heidegger's assertion that being-toward-death is essentially anxiety. Anxiety is not the dread of dying; it is the disclosedness of the Being of Dasein as being-in-the-world. Indeed it is the preeminent mode of such disclosedness. Anxiety is the experience of the beings of the world as insignificant; it thereby throws Dasein back on his or her own resources in order to come to self-understanding. Anxiety thereby pursues Dasein with a motive to authenticity. Inauthentic being-toward-death flees this pursuit; authentic dying embraces it. But both the authentic and the inauthentic take their direction from what is disclosed in anxiety; both are thereby essentially anxiety.

Anxiety is phenomenal evidence of the unity of the Being of Dasein as being-in-the-world. It is phenomenal evidence—to someone who is already following Heidegger in asking the question of Being.

A life of constant anxiety, constant dying, constant wonder, constant philosophizing, constant authenticity, is possible. But such a life is rare, heroic, practically superhuman.

Anxiety requires courage, leisure, and openness to perplexity. Anxiety can be resisted, but it cannot be compelled. It is unmotivated. It is a gift.

ADDENDUM: POETIC EXPRESSION OF ANXIETY

[Untitled sonnet]

John Keats

When I have fears that I may cease to be
Before my pen has glean'd my teeming brain,
Before high-pilèd books, in charact'ry,
Hold like rich garners the full ripen'd grain;
When I behold, upon the night's starr'd face,
Huge cloudy symbols of a high romance,
And think that I may never live to trace
Their shadows with the magic hand of chance;
And when I feel, fair creature of an hour!
That I shall never look upon thee more,
Never have relish in the faery power
Of unreflecting love—then on the shore
Of the wide world I stand alone, and think,
Till love and fame to nothingness do sink.[12]

This poem expresses a transition from Heideggerian fear to Heideggerian anxiety. At first, the poet is attached to the world and is afraid of losing his hold on it. He fears he will die without filling volumes with his poetry and without attaining the person he loves. His demise is the before-which of his fear; fame and love constitute the about-which.

The last two and a half lines provide indications enough that the poet has become anxious instead of fearful. He is on the *shore* of the wide world; that means he stands at its edge, not involved in it but instead looking on from a distance. The world is *wide*; he is facing the world as such and not merely some definite things within it. The wide world is the indefinite one. The poet is *alone*; other Daseins have become insignificant. He *stands* there; it is not said that the poet *goes* there. He is *transported* there; anxiety has overcome him, he was not seeking it out. In anxiety, the poet *thinks*—presumably not of death, fame, and love, for worldly things and other people leave him untouched. He must be thinking of nothing; that is exactly what he says: worldly things have sunk into *nothingness*, that is, into uncanniness. The poet is not at home there on the shore. He is experiencing anxiety. The question is whether the poet will respond in an authentic way or will shrug off the anxiety and return to his everyday world of fears.

The evidence points to this experience as inauthentic anxiety. The poet will indeed return to everydayness, for he says he stands of the shore when—that is, *whenever*—he has these fears. The poem is in the present progressive tense. So he will return from anxiety to those fears. He is one of those persons who later say, "It was nothing." Nevertheless, he must retain some recollection of what was disclosed in anxiety. The anxiety has had some sustained effect, or else he would not recollect it in the poem and apparently find solace in it. The poet is therefore open to anxiety and has the courage for it. But he is not one of the rare Daseins who live in it constantly. Unlike Socrates and Husserl, this poet is not more than human.

Chapter 4

Conscience and Mortality

Hamlet:
Murder, though it have no tongue, will speak
With most miraculous organ.
. . . The play's the thing
Wherein I'll catch the conscience of the king.

Hamlet, II, ii, 630–42

CONSCIENCE AND THE BEING OF DASEIN

We have seen (chapter 1) that being-toward-death, authentic dying, anticipation, is not a matter of resolutely facing up to one's demise but is instead a matter of philosophizing, preoccupation with disclosure of the Being of Dasein. The experience of signs (chapter 2), which might seem to be a matter of one thing pointing to another, and today a matter of one thing pointing to the menace of death, is also a disclosure of the Being of Dasein. Furthermore, anxiety, which essentially characterizes being-toward-death (chapter 3) is not the dread of dying but is also the disclosure of the Being of Dasein. We are about to see in the present chapter that conscience as well, which is intrinsically connected to anticipation, that is, to authentic being-toward-death, is also nothing other than disclosure of the Being of Dasein, whereby it, too, is a matter of philosophizing.

CONSCIENCE AS CALL

Heidegger takes up the topic of conscience to provide, once again, phe-nomenal evidence. The evidence concerns anxiety and its role in authentic

being-toward-death. While reflecting on the experience of anxiety, the phenomenological philosopher sees an intrinsic connection between anxiety and
authenticity. For reflection, anxiety is a motive to authenticity, since anxiety,
the experience of the insignificance of the world, motivates individuation.
Moreover, the reflecting philosopher sees an *urge* toward authenticity in anxiety: anxiety is not simply disclosure of the opposite, inauthenticity, lostness
in the they, but also includes a positive impetus toward authenticity. But is
there phenomenal evidence that anxiety compels, even demands, authenticity? Heidegger finds the phenomenal, everyday evidence in the experience of
conscience.

Heidegger begins by setting out the problem (*SZ*, p. 258). We are seeking
phenomenal evidence for an urge toward authenticity. Authenticity is possible only as a self-recovery from lostness in the they. For that self-recovery
to be possible, the authentic self has to be disclosed to Dasein. It is not enough
that anxiety simply holds out the specter of inauthenticity, lostness in the
world. It is not enough that the world has been made insignificant. There must
be a positive disclosure of authenticity. Because Dasein is *lost* in the they, it
must first *find* itself. And in order to find itself, it must first be disclosed to
itself in its possible authenticity.

After identifying this disclosure of the authentic self as the voice of conscience, Heidegger then outlines the path the analysis will take. Conscience
is disclosive. Dasein's disclosedness is constituted by affect, discourse, and
understanding. The mode of disclosedness most proper to conscience is discourse. Conscience is a call. As a call, it is an appeal to the authentic self, by
way of a summons to accepting its most proper guilt. (It is in this summons
that Heidegger will find the phenomenal evidence for an urge toward authenticity.) Everyday understanding does take conscience to be speaking of guilt
but fails to see wherein Dasein is primordially guilty, guilty in its very Being.
The task is then to exhibit the connection uniting authenticity, conscience,
and primordial guilt, the guilt which attaches to the very Being of Dasein
rather than the one stemming from an actual transgression.

Dasein is lost in the they because Dasein *listens* to others and fails to hear
its own self. The voice of the they is constantly droning in Dasein's ears.
This hearing has to be broken off by a different voice, a different appeal, a
different call, that of conscience. If Dasein is to recover itself from lostness
in the they, then Dasein must find itself as the self which has turned a deaf
ear to itself and has done so by becoming all ears for what the *they* says.
This enthralled hearing must be broken off; that is, it must be interrupted by
a different kind of hearing, one which is given to Dasein by Dasein itself.
The possibility of such an interruption lies in an "unmediated appeal" (*SZ*,
p. 271). This call will break off Dasein's self-neglecting spellbound hearing of the they, provided this call awakens a hearing in every way opposite

to the hearing that is lost in the they. The hearing attuned to what the they says is captivated by the noise of the manifold ambiguity of everyday idle talk which is always buzzing about the latest; in contrast, the call must call noiselessly, unambiguously, and without providing any foothold for curiosity. According to Heidegger, *"What calls in this way is conscience"* (*SZ*, p. 271).

What does Heidegger mean by an unmediated appeal? Presumably a mediated appeal would be hearsay, an appeal passed along through a third party. So this appeal would have to stem from the same Dasein as the one to whom the appeal is addressed. If so, then we can understand how the appeal would dispel the *self-neglect* involved in listening to the voice of the they.

Heidegger proceeds to say that conscience is not simply *like* a call; this is not a mere image, a metaphor. That is how Kant did conceive of conscience: a law court, a tribunal. To speak of conscience as a call is not such a metaphor; conscience *is* a call, a discourse, it gives us something to understand. Nevertheless, it is not an utterance in words. Vocal utterance is not essential to discourse and so is "not essential to the call either" (*SZ*, 271). Conscience has no tongue but speaks with most miraculous organ.

Silence can be eloquent. The negative can be positive. Heidegger is *the* philosopher of negativity—that is, of the positive power of the negative. Self-concealing, irony, hiding behind a pseudonym—all these can be more revelatory than direct self-showing. The silent treatment can be more expressive than an insult. Others who appreciate the negative are dialectical philosophers. According to Heidegger, however, they do not see what is positive about negativity and invoke it merely to keep the dialectic ongoing.[1] For Heidegger himself, the preeminent disclosedness to Dasein is in fact by way of negativity, that is, through silence, concealment, absence, absconding. Thus, it will be no surprise if conscience discourses by keeping silent.

Heidegger proceeds to articulate the structure of any discourse. This structure consists of three moments (*SZ*, p. 272). Discourse includes an about-which, that which is *talked about*. Furthermore, discourse provides *information* regarding the about-which and does so in a particular respect. That is, out of the about-which, discourse draws what it actually says, the said as such. Finally, in discourse as *communication*, what is said is made accessible to others, one's fellow Dasein, commonly by way of utterance in language.

Thus, the three moments in any discourse are:

1) what is talked about (the theme)
2) what is said (the particular information regarding the theme)
3) the actual communication of the information (commonly to other Daseins and commonly by way of language).

Heidegger then applies this structure to the discourse constitutive of con-science. First, in the call of conscience, what is the about-which, the talked about, the theme? Since this is a call, the question means: toward what is the call aimed, what is appealed to? In the case of conscience, this is not a what but a who. *Dasein* itself is obviously the about-which of conscience. This answer, as incontestable as it is, is also unacceptable, for it is too indefinite. Conscience does not simply call on Dasein to be attentive to itself. The call is not about Dasein in general. Instead, the call is about the way Dasein under-stands itself, about Dasein in its self-understanding.

How does Dasein understand itself? In its everyday average immersion in the world, Dasein understands itself in a worldly way, taking direction from other Daseins. The self of everydayness is the they-self. Everyday Dasein understands itself as undifferentiated from the they. For Heidegger, the call is indeed about the they-self and affects the they-self but is addressed only to the authentic self latent in the they-self and passes over the they.

Dasein, in the guise of its worldly self-understanding, gets *passed over* in the appeal. The call to Dasein's self takes not the slightest cognizance of that worldly self-understanding. Because only the authentic self latent in the they-self is summoned and brought to hear, the they collapses. But the fact that the call passes over the they and the public way of interpreting Dasein does not at all signify that these are not affected. Precisely in passing over, the call thrusts the they into insignificance, the very they that is "intent on notoriety" (*SZ*, p. 273). The authentic self, which the appeal deprives of its refuge and hiding place, is thereby delivered to itself by the call.

We see an obvious similarity to anxiety, which also reduces the they to insignificance. But with conscience the thrusting into insignificance is more forceful and more effective. The call of conscience is *oblivious* to the they, but the they is thereby nevertheless touched to the heart. For the they is intent on notoriety; to undergo being passed over is the death of the they. The call of conscience gives the they the silent treatment, a more effective repudiation than any reasoned argument or even than the mood of anxiety. Conscience, in colloquial terms, touches the they right where it hurts, in the desire of the they for acclaim.

Anxiety is the experience of the entire world as insignificant, and that is the motive to authenticity. But the call of conscience does not turn the self inward, closing it off from the world. Conscience makes the they, but not the world, seem insignificant. The appeal to the authentic self latent within the they-self does not press the authentic self back upon itself into an interiority, as if it was supposed to close itself off from the external world. The call leaps over all that and dissipates it, in order to appeal solely to the authentic self, which nonetheless does exist in no other way than in the "mode of being-in-the-world" (*SZ*, p. 273).

Thus, the call of conscience in a sense dissipates anxiety; at least it dissipates the isolation of Dasein from the world, which is central to the experience of anxiety. The call of conscious "leaps over" all that. It does not appeal to authenticity by making the world insignificant; on the contrary, it appeals directly to the authentic self, without the mediation of the insignificance of the world. The call of conscience leaves untouched the world which is an essential moment of being-in-the-world. Anxiety seems to be summoning Dasein to a life of constantly experiencing the uncanniness of the world, whereby action in that world would be cowardice toward anxiety, a dissipating of the uncanniness.

The ideal of authenticity as provoked by anxiety would be the life of Socrates and Husserl, a life withdrawn from worldly affairs. But conscience is calling for a different life, a life of authenticity lived out in the world, not in one's interiority. According to Hamlet, "Conscience does make cowards of us all" (*Hamlet*, III, i, 83), holding us back from action. Admittedly, Hamlet is not using "conscience" in Heidegger's sense. Hamlet is referring to reflection, brooding, thinking too much. Nevertheless, Heidegger can be understood as claiming the opposite: conscience does make heroes of us all. As we will see, conscience urges Dasein to act in the world and even discloses the most proper action to take under the given circumstances.

Regarding the second moment of discourse: What is said in the call of conscience? What does the call call out? What does it tell Dasein? What particular information about the theme does conscience assert? Taken strictly, conscience says nothing. What does conscience call out to the one appealed to? The call expresses nothing, provides no information about worldly events, "has nothing to narrate" (*SZ*, p. 273).

The call of conscience is silent. But there can very well be a silent call, a silent summons in a specific direction. In everyday experience, a look of disapproval can be most effective and does not need words. But conscience is not a silent expression of *disapproval*; it does not dissuade. On the contrary, it summons forth, ahead. It shows the path to take rather than the one to avoid. Conscience is a "calling forth ('forward')" (*SZ*, p. 273). Accordingly, conscience is not the same as Socrates' *daimon*. Conscience is not the spirit that ever denies.

Heidegger takes pains to distinguish the summoning of conscience from a summons in the legal sense, the summons to stand trial. Perhaps Heidegger is purposely differentiating his view from that of Kant: conscience as tribunal. In any case, for Heidegger conscience is not the provoking of an inner debate. Conscience does not strive to open a self-dialogue in the self that has been summoned. "The intention of the call is not to place the summoned self 'on trial' in any sense" (*SZ*, p. 273). Heidegger's point is that conscience does not turn Dasein inward. He describes such a turning in very pejorative terms.

The self to which conscience appeals is not the self that can become to itself an object of judgment, not the self of curious dissection of its inner life, and not the self of an analytic gaping at psychic states.

Instead of all this, namely, conscience as a dissuading *daimon* or a deliberative tribunal, that is, conscience as provoking a turning back or a turning inward, for Heidegger conscience is a calling *forth* to possibilities. Conscience is an appeal to the possibility of being a self in the most proper sense, a calling of Dasein "forth (forward) to its most proper possibilities" (*SZ*, p. 273). For now in Heidegger's phenomenology of conscience, this is merely an allegation. Let us see how he works it out.

Heidegger's next step is to ask about the third moment of discourse, the mode of communication. How does conscience communicate its call? The call dispenses with utterance of any kind. The call does not place itself in words at all and nevertheless is anything but obscure and indefinite. Conscience discourses solely and constantly in the mode of silence. But it thereby not only loses nothing in the way of perceptibility but even compels into self-reticence the Dasein that has been appealed to and summoned. The fact that what is called out in the call lacks a formulation in words does not thrust the phenomenon into the indefiniteness of a mysterious voice but only indicates that the understanding of what is called out must not cling to the expectation of a "communication in the usual manner" (*SZ*, pp. 273–74).

Thus, the communication, the third moment, takes place entirely in silence. The call is silent, what is called out is silent, and the one who is called responds in silence. Silence does not simply mean that no words are spoken out loud; it means no words at all are involved in the phenomenon of conscience. The disclosure of conscience, although conscience is a mode of discourse, occurs at a more fundamental level of disclosedness, not that of language but of affect. Although not placed in words, what is disclosed is "unequivocal" (*SZ*, p. 274), and the target (*Einschlagsrichtung*, lit. "impact-direction,") is a sure one (*SZ*, p. 274).

Heidegger concludes the section on "The Character of Conscience as a Call" by maintaining that the next step toward an ontologically adequate interpretation of conscience will need to be clarification of the caller and called and the relation between them. The interpretation needs to clarify not only *who* is called by the call but also *who does the calling*, how the called is related to the caller, and how this relation is to be grasped ontologically as a "nexus of Being" (*SZ*, p. 274). These clarifications are the tasks of the next section of *Being and Time*, on "Conscience as the call of care." This section and the following, on guilt, constitute the heart of Heidegger's phenomenology of conscience, and I will follow the course of the analysis with close attention. For the first section, I will employ interpretive paraphrase, if you will pardon the somewhat self-contradictory expression, and then will return to the usual exposition with commentary.

CONSCIENCE AND CARE

Let us begin with the one who is called. Conscience summons the authentic self from its lostness in the they. This self is indefinite and empty in its "what"—versus the "what" of the they-self. That everyday self is not indefinite and empty; it possesses the definite content supplied by the world and other Daseins. The they-self is a present-at-hand thing in the world, with the content, the properties, appropriate to a present-at-hand thing. The call of conscience leaps over this thing and touches a self that lacks present-at-hand content. Yet, this authentic self latent in the they-self is touched unequivocally and unmistakably. Therefore, the one called is called irrespective of prestige as a person. The they-self lives on prestige, and if such prestige is passed over in the call, then the they-self becomes insignificant within the experience of conscience. The one called is not the they-self; for the rest, the one called is unfamiliar and indefinite.

The caller, too, is conspicuously indefinite. The caller is nothing worldly and so is unfamiliar to everyday Dasein. Yet the caller is not purposely in disguise; the caller simply refuses to be determined. And this indeterminateness has a positive character: it shows that the caller is entirely given over to the call and can only be heard, not idly chatted about. Therefore, the question of who the caller is is indeed not an appropriate question when actually hearing the call of conscience. The hearing should be given over entirely to hearing and not to asking theoretical questions. But the issue is legitimate within an existential analysis.

Is it at all necessary to ask explicitly who does the calling and who is called? Conscience is Dasein calling itself. It is insufficient to state that obvious fact, however, for the caller and the called are not simply identical. The caller is not someone other than myself and yet is not simply myself. The call is not in my power, not something I myself carry out, and it even calls to me against my will. Conscience comes from beyond me and yet indeed from me.

Everydayness recognizes only one mode of Being: presence-at-hand. Even tools are considered present-at-hand things; they merely possess additional properties, ones relating to usefulness. Thereby the voice of conscience is interpreted as some alien thing invading Dasein—God or some function planted in us in the course of our biological evolution. These interpretations explain away the phenomenon as experienced, but a phenomenological analysis is seeking phenomenal evidence and so must save the phenomena: the call comes from Dasein and yet from beyond Dasein. In other words, conscience is a peculiar phenomenon specific to Dasein and can be understood only through an adequate interpretation of the mode of Being of this being, a mode which is not presence-at-hand.

The distinctive mode of Being of Dasein is existence, being-in-the-world. Things present-at-hand do not exist; they are not *in* the world. Only Dasein is in the world disclosively; only Dasein is "into" the world, involved, interested. Only Dasein "exists," that is, takes some *stand* or other in regard to the world. Dasein has no choice in this matter; Dasein has been *delivered over* to being-in-the-world. Even to make no choice about a definite way to exist, that is, even simply to go along with the way the they relates to the world, is a choice. Therefore, Dasein is *thrown* into existence and does not by its own powers place itself in relation to the world or not. Dasein is free to choose its own way of existence, but this is a thrown freedom; Dasein is free by necessity.

This thrownness, this necessity of choosing, is ordinarily concealed to Dasein. Everyday Dasein takes the easy way out and drifts along with the crowd. Everyday Dasein does not realize it is then surrendering its freedom to the they. Anxiety, however, the experience of the insignificance of the world and of other Daseins, discloses the possibility of another way of existing, a deliberately chosen way, an authentic way. Anxiety is the experience of realizing that one has been fleeing from one's most proper possibility of choosing for oneself. Anxiety motivates a cessation of this fleeing.

Could not conscience then be the addition of an admonition to the opening up of the possibility of authenticity? In other words, the caller would be anxious Dasein, Dasein as facing the insignificance of the world and as motivated to individuation. Conscience would not be a mere *disclosure* of the authentic self but would also involve the authentic self *summoning* Dasein to actually be this possibility. Conscience would add to anxiety the experience of being admonished, Dasein being called forth to be what is opened up through anxiety. So anxiety would make the call of conscience possible. Anxiety would provide conscience with a voice, something to call out, namely, authenticity, and conscience would be the voice as actually calling. At least, that *could* be a way of understanding conscience, namely, the caller not simply as Dasein but as authentic Dasein and the called as everyday inauthentic Dasein, that is, the caller as anxious Dasein and the called as complacent Dasein. But does this understanding fit the phenomenal facts as we have laid them out? That is, does it save the phenomena?

The phenomenal characters to be accounted for are: the indefiniteness of the caller, its unfamiliarity, its repudiation of curiosity, its silence, and its assurance of striking the proper target. First, the caller is indefinite in its "who." That means the caller is nothing worldly; definiteness is a property acquired by circumscription amid other worldly things. If the caller is Dasein in its authenticity, then the caller is Dasein as uncanny, not at home, suspended in a void. Accordingly, in terms of the world, authentic Dasein cannot be made into something definite. Second, the caller is unfamiliar, something like an alien voice. But what could be more alien to the they than the authentic, individuated self which is constituted precisely by the call passing over the they as insignificant? Third, conscience offers no support for curiosity and idle chatter. That makes perfect sense if the caller is the authentic self, for this self has no content which could be spoken about in public. As a call to individuation, conscience offers nothing that could be shared in common; authenticity is the renunciation of everything common. Fourth, the call discourses in the mode of silence and is met with silence. The call has nothing to say which could be made public; that is the entire point of the call—to individuate rather than make public. But everything spoken out loud can be made public. The only alternative is to communicate by means of silence. Accordingly, both the caller and the called keep silent. Not only are the caller and the called not chatterers, they also have nothing to chatter about. Lastly, the call is assured of its target; it cannot be misunderstood as aiming at anything other than the authentic self. This assurance derives from the fact that the authentic self is radically individuated and cannot mistake itself for anything else. Authentic Dasein has nothing in common with anything with which it could be confused. Therefore, in summary, the phenomena can be saved by taking conscience as intrinsic to Dasein and not as the invasion of some foreign thing such as God or some process of evolutionary biology—provided the caller is authentic Dasein and the called is the same authentic self, as called out from its latency in the they-self.

It is the affect of anxiety that opens Dasein to the call of conscience. Anxiety is a motive to individuation by disclosing the world as insignificant and Dasein as not at home there, as uncanny. It is conscience, however, that lends the motive toward individuation its motive power. Anxiety discloses the path to authenticity, to projecting one's self-understanding upon freely chosen possibilities, especially upon that preeminent of all possibilities, the indefinitely certain possibility of death. Conscience is the call to actually take that path toward authenticity, toward one's most proper possibilities understood as such, toward a freely chosen way of confronting one's mortality. It was said in the discussion of anxiety that uncanniness constantly pursues Dasein; conscience is that pursuit in full force. Inasmuch as the voice of conscience can never be totally suppressed, uncanniness constantly pursues Dasein, constantly motivates Dasein toward authenticity and away from lostness in the they.

The sameness of the caller and the called in conscience is now shown to be ontically possible. The ontological grounding requires understanding conscience in terms of Dasein's own peculiar mode of Being. The Being of Dasein is care. Conscience is the call of care. That must now be clarified.

The fundamental ontological characters of Dasein are existence, facticity, and fallingness. These form a unity, and the question is how to characterize the unity. In what phenomenon are they unified? The characters are not different from the moments of being-in-the-world; they simply make more explicit the characters of facticity and fallingness. The basic understanding of Dasein as in immediate contact with the world remains.

1) The moment of existentiality refers to the circumstance that Dasein always understands itself in terms of possibilities. Dasein projects itself upon possibilities, and so Dasein is always already ahead of itself. This moment (ahead of itself) expresses an openness to the future.
2) Facticity is the same as thrownness. Dasein is thrown into a world; as anxiety shows, Dasein is abandoned to itself and already finds itself in a world not of its own making and in that world not by its own choice. Dasein is always already in the world and yet cannot rely on that world to understand itself, as anxiety also shows. This moment (already in) expresses an openness to the past.
3) Fallingness is equivalent to everydayness, inauthenticity. Dasein is always absorbed in the world, fleeing from the uncanniness of its authentic self into the familiarity of the busy public world. Dasein is always "into" the ready-to-hand things of the world. This moment (being into) expresses an openness to the present.

The three moments joined together yield the structural whole of Dasein. The Being of Dasein then signifies "ahead-of-itself being-already-in (the world) as being-into (the beings encountered within the world)" (*SZ*, p. 192). This structure (ahead of itself, already in, being into) is the fulfillment of the meaning of the term "care." Care is the phenomenon unifying the ontological characters of Dasein. Care names the Being of Dasein.

Why the term "care"? It is appropriate, provided the term is understood ontologically rather than ontically. Thus the term does not refer to care in the sense of solicitude, nurturing, love (hate is an example of care; it is taking interest in someone versus total indifference). Nor does it mean practice versus theory (theory is care; it is taking an interest, thematizing). Nor does it mean apprehensiveness (in the sense of having cares versus being carefree). Nor does it signify gloom, melancholy.

Ontologically, as unifying the moments of the Being of Dasein, care means any way of being interested in anything, even if the interest is negative and manifested by turning one's back on a threat or on something uncomfortable. The only opposite to care is utter indifference to everything. Care is exactly equivalent to intentionality in Husserl's sense; consciousness is always directed to something. Life is relational. A Dasein without a world, even a world to turn its back on, a Dasein that is utterly carefree (in the ontological sense), a Dasein that needs some bridge to escape from its own interiority, is a contradiction in terms.

How does this structure make conscience the call of care? How does conscience take its ontological possibility from the fact that the Being of Dasein is care? The answer is that conscience is structured the same way as is care; conscience can therefore take on the structure it has because Dasein is already structured in the exact same way. Conscience is the call of care: the caller is Dasein in its thrownness (as already being in) and anxious about its possibility; the one appealed to is precisely this same Dasein, summoned to its most proper possibilities (as being ahead toward); and the called is Dasein as summoned out of its fallingness in the they (as being into the world of its concern).

Put schematically, the three moments of care (thrownness = already being in; falling = being into the world; existence = being ahead of itself) correspond to the moments of conscience (caller, called, call) as follows:

1) Caller: thrownness (facticity). The caller is Dasein which in its thrownness is anxious about its authenticity. The caller is authentic Dasein as latent in the they-self.
2) Called: falling (inauthenticity). The called is Dasein as falling, as lost in the they-self.
3) Call: existence (possibility). Dasein is called to its most proper possibility, as individuated from the they-self.

This analysis of conscience has saved the phenomena inasmuch as it has recognized conscience as a phenomenon intrinsic to Dasein and has not had recourse to outside powers. Conscience has been traced back to the ontological constitution of Dasein, to the structural moments of the Being of Dasein as care. But many misgivings now arise in regard to this interpretation which seems so far removed from "natural experience." How can conscience be understood as a summons to authenticity when in ordinary experience it merely reproaches and warns? Also, does conscience in fact speak so indeterminately and emptily about a possible way for us to be in the future? Does conscience not speak determinately and concretely about our failures, both those we have already committed and ones we are contemplating? Does conscience offer anything positive at all? Is it not rather merely critical? Even a "good conscience" is only a judgment about the legitimacy of some action, and in that sense is positive, but is not itself a *disclosure* of what action to take.

These misgivings are legitimate, although they do not mean that the ordinary understanding of conscience has the final world concerning an *ontological* interpretation. Furthermore, the misgivings are premature inasmuch as the analysis of conscience has not reached its goal by merely grounding the phenomenon in the Being of Dasein as care. What is still needed is an account of the hearing, the understanding, of the call of conscience. This hearing is intrinsic to the phenomenon of conscience and not an optional addition. To grasp conscience as a disclosure of and demand for authenticity, we need to delimit the character of the hearing of the call.

What is heard in the experience of conscience, what is given to understand, has something to do with guilt. That is what "natural experience" most insists on—conscience is a voice speaking of guilt. To save the phenomena, we must therefore turn our attention to guilt. The foregoing general ontological characterization of conscience will provide a ground for an existential grasp of conscience as a discourse that exposes Dasein as guilty.

GUILT

After the preceding interpretive paraphrase, I return now to exposition with commentary.

According to Heidegger, ontological investigations of phenomena such as guilt, conscience, and death must begin in everydayness (*SZ*, p. 281). What is the common understanding of guilt? It is basically understood as owing something, failing to fulfill some obligation, depriving someone of something he or she has a claim to. It is being responsible for a lack, a privation, something that should belong to another but has been stolen or was never supplied on account of one's failure to supply it (sin of omission). For everyday Dasein, what is owed is understood in terms of things present-at-hand. Even if what is lacking is something usually ready-to-hand, such as an automobile, it becomes an object present-at-hand to the one who has lost it.

Heidegger maintains that what an ontological investigation can derive from the everyday understanding of guilt is that this phenomenon is constituted by a lack, a negativity, and by the sense of some agent being responsible for that lack. An existential inquiry must take this ordinary understanding of guilt and place it in relation to Dasein's sort of Being, which is not presence-at-hand or readiness-to-hand but existence. Any guilt whatever harbors the character of a "not." So we need a way to understand the "not" as applied to existence. Also, guilt includes the idea of responsibility for the negativity, being the basis for it.

These moments in the structure of guilt occur very differently in the everyday understanding of guilt and in the ontological way appropriate to an analytic of Dasein. For everydayness, guilt means being the basis of a lack in the existence of another, such that this basis is itself determined as "lacking from the lack it has brought about" (*SZ*, p. 282). That is a typically convoluted Heideggerian way of saying that a thief is guilty only after thieving, not before. In everydayness, the lack, the negativity, the guilt residing in the one who causes a lack in another derives from the lack that has been caused. A thief is considered to be lacking in some way (the way that makes him or her be called by the derogatory name of thief) on account of the theft of the other's property. The negativity in the thief accrues to him or her from the negativity he or she has caused in another. It is not the other way around; we do not consider anyone a thief until he or she has stolen something. The thief does not steal because he or she is guilty; he or she is guilty because of the thieving. In summary, for everyday Dasein in concernful relations with the world and with other Daseins, the negative (the lack, the guilt) in the basis (the thief) for a lack in another (the neighbor who has been robbed) does not derive from the basis (the thief) itself but only derives from the negativity (the lack in the neighbor) brought about by that basis (the thief).

A phenomenological, existential analysis of guilt is not concerned with Dasein's relations to others and to the world. The call of conscience telling of Dasein's guilt applies to Dasein as such, not to thieves as such. Dasein is intrinsically guilty, and so the structure of the guilt is different from the one of everydayness. The moment of being the basis of a negativity remains, and so does the moment of bringing about a negativity. (These moments are for Heidegger *formal* ontological characters of any guilt.) But the essential difference between everyday and existential guilt is that in the latter case the negativity in the basis is not a mere reflection from the negativity it causes. The negativity in the basis does not derive from causing a lack. On the contrary, there is a lack, a negativity, intrinsic to the basis, which is the reason it causes the lack. Taken in terms of Dasein as such, a thief steals, so to speak, on account of being already guilty. Therefore, Heidegger characterizes the intrinsic, primary, ontological, existential guilt of Dasein as follows: it is being the "negative basis of a negativity" (*SZ*, p. 285). According to Heidegger, that means Dasein as such is guilty, but he wonders if this intrinsic negativity can actually be exhibited in the Being of Dasein.

Let us first take up Heidegger's attempt at exhibiting the intrinsic negativity, whereby his conclusion is supposed to follow: Dasein as such is guilty. We will then be in a better position to cast a critical regard at his phenomenology of guilt.

Heidegger returns to the three moments of the structure of care and shows how each moment is suffused with negativity. Then he shows how two of the moments are the basis for the third. Thereby care will be exhibited as structured in the manner of a negative basis of a negativity, which is the definition of existential guilt. Accordingly, Dasein as such is guilty.

Let us begin by reiterating, as does Heidegger, the ontological characters of care. The three moments are existence (projection toward the future), facticity or throwness (finding oneself already in the world), and falling (everyday preoccupation in worldly affairs, being "into" the world in the present).

Existence, projection upon possibilities, is negative inasmuch as these possibilities are not simply in Dasein's power to devise at will. Dasein's possibilities are *given*, and freedom amounts merely to appropriating and choosing among limited possibilities. Dasein's freedom is not infinite, and Dasein's power of imagining new possibilities is limited. Furthermore, Dasein is not free *not* to choose some possibility or other. Finally, choosing one possibility necessarily means forgoing others, *not* choosing them. Therefore, this first moment of care is permeated with negativity.

Throwness is negative inasmuch as Dasein has been brought into its "there," its disclosive relation to the world, but *not* by its own power. Dasein has literally been *brought* there; it did not *bring* itself. Dasein *finds* itself in the world but cannot account for how it itself came to be there. Being there was not the result of its own free choice or the exercise of its own powers. Facticity is negative precisely inasmuch as it is *thrown* and not something Dasein itself has undertaken. Dasein simply and inexplicable finds itself already in the world. Thus, this second moment of the structure of care is also permeated with negativity.

Two of the moments of care are negative. Heidegger now argues that these two moments, in their negativity, constitute the basis of the negative third moment, falling: "Negativity resides essentially in projection [first moment] as also in throwness [second moment]. This negativity is the basis of the possibility of the negativity of fallingness [third moment], that is, the negativity of *in*authenticity" (*SZ*, p. 285). Therefore, care is structured as the negative basis of a negativity, two negative moments forming the basis of the negative third one, corresponding to the definition of existential guilt. Accordingly, Dasein in its very Being, Dasein as such, is guilty.

This analysis is Heidegger's answer to his question of whether something like an intrinsic negativity, an existential guilt, can be exhibited in the Being of Dasein. It is the core of Heidegger's phenomenology of guilt, yet he treats this exhibition in a most casual manner. Heidegger offers no elaboration or evidence. He merely asserts in one brief phrase that projection and throwness, in their negativity, form the basis of the negativity of the third moment. Heidegger does not even say explicitly how fallingness is negative. He merely italicizes the prefix: *in*authenticity. So inauthenticity is negative inasmuch as it is *not* authenticity. Hardly enlightening. Since Heidegger offers no evidence, perhaps believing the matter is self-evident, let us attempt to think through the issues critically on our own.

An issue relatively easy to dispose of is the negativity of fallingness. Not only is fallingness *not* authenticity, it is also subject to the concealment, the *not* letting things be seen, that permeates all inauthenticity. The they is superficial, and idle chatter propagates the superficiality. Lostness in the they *prevents* looking for oneself, is a *surrendering* of freedom, and is *not* the full potential of Dasein. Therefore, the negativity of falling is self-evident.

What is not self-evident is how the other moments constitute the basis of fallingness. We might draw a clue from the temporality of the structure of care. Each of the moments has a temporal correlate. Existence is projection into the future. Thrownness is finding oneself already in the world and so is correlated with the past. Falling is current involvement in the world in the present. Therefore, Heidegger is describing a movement in the Being of Dasein as care: from the future, back to the past, and then into the present. Such a movement is the way that in general temporality temporalizes, according to Heidegger. Future, past, and present exhibit the phenomenal characters of out toward the future, back to the past, and involvement in (being "into") ready-to-hand things in the present. The future has the priority; it traverses the past and then awakens the present. For Heidegger, temporality temporalizes itself out of the future such that, by futurally taking up the past, it first awakens the present. *"The primary phenomenon of primordial and genuine temporality is the future"* (*SZ*, p. 329).

We see this movement of temporality again and again in *Being and Time*. For example, it is the structure of everyday concernful dealings with ready-to-hand things. These dealings begin with a projection of some possible product, such as a house to shelter Dasein, a projection which leads the carpenter back to the hammer which already exists and which is then used in the present to fasten boards. In terms of involvement, the movement is from a project, to a with-which, and then to an in-which: from a possible shelter, to the already extant hammer *with* which to fasten boards, and then to the actual involvement *in* hammering. It is also the movement from the for-the-sake-of-which to the in-order-to: from some possibility of Dasein as the for-the-sake-of-which to the hammer which is in order to fasten.

Signs possess this same temporal structure. The experience of signs proceeds from an indication to stop the car in the immediate future, back to the brake pedal which already exists, and then to the present engaging of a complex mechanism of interrelated worldly functions that brings the car to a halt.

The temporality of anxiety is admittedly an exception to the rule. Anxiety proceeds from the past, to the future, and then to the present. Anxiety begins with a disclosure of lostness in the world (thrownness, past), to a projection of authenticity (existence, future), to a taking of an actual authentic stance (falling, present). The first two moments are reversed. I surmise the reason is the circumstance that anxiety does not actually disclose authenticity; instead, it discloses the opposite, the inauthenticity Dasein is motivated to turn its back on. As Heidegger says, however, for Dasein to find its authentic self that self must first be shown to it (see above, p. 84). Anxiety does not disclose the authentic self; such disclosure is the work of conscience. The summons of conscience shows authentic Dasein to itself and thereby imparts motivating power to the indefinite motivation included in anxiety. Consequently, anxiety does not proceed from a future authenticity; it proceeds from a past inauthenticity. Nevertheless, for purposes of comparison to the temporality of conscience, the essential remains, even in anxiety: the first two moments combine forces to impose on the third, the present.

If temporality temporalizes from out of the first two moments toward the third, then it makes sense that falling (present) would be founded on the other moments (future and past), and not vice versa. But how does falling derive its negativity from existence and thrownness? Heidegger does not say, but the implication is that the future and the past lend their own negativity to the present. Dasein's projection upon possibilities is permeated with negativity, its thrownness is as well, and insofar as the present involvement is awakened by these, it cannot help but be flooded with negativity. Thus, there is evidence for Heidegger's basing the negativity of one of Dasein's ontological characters on the negativity of the other two.

Misgivings still abound, of course, ones Heidegger himself had raised. The main one concerns the demand that a phenomenology of conscience remain faithful to, though not be entirely judged by, "natural experience." Would everyday Dasein find that its experience of conscience is recognizable in Heidegger's analysis? The answer, at least at first view, is a resounding "No!" Heidegger's analysis is a highly artificial and abstract construct; no one would think of conscience in Heidegger's terms unless he or she had read, closely read, *Being and Time*. Nevertheless, if we generalize and attempt to see through the abstruse language, we might find that Heidegger is indeed touching on natural experience. As regards possibilities: we do all recognize that our freedom is limited and that we cannot bend the world to our will. We do all also recognize that we have to choose among possibilities and that we have to forgo some which will be lost forever. In terms of the world: we do find ourselves in one that is given to us without the rhyme or reason. We do not know how we came to be involved in the world and what we are supposed to do there. As for our actual present involvements, we find ourselves tempted by many superficial things and under enormous peer pressure. Thus, the negativities Heidegger speaks of are not foisted onto everyday consciousness. *Being and Time* offers a highly elaborated and obscurely presented view of natural experience, but it is faithful to such experience.

Yet even if natural experience recognizes the negativities Heidegger speaks of, how is their disclosure a matter of conscience? Does everyday Dasein recognize itself as guilty of these negativities? Does the voice of conscience heard by everyday Dasein speak of this sort of existential guilt? Again at first view the answer is a resounding "No!" Conscience speaks of actual transgressions; what brings guilt is stealing and not simply being-in-the-world as care.

Yet let us take a clue from Heidegger's characterization of existential guilt as "primordial" (*SZ*, p. 284, referred to above, p. 84). The clue is then to relate this guilt to original sin. Indeed Heidegger himself explicitly closes off this possibility: the primordial guilt attaching to the very constitution of the Being of Dasein is to be strictly distinguished from "the *status corruptionis* [postlapsarian state of corruption] as understood in theology" (*SZ*, p. 306n). Heidegger goes on to say that the ontology of Dasein, as a philosophical questioning, in principle knows nothing of sin. Indeed original sin in the theological sense, the inheritance of guilt from a transgression by remote ancestors, has nothing in common with conscience as understood by Heidegger. Nevertheless, I believe a fruitful comparison can be made.

Original sin can be understood as neither an actual transgression nor the inherited state of corruption from an actual transgression. Instead, let us understand it as a sin of *omission*. This omission would stem from the negativity in the Being of Dasein and would then relate to conscience in Heidegger's sense. What sin of omission are we all guilty of? Answer: the sin of *complicity* in the spirit of the age. Our age is the epoch of modern technology, and this technology is a matter of a certain outlook on things in general. Heidegger's compelling critique of technology demonstrates that technology is not primarily a matter of practice; it is a matter of theory, a way of looking upon nature. Modern technology in its essence is the view of nature as a storehouse of disposables. A certain practice follows from that theory, the practice of ravaging nature to produce disposable goods, but technology itself is the theory behind the practice.

The spirit of our age is that of disrespect for nature as material we are entitled to consume. That consuming, that ravaging, makes our age the age of consumerism. Is anyone today totally innocent of consumerism? Are we not all complicit in it? Does anyone have a perfectly clear conscience? Even if we have not stolen anything, are we not all guilty of omitting many steps that could be taken to resist the consumer mentality? And do not these omissions stem from a negative propensity in our makeup, the propensity to go along with the crowd? Therefore, does not everyday Dasein hear, as weakly and implicitly as it may be, the voice of conscience as set out, in a highly elaborate and abstract way, by Heidegger? Then does not Heidegger's onto-logical analysis of conscience save the phenomena?

Before taking up the other misgivings mentioned by Heidegger, we still need, as he said, a better grasp of the hearing of the call of conscience. What does the call give Dasein to understand? Answer: what is heard is that Dasein is guilty in its Being, that its Being as care is pervaded with negativity. Conscience calls Dasein *back* from its obliviousness of this guilt, an oblivi-ousness promoted by lostness in the they and the superficiality and din of everyday chatter. Conscience calls Dasein *forth* to appropriate itself out of the they-self, to appropriate itself as the being it genuinely is, to appropriate the primordial guilt attached to its very Being. In short, conscience summons Dasein to be guilty wholeheartedly.

This summons is not, of course, a call to commit evil (*SZ*, p. 287). It is a summons to *existential* guilt, not to the guilt that derives from stealing present-at-hand things. The summons to be guilty signifies a calling forth to a possible way of Being, namely, authenticity, which Dasein in each case already is latently. Conscience is not a summons to become guilty through transgressions and omis-sions; it is a summons to appropriate the guilt Dasein always already has and thus is a summons to be "authentically guilty" (*SZ*, p. 287).

Conscience is a summons to something positive, namely, authenticity. Authenticity is a projection upon possibilities that arise from the individu-ated self rather than from the they-self. This positivity, however, is the dis-closure of *being guilty* as the most positive, primordial way for Dasein to be. Although conscience does not give any information, it is nevertheless not merely critical; it is *positive*. It discloses that the most primordially possible way for Dasein to be is "as being guilty" (*SZ*, p. 288).

What is being guilty as Dasein's most primordial way to be? What does it mean to be authentically guilty? Heidegger says explicitly only that it is "equi-distant" (*SZ*, p. 288) from seeking out factual guilt and from the intention to be liberated from existential guilt. Presumably, although the passages in question are abstruse even by the usual standards of *Being and Time*, what lies equidistant is what Heidegger does eventually identify as the way the appeal of conscience is authentically understood (*SZ*, p. 289), what he now calls "wanting to have a conscience," *Gewissen-haben-wollen* (*SZ*, p. 288). So understanding the appeal of conscience, authentic guilt, is wanting to have a conscience. To hear the appeal is wanting to be appealed to. What could all this mean?

It does not mean wanting a clear conscience, and it does not mean deliber-ately fostering conscience, willfully provoking the call of conscience (*SZ*, p. 288). Right at the beginning of his phenomenology of conscience, Heidegger stressed that conscience is not in Dasein's power; conscience even speaks against one's will. Therefore, Heidegger declares that this wanting to have a conscience is simply readiness for the appeal. What is involved in this readiness? It seems to presuppose what it makes Dasein ready for. It presupposes what it itself is supposed to make possible. If understanding the appeal requires a readiness, and if that readiness itself *results* from hearing the appeal, then Dasein is entangled in a circle.

Although Heidegger makes no mention here of this circle, it would be an instance of what he calls the "hermeneutical circle." Such a circle is not a vicious one, for it is not sterile, leading nowhere. For Heidegger, the task is not to resolve the circle, to find an absolute starting point, but to leap into the circle in the correct way. How can this circle involving conscience be entered?

The readiness for hearing the appeal amounts to this: a breaking of the bondage to the they and openness for bondage to one's own proper possibility of existence. Such breaking off of the domination of the they is the work of anxiety. So anxiety is a way to break into the circle, and we see how anxiety and conscience are indeed related the way Heidegger had earlier intimated: anxiety makes the hearing of the call of conscience possible. Anxiety provides conscience with a voice, something to call out, namely, authenticity, and conscience would be the voice as actually calling. Therefore, wanting to have a conscience, wanting to be appealed to, is to be open to anxiety.

I believe *Being and Time* hints at another preparation for hearing the voice of conscience, a way of preparation more in Dasein's own power. This preparation and way of breaking into the circle would reside in philosophizing. When Dasein, "in self-understanding" (*SZ*, p. 287), lets itself be called to appropriate its guilt, that means Dasein has become free for the call, ready for the capacity to be appealed to. The implication is that Dasein's self-understanding is what constitutes readiness to hear the voice of conscience. Self-understanding is what lets Dasein be called. Self-understanding, however, preoccupation with the Being of Dasein, is philosophizing. So philosophizing, disclosure of the Being of Dasein and wonder about Being in general, is preparation for appropriating one's existential guilt. In other words, philosophical disclosure of the Being of Dasein as care, as suffused with negativity, is readiness for the call of conscience. Therefore, what it ultimately means to appropriate one's guilt authentically, to be existentially guilty, to want to have a conscience, is to philosophize, to be preoccupied with the Being of Dasein as care.

The circular problem, however, arises again immediately in regard to this way of understanding the authentic appropriation of existential guilt. According to Heidegger, conscience is what *first* discloses the Being of Dasein as riddled with guilt and negativity. In other words, hearing the voice of conscience is preparation for philosophizing, for philosophical disclosure of the Being of Dasein as care. Thus, hearing the call makes philosophy possible; it is the first disclosure of care. So how can philosophizing be preparation for hearing the call? Each presupposes the other. Philosophy is preparation for hearing the call; hearing the call makes philosophy possible.

Heidegger does not mention the circle in this form either, but *Being and Time* would surely allow the circle to stand. The proper response would be to leap in at whatever point one found oneself and let the two sides enrich each other. For the later Heidegger, however, I believe philosophy and the hearing of a summons do not form a circle at all. There is a first beginning; one of them takes the initiative and motivates the other. Expressed in terms of his later thought, the issue is the relation between Being and philosophy or between the gods and the philosopher. For the later Heidegger, these are related in the pre-Socratic way, whereby the gods have the priority. The philosopher does not take up Being as a topic; on the contrary, Being takes up the philosopher. Philosophy is a *response* to a claim stemming from something ascendant over Dasein. That is why, as noted earlier, Dasein comes to be characterized as steward and preserver rather than discloser.

Being and Time is the expression of a philosophy of rugged individualism. Not only is there the almost constant denigration of the they, the crowd, the everyday, but Dasein is also presented as self-sufficient in its disclosedness. The understanding of the meaning of Being is the accomplishment of Dasein's staunch exercise of its own disclosive powers. That self-sufficiency is the reason Heidegger keeps insisting that conscience is not to be understood as a voice arising from anything outside of Dasein. Conscience is a phenomenon running its course entirely within Dasein; it is merely the authentic self summoning the self that is lost in the they. For the later Heidegger, however, the disclosure of Being is primarily a gift offered by the self-showing of the gods (indeed a self-showing by way of absconding), of Being, of truth. There is something ascendant over the Being of Dasein, something that holds sway over Dasein's disclosedness. Dasein is not self-sufficient in its disclosedness. Dasein must to some extent *receive* the truth and not merely wrest it out. That is why eventually "truth" is given a new name, a negative and passive one: "unconcealment." This is not, Heidegger insists, a mere change in name; it represents a change in attitude: from a view of Dasein as discloser to the one of Dasein as shepherd.

Accordingly, the later Heidegger, looking back on *Being and Time*, writes in the margin of his copy of the book, at the passage concerning care as the structure of Dasein's disclosedness, "But care itself is under the sway of the truth of Being" (*SZ*, Gesamtausgabe edition, p. 252n).

Heidegger now turns to the misgivings he had noted earlier, the discrepancies between his ontological analysis of conscience and the everyday interpretation. He stresses that the way everyday inauthenticity understands conscience cannot be the "ultimate criterion" (*SZ*, p. 290), yet an ontological analysis has no right simply to disregard the everyday understanding. Indeed that understanding should now become intelligible, especially in the ways it misses the phenomena and the reasons it conceals them. Thereby light is shed back on the ontological analysis by contrast with the failings of every-dayness. Heidegger himself says that this confrontation with everydayness, while important, is a subsidiary one, whereby a cursory treatment will suffice. Heidegger lists four misgivings; I will let a look at his discussion of two of them suffice for present purposes.

The first misgiving has to do with time. The existential interpretation takes conscience as a calling *forth* to guilt, whereas the everyday understanding sees conscience only as following *after* an evil deed, a looking *back* on some-thing that has already occurred. Existentially, the call of conscience precedes the guilt; for everydayness, the guilt precedes the call.

The crux of the matter, for Heidegger, resides in the "ontological fore-having" (*SZ*, p. 290), that is, the presupposed understanding of what it means to be in general, which forms the background for the interpretation, whether existential or everyday. Everydayness recognizes only one mode of Being: presence-at-hand. Time is then conceived as a linear succession of present-at-hand events. Conscience, the call, guilt, the evil deed—these are all present-at-hand things, and they occupy a fixed position on the temporal series of present-at-hand events. Taken in these terms, the voice of con-science is indeed positioned after the evil deed; conscience is experienced as subsequent, as being called up by the past event. But—and this is the heart of the issue—the phenomena of conscience such as the call and guilt are *not* present-at-hand things. Their proper ontological context is not presence-at-hand but existence. They are phenomena pertaining to the Being of Dasein. Therefore, their proper temporality is the one of care. Such a temporality is not a linear one; it is a very convoluted one in which the future has the priority. Therefore, if taken in its proper context, it is possible for the call of conscience to be a calling *forth* to guilt, authentic guilt. Thereby the call of conscience precedes the guilt, rather than following afterwards. The call is one to appropriate authentically the Being of care, which means to appropri-ate care as guilty—as the negative basis of a negativity. In its most proper context, therefore, the call precedes the assumption of guiltiness; it is a call to *become* guilty, to take on explicitly what is latent in the structure of the Being of Dasein, namely, existential guilt. The call of conscience precedes existen-tial guilt, the guilt proper to the temporality of existence; only in the foreign context of presence-at-hand does the call of conscience follow upon guilt.

This misgiving has therefore been laid to rest. It depends on an inadequate understanding of what it means to be and is not a refutation of the existential interpretation. Furthermore, the everyday understanding, as Heidegger fore-told, has become intelligible, especially in the ways it misses the phenomena and the reasons it conceals them. It misses and conceals by not philosophizing, by preoccupation not with the Being of Dasein but instead with everyday affairs and with the loud chatter of the they.

The other misgiving I wish to take up questions whether conscience is entirely critical, entirely negative, as the everyday interpretation maintains, or whether it also has a positive content, as in the existential understanding. In other words, does conscience disclose positive possibilities for acting in the world, or does it merely pass judgment on already accomplished or proposed actions? Does conscience in any way tell us what to do?

In its denial that conscience has such a positive content, the everyday understanding, according to Heidegger, is indeed correct—within certain limits. Conscience has no positive content in the sense of providing useful information for calculating the advisability of some particular action. Conscience does not give specific advice or provide practical maxims. Conscience is not positive with regard to specific worldly concerns, for the simple reason that conscience is about a being of an altogether different ontological kind than such concerns, namely, Dasein. Yet in that ontological realm, conscience is the most positive of all: it summons Dasein forth to its most proper positivity of existence, namely, authenticity. It is a call for Dasein to become factically authentic, to exist factically as authentic being-in-the-world. "To hear the call authentically amounts to engaging in factical action" (*SZ*, p. 294).

Factical is a synonym for ontic, existentiell, phenomenal, worldly, practical. Thus, Heidegger is here envisioning a positive practical application of conscience. Since the world is essential to the Being of Dasein as being-in-the-world, the disclosure of the authentic self by conscience must also disclose something about the authentic way to be related to the world, thus about authentic factical action in the world. In this way, conscience might be *indirectly* disclosive of positive possibilities of action. At this point, Heidegger leaves this positivity undeveloped.

Heidegger concludes his engagement with the misgivings by discussing the moral implication of the everyday versus the existential interpretation of conscience. It might be thought that, since everyday Dasein does not experience conscience in the primordial, existential sense, then this Dasein is morally inferior. Such is not the case. Nor is a Dasein in possession of an existentially adequate understanding of conscience necessarily morally superior. Honorable action stemming from the ordinary experience of conscience is "no less possible" (*SZ*, p. 259) than is dishonorable action from a primordial understanding of conscience. Knowing the theory does not necessarily entail putting it into practice. Nevertheless, Heidegger maintains, the existential interpretation of conscience does disclose *possibilities* for a more primordial existentiell understanding. Existentiell understanding is understanding put into practice, as long as ontological conceptualizing does not allow itself to be "severed from ontic experience" (*SZ*, p. 295). Therefore, the existential interpretation of conscience does offer at least the *possibility* of actions that are more honorable. For now, Heidegger does not pursue the connection between conscience and these possibilities. He will soon come back to it.

PRACTICAL WISDOM

In the final section of the chapter on conscience and guilt, Heidegger seeks the full existential structure of hearing the voice of conscience. He termed this hearing "wanting to have a conscience." It is an understanding of oneself in one's most properly possible way to be, namely, authenticity. It is a *disclosedness* of Dasein to itself. All disclosedness is comprised of the moments of discourse, affect, and understanding. Accordingly, to unfold the full existential structure of hearing the call, which is wanting to have a conscience, those moments need to be made explicit.

Heidegger begins with understanding, which is always a projection on possibilities. What does Dasein project itself upon in wanting to have a conscience? We know the answer is that Dasein here projects itself on its most proper, existential guilt, upon the negativity in the structure of care. Heidegger now expresses the projection of wanting to have a conscience as a projecting of oneself, according to the respective case, on the most proper factical possibility of one's potential for being-in-the-world. This potential, however, is understood "only by actually existing in that possibility" (*SZ*, p. 295). This way of expressing the projection included in hearing the summons of conscience provides a first indication that Heidegger is linking conscience to ontic practice. He says that the projection is carried out according to the respective case, which means the projection varies, case by case. It is not an abstract universal projection that takes no account of the factical situation of the respective Dasein. Furthermore, the projection is upon a *factical* possibility. Since "factical" means "practical," "existentiell," Heidegger is here speaking of the possibility of *acting* authentically. Finally, Heidegger says that the potential for authentic being-in-the-world is understood only by actually existing in that possibility. In other words, it is understood in the course of actually existing as a being-in-the-world, as "into" the world in some definite way or other, acting practically in the material world.

With regard to the affect corresponding to this understanding, that is, the affect accompanying the self-disclosure of Dasein in existential guilt, Heidegger identifies it with anxiety, as we might expect. In understanding the summons of conscience, Dasein is individuated and as such is uncanny to itself. This uncanniness, Heidegger now says, is concomitantly disclosed in understanding but is genuinely disclosed "only in anxiety" (*SZ*, p. 296). This, too, expresses a distinction between theory (understanding) and practice (anxiety), and Heidegger is giving the priority to practice. That is not surprising and accords with Heidegger's general view that Dasein's prime mode of disclosure is affect. But the conclusion Heidegger now draws *is* surprising: wanting to have a conscience becomes "readiness for anxiety" (*SZ*, p. 295). It is surprising because previously the relation was the exact opposite—anxiety as readiness for the understanding that constitutes wanting to have a conscience. The affect was readiness for the understanding; now it is the reverse. Previously, the ontic, factical experience of anxiety was readiness for the ontological, theoretical understanding of the being of Dasein as care. Now the existential is readiness for the existentiell. Theory is yielding to practice.

The third intrinsic moment of disclosedness is discourse. We know that conscience in its entire structure (call, calling, called) discourses in the mode of silence. Therefore, Heidegger is saying nothing new here by identifying the mode of discourse as silence, except that he distinguishes this silence from being mute (*SZ*, p. 296). A person is mute from having nothing to say or from not being able to say anything. But silence implies "having something to say" (*SZ*, p. 296). Thus, the call of conscience does not strike Dasein dumb. It does give Dasein something to say, but Dasein does not say it. Heidegger intimated earlier that Dasein is silent in hearing the call of conscience because conscience gives Dasein nothing to say. Dasein is taken up entirely in the hearing and has nothing to say in reply. Now Dasein has something to say. What? What would Dasein, responding genuinely and factically to the call of conscience, talk about? It would certainly not be more of the idle chatter of the they. Furthermore, while the experience of disclosedness was actually under way, Dasein would not speak out. But Heidegger is presumably leaving open the possibility of a later ontic, though authentic, talk. I believe I would not be entirely reckless in suggesting that such talk would reach its highest state in philosophical discourse. In particular, *Being and Time* may be a prime instance.

Heidegger summarizes and gives a name to the disclosedness pertaining to the hearing of the voice of conscience as follows. Dasein's disclosedness that resides in wanting to have a conscience is constituted by the affect of anxiety, by understanding as self-projection on one's most proper guilt, and by discourse as silence. This preeminent, authentic disclosedness, attested to in Dasein itself by conscience, this silent, ready-for-anxiety self-projection of one's most proper guilt, "we will call *Entschlossenheit*" (*SZ*, p. 296).

Entschlossenheit would ordinarily be translated as "resoluteness," but I wish to leave the translation open until we examine Heidegger's characterization of the phenomenon he is naming with this term (*SZ*, pp. 296–301). It is preferable to allow the characterization to determine the translation, and not vice versa. But I will offer a hint as to the direction I believe Heidegger is taking.

The hint is provided by the German dictionary of the Brothers Grimm,[2] the dictionary favored by Heidegger. As with almost all the entries, the Grimms first provide the Latin equivalent, even for words that are not rooted in Latin, and then the German meaning. The Latin is *animi praesentia*, "presence of mind." The German is *Geistesgegenwart*, again literally "presence of mind." The entry does not offer any synonyms but includes a historical reference to Goethe, who used the term to mean "nimbleness of mind." Therefore, the meaning of *Entschlossenheit* is almost the opposite of "resoluteness," with its connotation of a closing off of possibilities. To be resolute is to be loyal to some course of action, whereas, according to the Grimms, *Entschlossenheit* means to have one's wits about one and be open to new possibilities. The Grimms are therefore taking the word in its etymological sense: *ent-schlossen*, "un-closed." "Resoluteness" bears almost the exact opposite sense.

Heidegger begins his characterization by asserting that *Entschlossenheit* is a preeminent mode of Dasein's disclosedness. Disclosedness has to do with truth, and so *Entschlossenheit* is a disclosure of truth. *Entschlossenheit* is even the most primordial disclosure of truth, the acquisition of the most primordial, most authentic truth concerning Dasein. Resoluteness might indeed consist in steadfast *adherence* to the truth, but it has nothing to do with a *disclosure* of truth.

To disclose the truth of Dasein is to disclose being-in-the-world, including all three moments: the who, the world, and the affective being-in. Heidegger now fills a long paragraph with an overview of his understanding of the world of everyday concern, the world structured according to the for-the-sake-of-which, the in-order-to, the ready-to-hand, the co-Dasein of others, the they, and so on. His conclusion is that this entire world is transformed by the disclosedness of *Entschlossenheit*. The ready-to-hand world does not become another one in terms of content, nor is the circle of relations with one's fellow Dasein exchanged for another circle. Nevertheless, Dasein's way of relating to ready-to-hand things in dealing with them concernfully as well as Dasein's relation to others in being with them solicitously—these relations are now first determined on the basis of what "they most properly could be" (*SZ*, p. 298).

Accordingly, *Entschlossenheit* has a radical, although subtle effect. It does not change the content of one's relations, does not substitute one set of things and other Daseins with another set, but those relations now become authentic. Heidegger does not say exactly what this transformation is, but presumably these relations are in some way, some radical way, improved. They become all that they could be.

Heidegger continues to determine *Entschlossenheit* by saying that insofar as it is authentic disclosure of the self of Dasein, it does not detach Dasein from the world. How could it, since *Entschlossenheit* is *authentic* disclosedness and so illuminates nothing other than genuine being-in-the-world? *Entschlossenheit* points the way to authentic dealing with things and authentic relations with others. For the first time, these relations become genuine and not ones ruled by the ambiguity, jealously, and idle chatter that characterize lostness in the they.

Entschlossenheit is not a seizing upon possibilities, not a remaining faithful to some chosen project. On the contrary, *Entschlossenheit* is itself the disclosive projection and determination of what is practically possible at any given time. This sense of *Entschlossenheit* as characterized by Heidegger could hardly present it in greater contrast to resoluteness.

The counter-concept to *Entschlossenheit*, as understood existentially, is not *Unentschlossenheit* as usually understood. *Unentschlossenheit* ordinarily means irresoluteness, indecision, being wishy-washy. But that is *not* the counter-concept to *Entschlossenheit* as existentially understood. The proper counter-concept to *Entschlossenheit* as Heidegger employs the term is everyday understanding, lostness in the ambiguous way the they discloses things. Accordingly, *Entschlossenheit*, in the existential sense, cannot mean resoluteness, as is evident by Heidegger's discussion of the counter-concept.

Heidegger concludes his characterization of *Entschlossenheit* by distinguishing the "situation" (*die Situation*) from the "general location" (*die allgemeine Lage*) (*SZ*, p. 299). Both terms, "situation" and "location," have a spatial connotation but, as Heidegger is using them, only the latter is predominantly spatial. The they lives in a location, more or less absent-mindedly walking through life, although possessing enough spatial orientation not to bump into things. *Entschlossenheit*, however, gives Dasein a situation, a *situs*, a site, a settlement, a place to be at home and dwell. Authentic Dasein is not merely spatially oriented in the world but is also disclosive of the most genuine possibilities for acting in that world. *Entschlossenheit*, authentic being-in-the-world, being-in-a-situation, is presence of mind, nimbleness of mind, wisdom in regard to practical things.

How then to translate *Entschlossenheit*? What is Heidegger characterizing with this term? Certainly not "resoluteness." Heidegger is referring to something almost the exact opposite of what we mean by resoluteness or perseverance, tenacity, single-mindedness. Heidegger means some kind of open-mindedness, some kind of disclosure of possibilities, specifically ones having to do with practice.

For the translation I am about to propose, I will take a clue from Heidegger's discussion of the Aristotelian intellectual virtues. The particular virtue relevant for my purpose is φρόνησις, *phrónesis*, "practical wisdom."

I do not need to rehearse Heidegger's lengthy commentary. At the end, he focuses on a peculiar property noted by Aristotle: "there is no forgetting with regard to phronesis" (*Nicomachean Ethics*, 1140b28). The reason is that phronesis is in each case new; phronesis does not merely repeat a judgment made earlier, a judgment which could be forgotten. Circumstances are always different, and phronesis is the nimbleness of mind to make the correct judgment concerning what should be done here and now.

Heidegger's conclusion is that Aristotle has in this way turned phronesis into conscience: "Certainly the explication Aristotle gives is very meager. But it is nevertheless clear from the context that we would not be going too far in our interpretation by saying that Aristotle has here come across the phenomenon of conscience. Φρόνησις is nothing other than conscience set into motion, making an action transparent. There is no forgetting in regard to conscience; it always announces itself."[3]

I believe that in the existential analyses of *Being and Time*, Heidegger has carried out the corollary: he has turned conscience into phronesis. Conscience set into motion, conscience as heard authentically, is *Entschlossenheit*, which, as characterized by Heidegger, is practical wisdom, phronesis. Therefore, deriving the translation from the characterization rather than vice versa, I propose phronesis as the proper word to render the meaning of *Entschlossenheit*.[4]

If Heidegger is speaking of phronesis, the various characterizations now make sense, whereas they are inexplicable if thought in terms of resoluteness. In all cases, Heidegger is referring to a disclosure of the correct choice of action at any given time, and that capacity is phronesis, not resoluteness.

The strangest of the characterizations had to do with the way *Entschlossenheit* brings about a radical change in Dasein's relations to the world and to other Daseins. Heidegger said that these relations are now first determined on the basis of what they most properly could be. Resoluteness would not be able to bring about such a change, but phronesis does have the power to do so. If Dasein's relations were infused with practical wisdom, rather than being ruled by the ambiguity, jealously, and idle chatter that characterize lostness in the they, then a new world would indeed open up.

What is the justification for Heidegger's turning conscience into phronesis? There are two main problems. The first concerns the practical applicability of conscience. How does it come to have any applicability to the world at all? Heidegger has stressed that conscience has no positive content in the sense of providing useful information for calculating the advisability of some particular worldly concern, for the simple reason that conscience is about a being of an altogether different ontological kind, namely, Dasein. Furthermore, anxiety is essential to conscience, is readiness for hearing the voice of conscience, and anxiety involves a sense of affective detachment from the world. How is conscience supposed to undo this detachment when all that is supplied by conscience is a summons to understand the structure of care?

The second main problem concerns the vast scope of phronesis as described by Heidegger. Phronesis is such an all-encompassing nimbleness of mind that it discloses the best possible action to take in any given situation. Even if some practical applicability of conscience can be demonstrated, how could this applicability be so universal as to be capable of transforming the whole world into what that world most properly could be? The voice of conscience summons Dasein to an appropriation of guilt. How could guilt be connected to the kind of practical wisdom Heidegger is describing?

With regard to the first problem, let us begin by noting a trade-off, as it were, between conscience and guilt. They are completely incompatible and cannot both be present in the same Dasein. One drives out the other. Anxious Dasein feels detached from the world because the relation between the in-order-to and the for-the-sake-of-which has been severed. Anxious Dasein does not sense itself as a for-the-sake-of-which. The functional relations among things in the world proceed normally, but these relations do not appear to be for sake of this Dasein. Hence, the affective detachment. To appropriate existential guilt is to accept the entire structure of care, the entire structure of being-in-the-world. The world is an essential moment of care. And an essential moment of the world is the for-the-sake-of-which. Consequently, to appropriate guilt is to accept the role of the for-the-sake-of which. Thereby guilt dispels anxiety; it reunites Dasein to the world.

Anxious Dasein feels no guilt for the events occurring in the world. That is a consequence of experiencing oneself as detached, as looking on from a distance at the world as an alien place, as leaving the particular Dasein untouched. Conscience is the voice telling Dasein that such detachment is a lie. We *are* attached to the world, responsible for what is going on there. We *are* guilty. There is no escaping this guilt; even to do nothing and claim no responsibility is a way of acting, and we are necessarily responsible for what results from this supposed inaction.

Guilt dispels anxiety. By the same token, guilt profits from anxiety. Because anxiety took away a sense of attachment and responsibility, the restoration of these in guilt is all the more impressive. Without anxiety, there would be no authentic sense of guilt. Without anxiety, the connection of Dasein to the world would be taken for granted, and Dasein would remain in its everyday absent-mindedness. Everyday Dasein lives in a state of neutrality with regard to guilt and anxiety, with no sense of either. That neutrality could be offered as an excellent definition of inauthenticity. Authentic Dasein is one that passes through a strong sense of one to a strong sense of the other. Anxiety is a gift and not entirely negative, but conscience, guilt, attachment, responsibility—these have the final word.

Conscience makes heroes of us all. At least it would have compelled the brooding Hamlet to stop behaving as if he were an outside spectator of his own life and begin to act.

The second main problem flows from the first. Granted that conscience can have practical applicability, at least inasmuch as it motivates some action in the world, how can it turn into the phronesis characterized in *Being and Time*? To answer, we need to examine exactly what is disclosed in the appropriation of existential guilt.

To hear the summons of conscience is to appropriate the full structure of care, the full structure of being-in-the-world. The moments of care are the who, the world, and affective being-in. Conscience calls on Dasein to appropriate, but appropriation requires understanding. Therefore, conscience is calling on Dasein to understand care (existentially) and then appropriate it (existentielly). This summons to understanding is left implicit in *Being and Time*. But it is self-evident; Dasein cannot *blindly* appropriate its own Being. It must have some sense of what it is appropriating. So conscience is a summoning of Dasein to self-understanding, specifically to self-understanding as care. Included in the self-understanding of care are all the moments. Conscience is summoning Dasein to understand all the moments, the who, the world, and the being-in, in their unity. The point I am arguing toward is that there is nothing else left to understand. Furthermore, to understand everything in its unity is to understand the Being of beings. It is to philosophize. Therefore, conscience is a summoning of Dasein to philosophy.

Conscience is a summons to contemplate the meaning of what it means to be *tout court*, a summons to phenomenological ontology. Now, our sense of what it means to be has enormous practical significance. For example, as already mentioned, if Dasein understands what it means to be as amounting to disposability, then the instruments to turn nature into disposables will be produced and the actual ravaging will be carried out. *Being and Time* does not suggest what will be disclosed by authentic Dasein, while contemplating care in all its moments, as the meaning of Being. Presumably, such Dasein will resist the outlook of modern technology, the view of Being as equal to disposability. Then nature might be spared the ravaging, and the entire world might indeed be changed for the better.

In summary, philosophy, inasmuch as it discloses what it means to be, does turn into phronesis. Indeed philosophy, ontology, leads to practice only indirectly. It provides no specific practical maxims, but it does lead to a specific practice, since how we look on things determines what we do with them and do to them. Accordingly, conscience, the summons to appropriate one's guilt, to understand the structure of care, to contemplate what it means to be in general, to philosophize, does amount to phronesis and even to a universal phronesis.

What Heidegger is saying, in Socratic terms, is that virtue can be taught, virtue is a matter of knowledge. Socrates does not mean that if we truly and genuinely know the right thing to do (or to avoid), we will do it (or avoid it). Socrates is not referring to such a simplistic connection between virtue and knowledge. To understand the Socratic connection, we need to begin with the distinctive Greek conception of virtue. The Greeks can and do speak of the virtue of a *thing*, such as an axe. The virtue of the axe is its sharpness, that which allows it to go on functioning as an axe, that which keeps it same with itself. Human virtue is then not some moral quality added on to human nature; human virtue is that which keeps a person same with human nature, same with himself or herself. In general, for the Greeks, virtue means self-sameness. The connection between virtue and knowledge is this: in order to institute a self-sameness in ourselves, we need a paradigm to live up to. We need a shining example of self-sameness to emulate. This example is supplied by the Ideas. As was mentioned earlier, the Ideas are radically self-same. It is by recollecting the Ideas, therefore, that we acquire the paradigm that makes it possible for us to institute a self-sameness in ourselves, which amounts to being virtuous. For Socrates, the Ideas and especially the Idea of beauty can be taught; there is a method to recollect them. That method is Socratic love. By intimate contact with a beautiful thing, we are provoked to behold the Idea of beauty appearing through. That intimate contact, however, cannot remain at the level of mere carnality; it must be open to philosophy. Socratic love can be generalized; it then refers not to aphrodisial relations but to any intimate, personal knowledge. To practice Socratic love is to look and grasp some being for oneself and not rely on hearsay. Socratic love is then a separating the soul from what *they* say about a thing. To practice Socratic love is thus equivalent to dying. And dying is equivalent to philosophizing, disclosure of the Ideas, disclosure of Being as such. This knowledge is the one that really matters, the one connected to virtue. How we understand what it means to be determines how we comport ourselves toward beings. Therefore, as Heidegger says, what is revealed in conscience, the whole of Being in general, does have radical practical potential. Our practice in regard to beings depends on our understanding of what it means to be in general, and inasmuch as this knowledge is provided by conscience, Socratic love, recollection of the Ideas, philosophizing, then ontology is a radically transformative phronesis.

Let us return to the caller. For *Being and Time*, the caller is the authentic self summoning itself out of its latency in the they-self. Yet does not the authentic self that does the calling also need to be called? Can the phenomenon of conscience remain entirely within the compass of Dasein? For the later Heidegger, it cannot. Dasein does not call itself to philosophy; something ascendant, Being, does the summoning. The philosopher is one who is claimed, and philosophy is a response. In *Being and Time*, Heidegger dismisses any sort of outside caller. But I believe the book does contain an adumbration of the later view. The adumbration consists in an obscure reference to the "voice of the friend."[5]

The topic of the voice of the friend arises in a discussion of hearing as the basis of discourse: our speaking is a response to something we have heard. Heidegger at first relates hearing to other Daseins, friends (or enemies) in the usual sense and maintains that hearing is the existential openness of Dasein as Being-with in relation to others. Heidegger immediately goes on to expand the role of hearing in a most surprising manner: hearing even constitutes the primary and authentic openness of Dasein for its "most proper possibility with regard to Being, by way of hearing the voice of the friend whom every Dasein carries with it" (*SZ*, p. 163).[6]

The most proper possibility of Dasein with regard to Being is simply Dasein's understanding of what it means to be in general. So the hearing at issue here is not merely an openness to other Daseins but is an openness to the meaning of Being. That is why Heidegger says that this hearing *even* constitutes such openness; it goes beyond interaction with other people.

Therefore, the friend at issue here is Being itself, its "voice" is the self-disclosure of Being to us, and "hearing" this voice is understanding what it means to be in general. Heidegger is employing figurative language to express what makes Dasein Dasein, namely, an understanding of Being.

If we take the voice of conscience to be a caller that is ascendant over Dasein and not simply the authentic self, then the voice of the friend and the voice of conscience are one and the same. This voice is a summons to philosophize, to hear the self-disclosure of Being. And such hearing would indeed have practical effects, for it would turn into phronesis.

AN ANTICIPATING PHRONESIS

At the end of the chapter on conscience in *Being and Time* and at the beginning of the next chapter, on Dasein's temporality, Heidegger finally raises the issue of the connection between conscience and being-toward-death. Is there an *intrinsic* connection, such that conscience by its own internal logic is brought into connection with anticipation, authentic dying? Heidegger finds this connection in what he calls an "anticipating phronesis" (*SZ*, p. 302).

The general idea is as follows. Phronesis obtains its capacity to disclose practical possibilities from the ontology that lies behind it. The more adequate the ontology, that is, the understanding of the meaning of Being in general, the more genuine will be the phronesis, the disclosure of the concrete situation for taking action. Therefore, phronesis must be based on an adequate understanding of the Being of Dasein. To be specific, it must be based on an understanding of Dasein as a whole.

The wholeness of Dasein has two aspects, which could be called the structural and the temporal, the synchronic and the diachronic. Structural wholeness refers to the unity of the moments of care, the unity of the moments of being-in-the-world. The diachronic wholeness is the unity of Dasein in its extension through time, all the way to death. Conscience discloses the structural wholeness; anticipation, the temporal.

Therefore, phronesis must of its own internal logic become an anticipating phronesis. In other words it must be based on an ontology of Dasein that includes the temporal wholeness, the wholeness supplied by anticipation, authentic being-toward-death.

We have seen that anticipation is not preoccupation with dying; it is neither a fleeing from death nor a resolute facing up to the end. Anticipation is a way of understanding the possibility of death as a most proper possibility. Such a possibility is distinctive of Dasein, and thus anticipation is an understanding of the Being of Dasein. Anticipation is equivalent to philosophizing.

Phronesis is the application of ontology. Conscience is the call to appropriate one's existential guilt, which means to understand the structure of care, which means to understand the Being of Dasein as being-in-the-world, which means to understand the meaning of Being in general, which means to philosophize.

Accordingly, the intrinsic connection between conscience and authentic dying, between phronesis and anticipation, derives from their common ground. That ground is philosophy. Phronesis and anticipation are unified by converging on the same point: an understanding of what it means to be in general.

CONCLUSION TO THE FIRST FOUR CHAPTERS, ON THEMES FROM *BEING AND TIME*

The themes of these four chapters have been death, signs, anxiety, and conscience. As disparate as these might seem, they are all of them about disclosing the Being of Dasein, philosophizing. They are all of them about hearing the voice of the friend, a hearing that makes Dasein be Dasein, a place where Being discloses itself, a place where resides an understanding of what it means to be in general. They have all of them also been about the hearing of the voice of conscience, for to hear that voice also means to understand the Being of Dasein, specifically as care, as being-in-the world.

There is another voice which figures very largely in *Being and Time*, the voice of the they. That voice constitutes a radical negativity in Dasein. It is the voice of mediocrity, ambiguity, complacency, inertia. It is a constant menace to philosophy, since it is satisfied with the average everyday superficial understanding of what it means to be, self-satisfied in its lack of perplexity over the question of Being. This voice spells the death of philosophy.

The voice of the they is the loudest of all the voices mentioned in *Being and Time*. We all hear it loud and clear. It is a voice that constantly pursues us. This voice which would strangle the call to authenticity and to philosophy is what is most morbid about our lives. This voice, even more than the menace of death, makes our atmosphere a mortal one. The voice of the they does not threaten life as such, but it smothers anxiety and existential guilt. It separates the soul—not from the body but from autonomous existence. It divides us from ourselves, that is, from our "fair judgment, without the which we are pictures, or mere beasts" (*Hamlet*, IV, v, 86).

Chapter 5

Music of Mortality

Orsino:
That strain again! it had a dying fall.

Twelfth Night, I, i, 4

BEETHOVEN'S KREUTZER SONATA

When in the first chapter I compared *Being and Time* to a Platonic dialogue, I stipulated, although it was hardly necessary, that I was not referring to style. *Being and Time* is prose and, even more than that, belabored prose. To work one's way through it is to tread over rocky ground indeed. Yet Heidegger could write artistically, and in this chapter, as promised, I will produce evidence.

Heidegger's small book *Gelassenheit*[1] does, I believe, qualify to be called art. As I attempted above in regard to the *Timaeus*, I will again emulate Agathon (*Symposium*, 197E) and blend play and seriousness, this time with a view to demonstrating that Heidegger's *Gelassenheit* is a sort of music and indeed music specifically about death.

Heidegger himself seems to have been attuned much more to the sounds of nature than to music. I can offer excellent anecdotal testimony, deriving from a late teacher and colleague of mine, André Schuwer, OFM. This Franciscan friar enjoyed a personal relationship with Heidegger and was one of the very few regular visitors allowed at the philosopher's rustic chalet in the Black Forest. Schuwer visited Heidegger every summer for many years. On one occasion, in the midst of a conversation about St. Bonaventure, Heidegger suddenly broke off the discussion and led Schuwer outside to hearken to the sound of sheep and sheep bells off in the distance. Schuwer said the sounds were only faintly audible, with the sheep themselves not even in sight, but the disordered jangles and bleats caught Heidegger's ear and brought him great delight. According to Schuwer, he and Heidegger never discussed music.

Of course Heidegger did know and appreciate classical music and must have listened often, considering his extensive record collection. But Heidegger did not play an instrument, and musical references are extremely rare in his writings. He seldom thematizes music as an artform, and when he does, his purpose is to denigrate it, as we are about to see. In referring to things heard, Heidegger's typical examples are not musical sounds but the creaking wagon, the north wind, the rapping woodpecker, the crackling fire (*SZ*, p. 163). These are quintessential examples taken from the world close to Heidegger's heart.

In downplaying music, Heidegger stands in stark contrast to Husserl. The founder of phenomenology was a virtuoso on the violin and in his writings often refers to music and especially to his favored instrument. He takes up the violin not only when discussing sound; he also has recourse to it in terms of its elegant shape and even in terms of monetary value.[2] Furthermore, the hearing of a melody is for Husserl the prime illustration of the synthesis of time, whereas Heidegger, although he writes extensively on temporal experience and as Husserl's assistant even edited for publication Husserl's lectures on the consciousness of internal time, does not ever appeal to music in this context.

Heidegger nevertheless did enjoy classical music and apparently had a broad taste, but I believe I can identify the one piece he knew best and heard most often. That is Beethoven's Violin Sonata No. 9, op. 47, the Kreutzer Sonata. It is what Husserl, in some variation without the piano accompaniment, liked to play to guests after dinner. And there was a time, when Heidegger was Husserl's assistant, that he was a frequent visitor at the Husserl home. Heidegger even writes letters, ones we would call bread-and-butter letters, thank you's, expressing gratitude to the Husserls for allowing him to dine with them and for treating him like a son. No doubt there were also other guests on many of these occasions, and so Heidegger would have heard Husserl playing the Kreutzer Sonata often.

Therefore, it is with some evidence that I venture to say Heidegger knew the Kreutzer Sonata well. If there was any classical music that haunted Heidegger in phantasy (this haunting in phantasy is how Husserl describes the tunes we usually have playing in our head), it was the Kreutzer Sonata. Furthermore, it is likely that Husserl, an extreme *semper docens*, someone "always teaching," would not have been content with merely playing but would also have analyzed the musical composition for the education of the audience. Therefore, Heidegger might very well have known some musical theory, at least in regard to sonata form. That form is composed of four moments: melodic theme, counter-theme, resolution, and coda or tailpiece. I am proposing that Heidegger knew something about this form and had special familiarity with the Kreutzer Sonata.

GELASSENHEIT

I turn now to Heidegger's little (seventy-five pages) book *Gelassenheit*, which has at least this extrinsic connection with music that it contains a lecture offered in commemoration of a composer, Conradin Kreutzer. I wish to show an intrinsic connection with music. That is, I wish to show that the book needs to be understood in musical terms and is in fact Heidegger's version of the Kreutzer Sonata.

The book as a whole is called *Gelassenheit*. It has two parts; the first is also simply called "Gelassenheit," and the second is "A discussion of Gelassenheit." Heidegger will put his own construction on the word "Gelassenheit," but in any case it is what unifies the book. Judging by the titles, the book is as unified as can be; it is all about Gelassenheit. By way of preliminary orientation, it could be said that this word, derived from *lassen*, "to let," in general means "letting things go."

The unity of the work is very difficult to see in the published English translation. The entire book is called *Discourse on Thinking*, and the two parts are "Memorial address" and "Conversation on a country path about thinking." What unifies the book and is mentioned three times in the German titles receives no mention at all. In particular, what is nearly impossible to see is the connection between the two parts, how the second flows from the first. Indeed a reader can gather from a translators' footnote on the very first page of the "Conversation" that it *antedated* the memorial address.[3] The order as published and the intrinsic connection between the two parts will prove crucial for my interpretation of the artistry of the book.

The first section of *Gelassenheit* is indeed a memorial address. It was delivered by Heidegger at a public commemoration of the 175th birthday of the composer Conradin Kreutzer. This Kreutzer was one of a family of prominent German musicians active at the time of Beethoven. Conradin was not the Kreutzer to whom the sonata is dedicated. That is his cousin Rodolphe, himself a composer and by all accounts the finest violin player of his day. As for Conradin as a composer, he was especially known for his part-songs for male chorus.

At the commemoration, Heidegger begins his remarks by saying that the only proper way to honor a composer is to listen to his works being performed. Heidegger says he himself is on the program only to make it a thoughtful commemoration: an *Andenken* is supposed to be a *Denken* (*G*, p. 13/44). But the genuine commemoration will follow immediately afterward in the musical performance. Presumably, then, there is a male chorus waiting in the wings. There are three male voices, tenor, baritone, and bass, so there is at least a male trio ready to sing works by Conradin Kreutzer. That will be the important event of the day.

Heidegger then presents his talk about Gelassenheit. In point of fact, he says very little about Gelassenheit. His main concern is to distinguish two ways of thinking, and that presumably is the reason the English translation of the title and subtitles ignores the term "Gelassenheit" and focuses on thinking. So I do concede that the English translation has motivation; I believe it is mistaken, but at least it is a motivated mistake.

Heidegger's procedure regarding the term "Gelassenheit" is the one I followed with regard to Entschlossenheit. First he characterizes it, and then he finds the fitting word. The characterization is couched in terms of our relation to the devices of modern technology and consists of two paragraphs as follows:

> We can use technological things, indeed use them just as they are meant to be used, and yet we can at the very same time keep ourselves so free of them that we let go of them. We can take up technological things just as they were designed to be taken up, and yet we can do so such that at the very same time we are letting them alone as things which do not touch us in what is most inward and proper to us. We can say "Yes" to the unavoidable use of technological things while at the very same time saying "No" to them inasmuch as we repudiate their claim to exclusivity, whereby they would distort, confuse, and ultimately devastate our essence.
>
> Yet if we in this way say "Yes" and "No" simultaneously to technological things, will not our relation to the technological world become ambiguous and insecure? Quite to the contrary. Our relation to technology will become marvelously simple and serene. We will let technological things into our daily world and at the very same time keep them out, that is, let them alone as things that are not absolute but are instead dependent on something higher. I would call this attitude of a simultaneous "Yes" and "No" to technology by an old word: detachment [*Gelassenheit zu den Dingen*]. (*G*, pp. 24–25/54)

Heidegger's word is an "old" one inasmuch as it figures in medieval spirituality. Detachment means to live in such a way as to be *in* the world but not *of* it, detached from the world in spirit but not in body. Such a way of life brings *serenity* (a possible translation of "Gelassenheit," naming its result). Detachment is not renunciation of the world and withdrawal into a cloister, and it is not wholehearted abandonment to worldly concerns either. In regard to the root *lassen*, it means to let the world go. But this letting go must be understood in a double sense. It means to let the world go on and also to let go of it.

In relation to technological things, detachment means to let these go on, not fight against them in the manner of the Luddites, smashing them, or even simply attempting to refrain from using them or using them in some idiosyncratic way. Heidegger says they are to be used the way they are meant to be used. They even call us to ever greater achievements (*G*, p. 24/53). So they can go on. But the attitude of detachment also means letting go of them, not putting one's heart and soul into them and becoming dominated by them. Heidegger says they are not absolute since they depend on something higher. In Heidegger's philosophy of technology, technological things indeed depend on how *Being* reveals itself. But in this context of a public discourse, I believe Heidegger means something more mundane. He had already referred to our freedom, and so he might be implying that that is what technological things depend on. They depend on our freedom to allow them into our lives or not. So they are not absolute; they depend on "something higher," namely, our freedom. Technological things would be nothing without our consent. If we remember our freedom in relation to them, then we can use them and yet recognize their subordinate place and take distance from them. That is how detachment is a simultaneous "Yes" ("I let them go on") and "No" ("I let go of them").

There is another old name for the attitude of detachment—old at least in the sense that we have come across it earlier in our discussion of Heidegger on authentic being-toward-death. That word is "anticipation." Anticipation, too, is a simultaneous "Yes" and "No"—in this case, spoken in relation to death. Anticipation recognizes the constant possibility of death and even enhances that possibility, thereby saying "Yes." But anticipation also says "No" to death, does not let death dominate one's being-in-the-world. Anticipation does not exhaust itself in fleeing death or calculating about it. Anticipation recognizes death as a most proper possibility, that is, as one which leaves us our freedom in choosing our own way to live with the menace of death. For Heidegger, anticipation says "No" to death not by attempting to avoid it at all costs or control it but by philosophizing, by preoccupation with Being.

In the book *Gelassenheit*, Heidegger describes the attitude of detachment as equivalent to a certain kind of thinking. Indeed most of his commemorative speech is devoted to distinguishing two ways of thinking: calculation versus contemplation. Calculative thinking is not necessarily computational in the sense of using mathematics. It is calculative the way an insincere person is calculating. This attitude sees in nature only what can be derived from it for one's own benefit. This attitude sees in nature only disposables.

So calculative thinking is identical with the attitude toward nature that defines modern technology. It sees in beings only other beings, disposable ones.

Contemplative thinking sees in beings the handiwork of Being, that is, sees beings as having been granted presence by an understanding of what it means to be in general, by the self-showing of Being to us. Con-*templ*-ation is what is carried on in a templum, the space in the sacred precinct reserved for observing auguries, that is, for seeing the work of the divine in worldly things, for a raising of the sight toward the gods. An augury is an omen, a being which bears a divine message, a being through which the gods speak to us, a being in which we can see Being rather than a disposable. Thus contemplative thinking, as attuned to the Being of beings, is philosophizing. Therefore, contemplative thinking is equivalent to anticipation, authentic dying.

In musical terms, anticipation (authentic being-toward-death, philosophizing, contemplative thinking) would be the main theme (Being) played over a ground bass (the menace of death constantly making its presence felt underneath). That, I wish to show, is exactly how the trialogue composed by Heidegger, if interpreted as music, plays out.

"DISCUSSION OF GELASSENHEIT"

We arrive now at the second part of the book *Gelassenheit*, remembering that what was to follow Heidegger's memorial address was a performance by a male chorus in close-part harmony. In the book, what follows is "A discussion of detachment." It is a trialogue, and in the published English translation, it simply follows on the next page. But in the original German, what immediately follows the memorial address is a title page by itself and then an almost blank page (*G*, 50) listing the cast of characters in the trialogue:

Forscher

(F)

Gelehrter

(G)

Lehrer

(L)

The German prelude to the trialogue resembles the program to a play or musical performance: first the title[4] by itself, then a page listing the cast of characters or performers. It is as if we are being introduced to a performance.

What follows is then the trialogue—not a narrated one, but one in which the lines are assigned to the various speakers themselves.

The players will be: Scientist, Scholar, Teacher. Furthermore, since the German language has masculine and feminine forms for the individuals who pursue these occupations, the players are identified as all males. What is announced, therefore, is that a male trio is about to perform. Accordingly, what in the book follows the memorial address is exactly what Heidegger said would follow on the day of the actual commemoration—a male chorus in close-part harmony. This chorus will perform what could be called Heidegger's Kreutzer Sonata.

Moreover, I wish to show that the trialogue, if interpreted as music, will not only be a *discussion* of detachment but will also be an example of it. In other words, it will be an actual example of contemplative thinking, anticipation, detachment, authentic being-toward-death, preoccupation with Being—all the while sensing the menace of death in the background. It will concretize what the memorial address could only speak about in the abstract. Thereby the trialogue might be seen as Heidegger's concession to the power of music, a recantation of his usual derogatory remarks. Music brings home what the philosopher can only show from a distance. The philosopher can only *discourse* about Being; music, in a way to be worked out below, lets us hear its voice.

Music is thereby an additional voice in the atmosphere we breathe. In the air are not only the voice of the friend, the voice of conscience, and the voice of the they. Music, too, is in the air; if music is the voice of Being, and Being provokes wonder, then this voice might be able to drown out the voice of the they, the voice that is the death of philosophy. Indeed, we all usually have some tune or other haunting us in phantasy; perhaps music is then that very friend whom "every Dasein carries about." Thereby Heidegger's denigration of music will, by the logic of his own thinking, be overturned: music might show itself to be the primordial art form, the one wherein Being most reveals itself.

PHILOSOPHY OF MUSIC

Before proceeding to the actual musical interpretation of the trialogue, I will set the stage by discussing the philosophy of music in general. I will first explicate Heidegger's disparagement of music and will then appeal to two other phenomenologists, Maurice Merleau-Ponty and Husserl.

Painting in very broad strokes, philosophy can be portrayed as always having denigrated music. Music is inferior to the other arts because it cannot represent any definite beings. Accordingly, it cannot be conceptualized; it offers nothing from which to abstract and discover the universal. Therefore, music is far removed from thinking and can contribute little or nothing to the project of philosophy. Music can only excite the emotions.

This last paragraph expresses roughly Heidegger's view. To understand his position more precisely, we need to situate music within Heidegger's general philosophy of art. The most convenient way to do so is to distinguish Heidegger's thinking on art from aesthetics.

Aesthetics, for Heidegger, is not equivalent to the philosophy of art. Aesthetics is only the metaphysical approach to art. Thus, aesthetics arises with the beginning of metaphysics; prior to that, in the pre-Platonic era, there was no aesthetics:

> The aesthetic consideration of art commences precisely with the inception of metaphysics. That means the aesthetic attitude toward art begins the moment the essence of ἀλήθεια [*alétheia*, "unconcealment"] is transformed into ὁμοίωσις [*homoíosis*, "homogenization," "assimilation"], the conformity and correctness of perceiving, presenting, and representing. This transformation starts in Plato's metaphysics. In the time before Plato, a consideration "of" art did not exist, and so all Western considerations of art from Plato to Nietzsche are "aesthetic."[5]

The difference between Heidegger's "philosophy of art" and aesthetics can be seen in the transformation from *alétheia* to *homoíosis* as definitions of truth. In the pre-Socratic era, truth was a goddess, one who took the thinker by the hand (although of course the thinker still needed to reach out a hand to the goddess for her to take up). In the post-Socratic era, truth is an agreement or conformity instituted by the subject. In other terms, the difference between the two eras is that between an understanding of Dasein as discloser rather than steward, shepherd, preserver. Therefore, even *Being and Time* has not completely broken with metaphysics. Dasein is still thought of as subject, as discloser. Accordingly, the later Heidegger writes: "In *Being and Time*, Dasein still has an 'anthropological,' 'subjectivistic,' 'individualistic,' etc. appearance, and yet the opposite of all this is in view in that work. To be sure, it is not in view as the sole or even primary focus."[6]

Aesthetics, the subjectivistic, metaphysical outlook on art, takes its orientation precisely from *aísthesis*, the sensory impression on a subject. Art is there to deepen our lived experience. Before we consider Heidegger's contrasting approach, let us see how music fits into aesthetics. Indeed it is the pinnacle of the arts from an aesthetic point of view, because it is most immediately about *aísthesis*, lived experience, feeling. I will provide what I believe is Heidegger's most complete and explicit denunciation of music in its association with feelings. The passage is intricate but requires only a little commentary to become clear. Heidegger himself provides a succinct summary, one which says it all: "To feel the feelings counts as the high point of lived experience: music therefore the absolute art." The extended discussion derives from the same entry as the summary in the *Black Notebooks*:

> "Art" is currently undertaking the management and the corresponding organization of lived experience (as a feeling of the feelings), whereby the conviction must arise that now for the first time the tasks of calculation and planning are uncovered and established, and thus so is the essence of art. Since, however, the enjoyment of the feelings becomes all the more desultory and agreeable as the feelings become more indeterminate and contentless, and since music most immediately excites such feelings, music is thus becoming the prescriptive type of art (cf. Romanticism, Wagner and—Nietzsche). Music bears in itself a proper lawfulness and also a calculability of the highest kind, yet that does not at all contravene—but merely manifests—how decisively it is that pure number and the sheer feeling of the feelings are compatible and require each other. All types of art are being apprehended musically, in the manner of music, that is, as expressions and occasions of the enjoyment of the feelings (feelings of achievement, glory, power, communion). Poetry, in case such ever arises beyond mere ink–slinging, is becoming "song" and the word merely a supplement to the sound and to its flow and rhythm. "Thoughts," especially if they disturb contemplationlessness, are prohibited; moreover, one disposes of the genuine thoughts (λόγοι) in the calculation and planning that can "effect" something. The interpretation of art in terms of lived experience is being elevated to the role of the measure for all active and productive human comportment (τέχνη); comportment is most highly honored when judged to be "artistic."[7]

Heidegger is saying that "art" (in quotation marks as not actually deserving the name in the context of aesthetics) is now viewed aesthetically (that is, in terms of lived experience, feeling), and therefore music is becoming the "prescriptive type of art," "absolute art." The reason is that music most immediately excites the feelings. In music, the feelings are "contentless." Presumably, Heidegger means that these feelings are not tied to any particular being exciting them. We can see why Michelangelo's *Pietà* arouses feelings of compassion, but music arouses tenderness or any other feeling for no reason other than to arouse it. Yet it might seem that music should be foreign to feeling, since music is ruled by a strict lawfulness and a calculability. Heidegger must have learned, perhaps from Husserl, how very mathematical music is; to compose music requires a strict adherence to mathematical rules. But that relation to number, as abstract and removed from concrete feelings as numbers might seem, only shows how compatible mathematics and feelings actually are. Heidegger goes on to say that all art is being viewed in the manner of Romanticism—as giving priority to the feelings. Poetry is becoming song; that is to say, what matters is not the thoughts but only the musical quality of poetry, namely, the sounds and rhythm. (I do not believe this critique of poetry would apply today. Poetry has indeed more and more become ink-slinging, and almost any expression of anything, as long as it is chopped up into lines, now counts as poetry. Thoughts are certainly absent from the vast majority of today's so-called poetry, but so is any sort of sound or rhythm that could turn the poetry into song. Yet Heidegger is surely correct that contemporary poetry, nearly all of which is composed in the diction of a grammar school child, does not disturb contemplationlessness. Today, any poetry that challenges the reader to think or that even uses words of more than two syllables is branded elitist.) According to Heidegger, thought that transcends everyday comprehension is assigned not to the poet but to the inventor of new technological devices. But even these devices are ultimately meant to enhance our lived experience, whereby the inventions that are most highly honored and are called artistic are the ones that are most closely applicable to the exciting of the feelings. Heidegger's implied conclusion is that these inventors and inventions should, in the metaphysical–aesthetic age, not only be called "artistic" but also "musical."

In the "philosophy of art," that is, the approach espoused by Heidegger, art has a higher vocation than the mere excitation of feelings and the deepening of lived experience. In a sense, art is indeed there to excite the feelings, but these are not feelings as usually understood. Art is there to jolt us out of our complacency over the fact that there is something rather than nothing. Art for Heidegger does not portray present beings; it portrays the presence of those beings, the astounding fact that beings have emerged into presence, have had a presence bestowed on them. In other words, art is there to jolt us into wonder, to make us contemplate, to philosophize about Being. The function of art is not to confirm us in our subjectivity; it is to make us less of a subject in control and more of a reverential wonderer. The experience of art is then something very close to anxiety or the hearing of the voice of conscience. Art is a hearing of the voice of the friend, the voice trying to make itself heard over the everyday clamor of the they. It is a voice calling us to contemplation instead of calculation. It is a voice calling us to individuation in the sense of becoming shepherd, steward, preserver of "something higher," of Being, of that which bestows presence. Thus, according to Heidegger, if art ever attains "the highest possibility of its essence," it will "awaken and found anew our vision of, and trust in, that which bestows."[8]

Presumably, for Heidegger, music in a post-metaphysical age will descend from the zenith to the nadir. If music is so strictly tied to the arousing of feelings, and if contentless feelings are what counts least, then music could no longer be the paradigmatic art. Is that true? Does music say nothing about Being and merely arouse subjective feelings? I am about to challenge Heidegger's view, indeed from Heidegger's own perspective.

MERLEAU-PONTY

Merleau-Ponty, like Heidegger, mostly disparages music and links it to feeling and lived experience. There could not be a more exact and striking description of the effect of music on lived experience than the following: "Music is not in visible space; on the contrary, it undermines that space, besieges it, and supplants it. People waiting to hear a concert are overly composed for what is to come; they take on the disinterested air of judges and exchange smiles and a few words, oblivious to the fact that the ground is about to quake beneath them and that they will soon be like a ship's crew tossed about on the surface of the sea by a storm."[9]

Merleau-Ponty maintains that the space of music is not that of visual perception. Music has its own spatiality, although the spaces of the various senses are merely "moments of a global configuration which is the one space, and I can understand that my power to attain this one space is inseparable from my ability to sever myself from it by ensconcing myself in a single sense."[10] What then happens if I ensconce myself in hearing, specifically hearing music in a concert hall? According to Merleau-Ponty, "When I reopen my eyes in a concert hall, visible space seems to me very confined in comparison to that other space in which, a moment ago, the music was breaking forth. Even if I keep my eyes open during the whole performance, it seems that the music is not truly contained in this precisely delimited and paltry space I see before me. The music insinuates a new dimension into visible space, and it is there that the music ebbs and flows."[11]

The space of music is more encompassing than visually perceived space. Music opens up a space from which the other spaces are broken off. Visual space is paltry in relation to musical space. If all this is so, then precisely as more encompassing, musical space is apriori, the condition of the possibility of experiencing individual spaces within it. Musical space is a condition of the possibility of visually perceived space. Let us establish this apriori character by appealing once again (see above, p. 59) to Kant's metaphysical exposition of space.

Kant attempts to demonstrate that space is an apriori intuition. As an *intuition*, space is distinct from a concept; as *apriori*, space is a condition of the possibility of experience. Kant argues (*Critique of Pure Reason*, A25/B39) as follows. Both space and concepts involve a one–many relation. In the case of concepts, the real things are what must undergo limitation. In order to arrive at the concept, we must consider a thing in a limited respect, the respect which the thing has in common with other such things. In the case of space, it is the other way around; space itself must be limited to arrive at the parts that fit within it. So space is an intuition. It follows then, that space is also apriori, for if the parts are broken off *from* it, then in regard to space, the whole is "absolutely prior to the parts."

But how is this possible? How could anyone experience the whole of space, especially as prior to the parts? It is possible, according to Kant, if space is considered an "infinite *given* magnitude." That does not mean space is an infinitely large container; such a container could not be given. Space is given as a whole inasmuch as it is the *realm* of extensiveness, the realm that makes possible any delimited quantitative extension.

In more Heideggerian terms, space is the realm individual beings must step into in order to appear as spatial beings. Space is the clearing that provides beings their possibility of coming to presence. Space, specifically the most encompassing of all spaces, is what allows beings to be present to "essentially *spatial* Dasein" (see above, p. 59).

We saw in chapter 1 that Heidegger compares the most proper phenomenon of phenomenology, namely, Being itself, to space and time for Kant. Now we see the corollary: space is comparable to Being. For essentially spatial Dasein, space *is* Being. That is to say, the most encompassing space, the space that is prior to its parts, the whole of space as the realm of a clearing, is Being. But—coming to the point of this entire disquisition on space—*music* is our access to that most expansive space. Thereby music is the voice of Being. In listening to music, what is disclosed to us is Being as making possible an experience of beings.

Certainly some qualifications would be needed here. For instance, it would not seem that all music could carry out this function. The full effect of hearing the voice of Being in the guise of the most expansive space is possibly limited to symphonic music in a large concert hall. Furthermore, it does not follow that no one has an experience of spatial beings before attending a classical concert. There are of course other modes of access to space itself, but music might be the most *striking* mode of access. It might indeed require music for us to be jolted out of our complacency and actually wonder how beings come to presence. Music is the voice of Being calling *over* the voice of the they and even over the voice of conscience that tells us of our guilt. Thereby music provokes—or at least *might* provoke—wonder in a positive way: wonder not simply at the inexplicability of the presence of things but wonder as exuberant joy that we have been gifted with a world. Great music, whether Beethoven's Ninth or not, tells us that "above the starry firmament a loving parent must dwell."

Merleau-Ponty comes to something like this conclusion himself, in his discussion of art in a book called *L'Oeil et l'Esprit*. *The Eye and the Mind* is devoted almost entirely to visual works of art and contains many reproductions of modern artworks, such as drawings by Matisse and paintings by Klee. Merleau-Ponty is here mostly in dialogue with Descartes on the issue of visual perception. But Merleau-Ponty does turn to music, again with what might seem a disparagement: "Music is too far on this side of the world and of what can be designated in speech to be able to represent anything but beings as sketched out in advance, Being as surging and ebbing, as expanding, as bursting forth and eddying."[12]

Merleau-Ponty takes this characterization of the power of music to be a reproach: music does not depict the things in being, namely, the world and what can be designated conceptually. Music can represent only Being, the dynamism of Being. But is that not rather praise of music instead of censure? At least from the viewpoint of the capacity of music to provoke wonder, Merleau-Ponty is heaping the highest honor on music. Music is indeed on *this* side of the world and of conceptuality. But that means music is apriori. It opens the listener to the sketch in advance, the paradigm, the matrix, from which all beings emerge. As residing on *this* side, music opens up what is closer to us than the beings in the world. What resides closer than beings is Being, and accordingly music is the voice of Being, calling on us to contemplate in wonder what we might otherwise take for granted: beings are present on account of "something higher."

HUSSERL

Husserl did not elaborate a theory of music or of art in general. He does see, however, the crucial role of art in the practice of phenomenology. The phenomenological method is one that operates on examples, and these examples need to be as varied as possible. Our own experience and the offerings of history are limited, and our imaginations are sluggish, preventing us from devising original examples in phantasy. Therefore, the phenomenologist must rely on great imaginative art, especially as present in poetry, to supply the required examples and to fertilize our own imaginative powers. The "purely fictitious" thereby becomes the "element in which phenomenology lives and breathes."[13]

Husserl mentions music often enough, but he does not thematize it. Nevertheless, he proposes a theory of passive synthesis that applies to music and that applies especially to music about death. Husserl's understanding of passive synthesis will prove to be an essential basis on which I will build my claim that the experience of music is a mode—perhaps the best mode—of anticipation, authentic being-toward-death.

Basically for Husserl the difference between active and passive synthesis amounts to this: in cases of passive synthesis, the material to be synthesized has already undergone synthesis prior to being apprehended, whereas in cases of active synthesis, the material is first apprehended discretely and only afterwards synthesized. A discursive concept is a prime example of something actively synthesized: first we must run around (dis–curs) collecting the discrete examples and then abstract out what they have in common. First we must experience individual trees and then subsequently synthesize them into a concept. In passive synthesis, however, there are no discrete elements; the elements are already synthesized when apprehended. What we immediately apprehend is the *result* of a synthesis already performed.

Passive syntheses are perceptual rather than discursive ones and have two modes, applying respectively to spatial and temporal experience. Let us begin with the passive synthesis involved in spatial perception. A profile of a perceived thing is surrounded by an inner and an outer horizon. The profile looks the way it does partly on account of the influence of these horizons. For example, to consider the outer horizon, a gray object on a white background looks much darker than the same object on a black background. The appearance of the object has already been synthesized with the background when we apprehend it. We do not first see the object and then the background and then by reasoning deduce how the one influences the other. In our very apprehension of the object, the background has already done its work. That is the sense of passivity. It does not mean spatial perception is a matter of passive undergoing, as if it were the reception of some blunt force. We must be engaged in attempting to see in order for the passive synthesis to operate. We must be active perceivers.

The same passive synthesis is involved in the inner horizon, namely, the other profiles of the object I am looking at, the profiles now hidden from view. The way I protend these other profiles is passively synthesized with the given profile. For instance, if I am walking along a city street, the fronts of the houses look like the fronts of real houses; the fronts have a solidity about them. But if I am walking on the set of a movie production, where I surmise that the fronts are mere fronts with nothing but scaffolding behind then, then the fronts will appear differently. The projected back of the house influences passively the way the front appears. In general, if I believe something exists in reality, it will appear differently than it does if I believe it is only imaginary. This circumstance, the dependence of an appearance on the projected inner horizon, is the one and only motive behind Husserl's transcendental reduction. If the reflecting phenomenologist wants to describe phenomena, appearances, just as they are given, without the influence of the projected inner horizon, then that inner horizon has to be put out of play. That is to say, judgments about reality or non-reality must be suspended. The phenomenologist must refrain from any judgment about whether this is a front of a real house or a movie set house; the phenomenologist must describe how the font appears by itself and so must abstain from any judgments about the inner horizon, about that which makes something real or not.

As to the passive synthesis of time, Husserl's prime example is the hearing of a melody. In order to hear a melody as a melody and not as one single chord of notes or at the opposite extreme as discrete notes without inner connection to one another, the notes need to be synthesized in a certain way. The listener to the melody must retain the past notes (yet retain them *as* past, with a sense that they are slipping away) and protend the future notes (*as* future, with a sense that they are still approaching). If the notes were all to be apprehended without any differentiation of past, present, and future, then the notes would seem to be sounding all at once, and that is not a melody. On the other hand, if the notes are apprehended discretely, as totally differentiated into past, present, and future, that is, totally outside the horizon of the other notes (perhaps one note now, another an hour later), then the melody again breaks down. In the case of discrete notes, they would have to be actively synthesized by recalling them in deliberate memory; the notes would no longer influence one another and the melody would vanish. The notes must be *passively* synthesized in a melody: that means the notes must be heard as already synthesized with the other notes but not so united as to be one with the sounding note. While hearing the present note, we must have some vague expectation of what is coming and must possess a vague retention of what has passed—without the effort required to remember explicitly. The future and the past must be to some extent, and only to some extent, present in the current note heard.

Especially with respect to the passive synthesis of a melody, the term "passive" is misleading. A lackadaisical, totally passive listener will not hear a melody; if I let my attention wander while listening to music, the melody is lost. The passive synthesis of music requires an *active*, engaged listener. Passive synthesis, the actual hearing of a melody, is a favor granted to someone who is actively listening.

Any note, in order to be heard as the note of a melody, must be involved in complex temporal relations. The future must already—to some extent—be present in it, and the past must still—to some extent—be retained in it. Taken out of this temporal horizon, a note is just a discrete note. The crucial point for my purposes is that this temporal complexity involved in music is precisely the one that constitutes the meaning of the Being of Dasein. It is the exact same complex temporality as the one that must be projected in order to make the Being of Dasein comprehensible. The passive synthesis of the notes in a melody is thus made possible by the *meaning* of the Being of Dasein.

Music, melodies, can be heard because Dasein's possibilities are most proper ones. Past possibilities, ones already chosen, are still to some extent open possibilities, and future possibilities are already to some extent actual in the present. Death is *the* future possibility. Music therefore is structured like being-toward-death.

Death may not explicitly lie on the horizon of all musical experience. But all such experience does include at least some expectation that the melody will end. Thereby, the listener has a sense that not only is the forthcoming note already present, but so is the next one and the next, all the way to the end. Music involves at least implicit awareness that the end is already present and is not utterly outstanding. Bringing Husserl and Heidegger together, it can be said that Dasein's death is passively synthesized with his or her present. Music, inasmuch as it involves the same passive synthesis, is at least implicit disclosure of authentic dying.

HEIDEGGER'S KREUTZER SONATA

With all of the above as preparation, we come finally to the second part of the book *Gelassenheit*, the "Discussion of detachment," the trialogue. My intention is to interpret it as music, specifically as voices raised in three-part harmony. That is precisely what Heidegger said would follow his speech. If it can be shown that the trialogue is also in sonata form, then it could be called Heidegger's Kreutzer Sonata. If it can be shown that the theme of this sonata is being-toward-death, then this sonata might be music about the Being of Dasein. It might be a carrying out of contemplative thinking, anticipation, hearing the voice of conscience, hearing the voice of the friend, philosophizing. Music might even show itself as more appropriate to what philosophy attempts to accomplish than is abstract thought.

The first step is to see how the roles are distributed to the three male voices. The lead tenor is obviously the teacher. He directs the discussion, and the other participants defer to him. This teacher is not explicitly identified as Heidegger, but it could be no one else. The teacher speaks in the vocabulary and from the general outlook of Heidegger, but the teacher proposes so many paradoxes that he might be some Zen Master parading as Heidegger—or vice versa.

The baritone (or second tenor) is the scholar. He mostly remains subservient to the tenor but does at times take the lead. To him is assigned the all-important theme of the coda. He is a typical pedantic scholar, with a memory for the history of philosophy. He knows all the right words to say, all the formulas, but it is not certain he knows what they actually mean.

The bass is the scientist. He is the dullest and mostly just reverberates the words of the others. He is versed in the natural sciences and has only half shaken off the objectivistic attitude. Nevertheless, he is completely open to the new way of thinking proposed by the teacher.

In order to interpret the trialogue as a sonata, three aspects must be accounted for: harmony, florid passages, and sonata form. Eventually, this sonata will also be tied to death.

As to harmony, it is possibly the most striking aspect of the entire discussion. The participants stem from very different backgrounds. What should a Zen Master, a pedant, and a natural scientist have in common? Almost nothing. And yet, except for some minor disagreements which are soon resolved, the three voices speak in perfect harmony. They agree about everything. In music, harmony requires two or more notes sounding together. That is not possible in a written trialogue, but I believe Heidegger simulates such harmony by having the participants very often finish one another's sentences. That is as close as a trialogue can come to sounding a chord. Many sentences involve the contribution of all three choir members. One sentence is even composed of five separate contributions. These voices are in total close-part harmony.

A sonata is designed to showcase virtuosity with florid passages. In the trialogue, nearly every sentence is a florid passage. The trialogue is as far from dull logic-chopping as could be imagined. The voices all speak in elaborate, enigmatic, esoteric language without actually making any conceptual advancement. They rehearse some themes from Heidegger's later philosophy, and Being is given a new name, "region." But the reader will find nothing to learn here. No new insights are gained, and no phenomena are clarified. The participants are engaged in philosophizing, but they settle no issues definitively. They open themselves to where their contemplative thought is directing them, but it leads nowhere in particular. The participants have definitely taken the first philosophical step, but the second eludes them. They are mired in wonder, wallowing in wonder, and do not accomplish anything that could be set down as a philosophical thesis. The trialogue remains "on this side of what can be designated in speech."

With regard to sonata form, the first three moments are more or less clearly marked in the trialogue; the coda definitely is. After an introductory section, the first theme is voiced by the lead tenor. It is the theme of "region" as a name for Being (*G*, p. 40/65). The counter-theme is assigned to the bass: the theme of "waiting" (*G*, p. 46/69). The resolution is accomplished by the tenor again: "appropriation" (*G*, p. 52/73). As in Beethoven's Kreutzer Sonata, the themes are not precisely distinct and appear and reappear in various guises.

The coda of the trialogue is the most significant section of this sonata. Its theme is assigned to the pedantic scholar, who offers a pedantic word, a Greek word standing alone as one of the fragments of Heraclitus: Ἀγχιβασίη (*G*, p. 71/88). The coda itself is in sonata form: the baritone offers one meaning of the term, the bass offers a counter-meaning, and then the tenor finally resolves the issue.

Heraclitus' word ἀγχιβασίη (*anchibasíe*) is a nominative singular feminine noun formed from the roots ἄγχι, "near," and βαίνω, "to go." Accordingly, the basic meaning of the word is "approaching." The scholar proposes the meaning "going forth," the way knowledge is a striking out in search of the truth. The scientist, true to his background, proposes the meaning "attacking forth," the way nature is attacked by the methods of science. The teacher reverses the direction of the motion and proposes the meaning "drawing near," not as something Dasein accomplishes toward the truth but as a movement of the truth toward Dasein. That in general would express contemplative thinking versus calculative thinking. Contemplation is the work of a shepherd, steward, preserver, in openness to the self-offering of Being. The other participants accept this meaning, and the trialogue ends, with harmony restored.

If we apply Husserl's understanding of passive synthesis to the end of the trialogue, assuming the discussion is a sort of music, then I believe we can see the coda on the horizon of the entire discussion. The word ἀγχιβασίη—its meaning—is in play throughout; at the end the word simply comes to be sounded explicitly. This word is comparable to the last note of a melody or like death; at the end, the last note and death arrive in their own person, but they were present beneath the surface all along.

The term ἀγχιβασίη does mean "drawing near," and the teacher correctly identifies the direction of the movement—an approach of Being toward Dasein. But the teacher leaves implicit the connotation of the term: an importunate pressing close. The Greek word was characteristically applied to the behavior of a creditor toward a debtor. This is not a neutral approach of one thing to another in objective space but is instead a "dunning," "buttonholing," "constantly pursuing." Therefore, what the teacher is leaving implicit is the application of the term to death. Death is *the* creditor, and we all owe it a debt. Death is constantly badgering us for payment. It is indefinitely certain in its possibility. The teacher is then correct to speak of the drawing near of Being, the uncanny; what he leaves implicit is that the most uncanny of all is death.

This sense of something constantly rumbling on underneath, threatening, pursuing, is not lost on the participants in the trialogue. The scholar (*G*, p. 69/87) says the word was pursuing him from the very beginning. The teacher (*G*, 70/88) says they have all along been confronted by something ineffable. The scholar (*G*, p. 72/89) concludes that ἀγχιβασίη is the most appropriate name for their conversation as a whole. What is most ineffable, what most pursues, what most confronts, what most draws near is death. Therefore, this theme, although announced explicitly only in the coda, is *the* theme of the trialogue, and it makes Heidegger's Kreutzer Sonata music about death.

What is the proper response to the menace of death? For Heidegger, authentic being-toward-death is not calculation about death, not preoccupation with death, but instead is contemplation of the meaning of Being. That is exactly what is transpiring in the trialogue: while sensing the menace of death, the dunning of *the* creditor, the participants engage in philosophizing and wallowing in wonder. The participants thereby say "Yes" and "No" to death. They allow death to pursue them, but they do not allow it to dominate. The trialogue is detachment in the guise of contemplative thinking, namely, philosophizing about the meaning of Being. The trialogue contains no conceptual determination of what detachment is. Instead, the trialogue *exemplifies* detachment.

The trialogue can be such an exemplification precisely if understood as music. In order to explain that, we need to bring together Merleau-Ponty, Husserl, and Heidegger on the theme of music. From Merleau-Ponty and Husserl, we learn that music discloses being-toward-death. From Heidegger, we learn of detachment as the authentic way of being-toward death, and in his trialogue we see that detachment in play.

Merleau-Ponty's phenomenology thematizes the spatiality of music. What listening to music discloses is that we are not secure in space. Music reveals a complex spatiality such that we can never be sure where we stand; while listening we are, as Merleau-Ponty says, tossed about with the ground quaking beneath us. And when we open our eyes and return to our ordinary world, space looks paltry and strange. Music disrupts our experience of space and shows us as insecure in space. Husserl's phenomenology thematizes the temporality of music. Listening to music discloses that we are not secure in time. Our temporality is a complex one, in which an end is always impending. Our present is always threatened, if not by the utter end then at least by something not wholly in our control. Therefore, from Merleau-Ponty and Husserl, we learn of music as disclosing the Being of Dasein as insecure, as being-toward-death.

From Heidegger we learn of detachment, contemplative thinking, as the authentic response to the constant threat of death. In the trialogue, this detachment amounts to the participants carrying on with the melodies of the sonata while the danger of *the* creditor drones on beneath. The melodies are in a sense sneering at the ground bass: the music will go on despite the threat beneath, aware of it but refusing to be dominated by it. The melodies are saying "Yes" and "No" to the ἀγχιβασίη.

If we generalize, then we can say that all classical music is structured like this trialogue; all classical music is in sonata form or at least in the form of a melodic line over a ground bass. Then all such music is structured like detachment, like the Being of Dasein as being-toward-death and as the refusal to be dominated by it. In addition, music is an even more effective disclosure of the Being of Dasein than is philosophy, because, on Heidegger's own terms, affect has a priority over rational understanding, which merely brings the more primordial disclosure to concepts. Then, in accord with Heidegger's own thinking, Being speaks in music more than in philosophy. Music is *the* voice of Being.

SOCRATES

Let the coda to this chapter—which attempted to mingle play and serious-ness on the theme of music and mortality—be a return to Socrates. We know him as the paradigm of authentic being-toward-death, constantly practic-ing Socratic love, constantly gazing through worldly beings to the Ideas in heaven. What is his relation to music?

In his prison cell, on the morning of his execution, Socrates tells of a recurrent dream. He says he heard many times in his past life a command in a dream to "make music and keep at it" (*Phaedo*, 60E). Socrates took the command to mean that he should keep at what he was already doing, namely, philosophizing, since "philosophy is the greatest music" (*Phaedo*, 61A). But now Socrates wonders if the command (not the voice of his exclusively dissuading *daimon*, so perhaps the voice of conscience, the summons of phronesis) might not mean to engage in music in the usual sense, and so he composes a hymn to the god whose festival was in progress. Socrates is refer-ring to Apollo, whose festival was the occasion for the delay in the carrying out of the execution.

Socrates does not here explain how philosophy is the greatest music, but in another dialogue, he does take up the relation between philosophy and the muses (*Phaedrus*, 259C–D). Philosophy is the province of the two greatest and oldest muses, Calliope and Urania. The pursuit of philosophy is an honor-ing of these greatest muses, and so is the greatest music, or at least it rivals the music of these muses themselves.

These muses are the patrons of philosophy because their province is the greatest things: heaven and reason (= the relation between Being and Dasein). The muses disclose these things, but the muses do not compose philosophical treatises; they merely make music and sing. According to Socrates, however, they make the most beautiful music. In other words, they offer the greatest disclosure of Being and of Dasein merely by making music; if the music is beautiful enough, it does not need conceptualization. It can disclose the meaning of Being and yet remain on this side of what can be designated in speech.

Socrates in the end turns to music; he composes a hymn to Apollo. Presumably, he made the hymn as beautiful as he could. He must have come to the realization that beautiful music is by itself a disclosure—indeed the best possible disclosure, a disclosure rivaling that of the muses themselves—of what philosophy is attempting to say in concepts. Thus, Socrates began by believing that philosophy is the greatest music, and in the end he senses that music might be the greatest philosophy.

Chapter 6

Corona-Virus-Disease-2019 and Mortality

COVID-19 SLOGANS AND HEIDEGGER'S VITAL CATEGORIES

We breathe an atmosphere of mortality inasmuch as death is in the air in the figurative sense. Death colors everything we do. Death is also in the air in the literal sense, inasmuch as music and the voice of the they resound in our ears. But the atmosphere today is mortal in another sense as well: it is contaminated with carcinogens and deadly viruses. What would a Heideggerian approach to philosophy and death have to say about the current corona-virus-disease–2019 (acronym: COVID-19) pandemic? Are there distinct possibilities in our current plight for philosophizing, that is, for disclosing the Being of the beings we ourselves are?

The air in this pandemic is filled not only with a new corona virus but also with new voices, slogans about the proper response to contain its spread. Four slogans have been drummed into everyone's consciousness. They take the form of commands: Lock down. Practice social distancing. Wash your hands. Mask up. From a Heideggerian perspective, what do these slogans, all of them reminding us of our mortality, offer as food for thought—specifically for thought in the sense of contemplation?

Dasein is not the human person as such. Indeed Dasein is always "mine" to some particular person, and there is no Dasein apart from a person. But Dasein is the person thematized in a restricted way. Da-sein is a person considered only with respect to *Sein*, Being. The concept of Dasein prescinds from everything about a person that is irrelevant to a disclosure of what it means to be.

Heidegger's analytic of Dasein is not a philosophical anthropology, not a theory of the human being as such, not a theory of human life. For example,

Being and Time says nothing about sexual difference, since that is irrelevant to the meaning of Being in general. It is not the case that only one sex understands Being within the horizon of temporality. It is not the case that for only one sex is discourse a middle-voiced phenomenon, a disclosure not simply to the outside but even to the very one who is discoursing. It is not the case that for only one sex is there a priority of the ready-to-hand over the present-at-hand. Nor does *Being and Time* say anything about many other human characteristics that would need to be included in a philosophical anthropology but are irrelevant to Dasein as the "there" of Being. Heidegger says nothing about eating and sleeping, as if he failed to recognize that a person has these needs. But these are physiological needs, and Heidegger's perspective toward Dasein is ontological, not biological.

In the period prior to *Being and Time*, however, Heidegger was indeed occupied with human life as such. He called it "factical" life, and he attempted to articulate its properties, which he called "categories." The perspective is still philosophical, not biological, but already we see a distinction from *Being and Time*, where Dasein is more radically differentiated from things and has to be characterized in terms of "existentialia" rather than properties or categories. Factical life is human life as lived not with respect to an understanding of the meaning of Being but rather with regard to life itself. The categories of factical life are the ways a human being comports himself or herself to his or her own everyday life amid everyday concerns. Heidegger's philosophy of factical life amounts to a prolonged reflection on inauthenticity. *Being and Time* will add authenticity.

Heidegger's most sustained discussion of factical life occurs in a lecture course from the winter semester of 1921–1922.[1] What I wish to exploit from this lecture course is the remarkable parallel between the categories of factical life and the slogans mentioned above:

Lock down: category of sequestration (*Abriegelung*)
Social distancing: category of abolition of distance (*Abstandstilgung*)
Wash your hands: category of frantic self-concern (*tolles Sorgen über sich selbst*)
Mask up: category of larvance (*Larvanz*) (Latin *larvatus*, "masked").

I will attempt to think the slogans in the direction of Heidegger's categories. Thereby the pandemic might be seen to offer distinct possibilities for contemplation, and we might uncover again an intimate connection between philosophy and death. My attempt was motivated by a recent poem about the COVID-19 pandemic and its "unexamined slogans." I will end this chapter with a close Heideggerian reading of the poem in full. But let us first turn to Heidegger himself.

RELATIONAL SENSE OF LIFE: CARING

In the lecture course on factical life, antedating *Being and Time* by five years, Heidegger is still seeking his genuine philosophical voice. But the vocabulary of his magnum opus is foreshadowed. Heidegger does not yet use "Dasein" in the technical sense; here it simply means "existence" and is equivalent to "life." It means "to be in and through life" (*PI*, p. 85/64). The basic idea of Dasein as a technical term, however, is already visible. Life, existence, is *relationality*, and what life necessarily relates to is the world. Heidegger takes "living" in a transitive sense: life lives something, and what it lives is the world. The world is not an optional accoutrement to life; life is always already involved in the world. Therefore, the concept of being-in-the-world is adumbrated as a name for the beings we ourselves are.

Furthermore, Heidegger already calls the essence of factical life "care." The term means basically the same here as it does in *Being and Time*, but Heidegger is more explicit that care simply means finding something to be of interest, to be meaningful, whether negatively or positively: "Living, in its transitive meaning, is to be interpreted according to its relational sense as *caring*: to care for and about something; to live as directed to something, which is to care for it. . . . In unrestrained excitement, in near indifference, and in everything in between—'to live' means to care. What we care for and about, what caring adheres to, is equivalent to what is meaningful" (*PI*, 90/68).

The difference from *Being and Time* is that the caring which characterizes factical life is primarily a caring for one's own continuance in life: "In its broadest relational sense, to live is to care about one's 'daily bread.' . . . Privation (*privatio, carentia*) is both the relational and the intrinsic basic mode and sense of the Being of life" (*PI*, 90/68). In this early lecture course, Heidegger has a much more jaundiced view of humanity than he does in *Being and Time*. Factical life is self-absorbed, a continuous attempt to satisfy a constant privation, a constant hunger. Caring is interested in the world primarily because that is where one's daily bread might be found. To flee from this hunger and possess many things that can satisfy it is not to escape privation. It is entirely to be preoccupied with it; to avert privation is, as always, to acknowledge all the more insidiously what one is turning away from. To stockpile provisions might seem to bring security, but it is actually all the more to acknowledge the privation that always threatens, no matter how full one's storehouse. The more one is preoccupied with security, the more insecure one becomes.

The caring which characterizes factical life is equivalent to inauthenticity, as it will later be called. Caring is relationality, and the general categories of the relationality of factical life are the following. In caring about meaningful things, life experiences an *inclination*, a pull toward something specific. This pull stems from life itself; it is its own *proclivity*. Such proclivity impels life into the world, rigidifies life, and petrifies its directionality toward the world. Life thereby takes from worldly things its directionality toward itself. Life experiences itself only in the form of its world; life is essentially experienced *as* world. Life is thereby *transported*, abandoning itself to the pressure exerted by the world. With the passage of time, the relationality of life becomes *disperse*, and newly awakened proclivities keep life increasingly disperse. Life becomes played out at random. Any claim of life to see itself as more than its world is contested by the diversions offered by the world, whereby life becomes *self-satisfied*. Heidegger concludes: "The more incisive interpretation of the relationality of caring has thus disclosed and set in relief the following general categories of life: inclination, proclivity, being-transported, dispersion, and self-satisfaction. Those are the phenomena which must guide the interpretation" (*PI*, 102/76–77).

What a jaundiced view of life! Heidegger is precisely describing complete inauthenticity: life not only *related* to the world, but life as under the complete dominance of the world, life as taking its self-understanding from worldly things, life *as* world. Furthermore, this is Heidegger's entire account of factical life. He does not see any motive toward authenticity. In particular, nothing in factical life corresponds to the experience of anxiety (disclosure of the *possibility* of authenticity) or conscience (disclosure of practical ways of making authenticity *actual*).

Death does loom over factical life, but this life is inauthentic being-toward-death. Factical life is preoccupied with death solely in the sense of *fearing* death, is concerned solely with averting death, prolonging life. As Heidegger says, the basic sense of factical is privation, concern with one's daily bread.

Nevertheless, in turning away from authenticity, factical life must sense at least implicitly what it is turning from. So there may be possibilities of a disclosure of authenticity. Insofar as the particular categories of factical life Heidegger is about to describe are equivalent to the slogans of the pandemic, these slogans may then offer an occasion for contemplation.

LOCK DOWN!

To lock down is to stay home, isolate oneself, barricade oneself. What constitutes the most fundamental barricading of oneself? For Heidegger, what is most fundamental is *self*-barricading: the sequestration (*Abriegelung*, from *Riegel*, "bar," "obstacle," "barricade") of life *against itself*. Such self-barricading constitutes the first specific category of factical life. Factical life *is* sequestration.

Heidegger draws on the general categories of factical life and argues as follows. In being transported by the meaningful things of the world, that is, in the hyperbolic development of ever new possibilities of diversion, factical life constantly eludes itself, nudges itself out of the way. Factical life, in constantly bustling about over worldly concerns, has no free moment to examine itself. But factical life knows very well, even if implicitly, what it is doing. In order to nudge itself out of the way, factical life must know where it itself is to be found. Eluding requires consciousness of what to elude. The more that life increases its worldly concerns and its proclivities toward worldly things, all the more certainly does life have to do with itself. But it has to do with itself in a negative way, as what is to be avoided. In caring for worldly things, life avoids caring for what is not one of things of the world, namely, itself, the authentic self (Heidegger does not use the term "authenticity" in this lecture course, but it is obviously what he means by the self that is eluded in worldly concerns). Factical life sequesters itself, barricades itself, from itself so as not to encounter itself; it desires to be diverted from itself. Life desires to be carefree, unworried about itself, assured of its own importance in worldly affairs, even if these are no great matter. For example, factical life busies itself with sharpening pencils and arranging paper clips so as to seem to itself engaged in meaningful activities, all the while eluding the actual tasks of writing and thinking. "In concernful sequestration against itself, factical life develops ever new possibilities of meaningfulness in which it can bustle about and thereby be assured of its own significance" (*PI*, p. 107/80).

In sequestration, factical life finds itself only in the world, only as engaged in busy-work. "Caring life indeed finds itself precisely in the mode of inclination within the world and has no inducement to seek itself in some other way" (*PI*, p. 106/79). Then what is it seeking in eluding itself? Heidegger's jaundiced answer: it is ever seeking to make things easy for itself. Heidegger explains the easiness in terms of Aristotle's distinction between the ease of vice and the difficulty of virtue (*PI*, p. 108/81). It is a matter of quantity. Vice is easy because there are many ways to go wrong; virtue is difficult because there is only one way to hit the mark. By multiplying hyperbolically the possibilities of diversion, it is easy for life to elude itself. It itself is only one mark out of a myriad of others. "Mundane difficulties are actually ways to take our ease" (*PI*, p. 108/81).

Factical life desires to be carefree. That is still a mode of care, a mode of the concern of life for itself, namely, "the assurance that nothing will be closed off to it" (*PI*, p. 109/81), that it can cope with any problem. Carefreeness is the security that derives from attending to life's superficial problems while eluding the decision regarding whether these problems, even if complex and challenging, are all that life is meant to accomplish. Factical life eludes the primal decision: "Carefreeness then shapes the world and, in order to be satisfying, must increase; it becomes hyperbolic and grants an easy concern and fulfillment . . . . At the same time, hyperbolic existence proves to be elliptical [harboring an ellipsis]: it eludes that which is difficult, that which can be attained in only one way. It recognizes no fixed limits, and it is unwilling to be posed *upon* a primal decision and *in* it" (*PI*, p. 109/81).

The primal decision, the difficult one, is that between authenticity and inauthenticity. Factical life contains no motive to pose this decision. Factical life, as described by Heidegger a hundred years ago, is not anxious; it contains no motive to be unsatisfied with worldly concerns. Nor are our own lives today anxious; we are too much caught up in the fear of corona-virus-disease-2019 to have a free moment for concern over anything but, as just quoted, "the conserving and preserving of existence." Nevertheless, the slogans drummed into our heads might give us food for thought.

If we examine the command to lock down in the direction of Heidegger's vital category of sequestration, we might disclose the *inauthenticity* of a life constantly bustling about over mundane matters. Thereby, the COVID-19 pandemic might be an occasion for contemplation. We might take some little thing, such as a slogan, and find in it a way to disclose the opposite of inauthenticity. Contemplation would then be directed at how we are actually locked down, actually isolated and sequestered—not from others but from ourselves, our authentic selves. Locking down amounts to busying ourselves with mundane practical affairs, trivial ones and even ones of supreme importance for the continuation of the life we have been living, inauthentic life. Contemplation might then, in the manner of anxiety rather than fear, show the path to a decision between authenticity and inauthenticity. That would amount to disclosing the Being of Dasein, philosophizing.

PRACTICE SOCIAL DISTANCING!

The command to social distancing is not well expressed. Social distance and closeness are matters of the affections and are unrelated to the spread of germs. I am socially close to the ones I love (or hate) even if an ocean rolls between us. The following poem could not express better the spatial experience of lovers:

Unforgotten

by Robert W. Service

I know a garden where the lilies gleam
And one who lingers in the sunshine there;
She is than white-stoled lily far more fair,
And oh, her eyes are heaven-lit with dream!

I know a garret, cold and dark and drear,
And one who toils and toils with tireless pen,
Until his brave, sad eyes grow weary—then
He seeks the stars, pale, silent as a seer.

An ah, it's strange; for, desolate and dim,
Between these two there rolls an ocean wide;
Yet he is in the garden by her side,
And she is in the garret there with him.[2]

Social distance cannot be measured by yardsticks, and so it makes no sense to maintain a social distance of six feet, as the slogan commands. What sort of distance is a category of factical life according to Heidegger? The lecture course describes a complex distancing, complex both in regard to things and other persons. In both cases, the complexity amounts to an establishing of distance and a simultaneous abolition of it.

With respect to other persons encountered in the world, Heidegger's jaundiced view sees factical life always seeking distance rather than equality or cooperation. The distantiation takes the form of a seeking of preeminence: "Factical life is intent on rank, success, position in life (position in the world), superiority, advantage, calculation, bustle, clamor, and ostentation" (*PI*, p. 103/77–8).

Is such seeking of differentiation from others a matter of authenticity, refusing to follow the crowd? Not at all. It is still taking one's bearings from others. It is in fact an abolition of the distance from others. To seek precedence is to let others determine what constitutes the order of importance and is then simply the wish to be first in that order. So such distancing is inauthentic being-with-others; it is taking direction from others. Furthermore, it amounts to abolishing the distance from others in the additional sense of doing exactly what everyone else is doing: to distinguish themselves from the they by seeking preeminence is precisely what they strive to do. Accordingly, with respect to other persons, factical life seeks a distantiation which is actually an abolition of distance.

With regard to things, the category of distance concerns the way meaningful objects stand "before" (*vor*) us. On the one hand, factical life takes the "before" in the sense of "not too close," "at some remove." Thereby things are held at a distance and can be viewed impartially, disinterestedly, as things that do not touch us personally. Thus is born the theoretical attitude, the stance of objective science: "The 'before' of the theoretical attitude presents itself as the highest value in the form of objectivity, scientificity, free intellectual honesty, impartiality" (*PI*, p. 122/91).

In adopting this theoretical attitude, however, life "mis-measures itself" (*PI*, p. 103/77). What is placed at a distance for impartial inspection is in fact closer than science believes. Factical life actually abolishes the distance between itself and the meaningful things of the world, or, better, factical life disperses itself into these things such that no distance ever arises. In other words, factical life abolishes the distance between itself and scientific objects inasmuch as it takes these objects to be primary. They are closest in the sense of what is first encountered, the foundation for the higher, supposedly more distant objects of value or usefulness. Thus, the scientific object is held at a distance and simultaneously placed closest.

As already quoted in chapter 2, Heidegger in this context scoffs at the notion that things are first bare objects (= present-at-hand) which then receive a garb of value so that they do not have to run around naked. He immediately proceeds to say that "the objectivity, 'nature,' first arises out of the basic sense of the Being of the things of the lived, experienced, encountered world" (*PI*, p. 91/69). In failing to recognize this order of priority, however, factical life relates to things as it does to other persons, namely, by way of an establishing of distance (from nature, nature as "before," not too close) which is actually an abolishing of distance (nature as primary, the closest).

If we think the command regarding distancing in the direction of Heidegger's category of factical life, then the question arises as to who—and what—actually is closest to us. If we do not wish to mis-measure, then we will need to contemplate.

With regard to things: if we contemplate closeness and distance, that is, think of them while attuned to Being, then we would have to say that Being is closest. Being is what must be understood in order then to encounter beings as beings. Yet Being is also what is most distant: always overlooked in favor of beings. Being imparts visibility to beings and then recedes in favor of those visible beings. Heidegger offers a simile: Being is like the eyeglasses sitting right on our nose. The glasses are spatially closest but recede in favor of the distant objects they bring into focus (*SZ*, p. 107). To realize this peculiar character of closeness and distance with respect to Being and beings is a way to take the first philosophical step. Consequently, the slogan, although not well expressed—or perhaps precisely because it is not well expressed—provides an occasion for philosophizing.

With regard to other persons: Who is close and who is distant? Those who are physically close may be like the eyeglasses on our nose: overlooked in favor of the distant one we are focusing on. The physically close are not necessarily first. Thereby we uncover something of the Being of Dasein, something of being-in-the-world. We uncover something of the moment of being-in. That moment names the modes of Dasein's disclosedness, which takes place through moods, discourse, and understanding. Heidegger stresses that moods are primary. To be in the world does not mean simply to be spatially present there; it means to be related emotionally—through love or hate or anything other than complete indifference. Thus, the slogan, as poorly expressed as it is, offers an occasion for thinking of what makes another person close or distant. Thereby the slogans of COVID-19 again prove an occasion for contemplating Being, the Being of Dasein as being-in-the-world with the moment of being-in made prominent.

WASH YOUR HANDS!

The command regarding frequent washing of the hands corresponds to the preoccupation of factical life with itself. According to Heidegger's analysis, the preoccupation arises because factical life "has no time" (*PI*, pp. 139–40/104), that is, no free time. Every instant of hyperbolically dispersed life is filled with some diversion or other. The consequence is that life becomes obsessed with itself, that is, with its own continuation. With no time to pause and reflect on its frenzied pursuits, factical life makes no decision on them except to desire them to go on. "Factical caring takes *itself* into care" and becomes "entrapped in itself" (*PI*, p. 140/104). Care "devotes itself more and more to the continuance of life and eventually becomes obsessed with living" (*PI*, p. 140/104). Factical life becomes "frantic self-concern" (*PI*, p. 140/104).

If we reflect on the slogan in the direction of Heidegger's analysis of factical life, we might indeed be led to contemplation—with regard to our frantic relation to time and thus with regard to temporality as the meaning of the Being of Dasein. We might also think of Lady Macbeth's obsessive handwashing in her futile attempt to cleanse away guilt. We could then contemplate our own existential guilt, one that has nothing to do with murder or stealing and that cannot be washed off in any way at all. We might also think of Lear, as quoted in the epigraph to this book, wiping the smell of mortality from his hand. We could then contemplate how death is in the atmosphere, namely, as something that can be smelled on a hand which is still alive. More fundamentally, however, Heidegger's philosophy offers resources for contemplating just what it means to be endowed with hands. What is the "essential realm" of the hand? How is the hand related to the Being of Dasein?

The motive for pursuing these questions lies in the full statement of the command: Wash your hands frequently and keep them away from your face! What is the relation of the hand to the face and specifically to the mouth?

For Heidegger, the essential realm of the hand is the word. But the human being is the being that by essence possesses words; accordingly, the definition of the human being as the animal possessing discourse is equivalent to defining the human being as the animal possessing hands. To possess words and to possess hands are equivalent. How so?

Heidegger's most sustained reflection on the hand occurs in a lecture course on Parmenides. Surprisingly, Heidegger's commentary on this pre-Socratic philosopher leads to the theme of the typewriter. Heidegger begins as follows:

> The human being acts [*handelt*] through the hand [*Hand*]; for the hand is, together with the word, the essential distinction of the human being. Only a being which, like the human being, "has" the word, can and must "have" "the hand." . . . The hand exists as hand only where there is disclosure and concealment. No animal has a hand, and a hand never originates from a paw or a claw or talon. The hand sprang forth only out of the word and together with the word. The human being does not "have" hands, but the hand holds the essence of the human being, because the word as the essential realm of the hand is the ground of the essence of the human being. The word as what is inscribed and what appears to the regard is the written word, that is, script. And the word as script is handwriting.[3]

Exactly how is the word the essential realm of the hand? How is the hand related so intimately to discourse that they arise together? Let us take a clue from a speech by King Claudius to Laertes. To express how very close Polonius is to him, the king says:

> The heart is not more native to the head,
> The hand more instrumental to the mouth,
> Than is the crown of Denmark to thy father. (*Hamlet*, I, ii, 47–9)

The king does not say how the hand is instrumental to the mouth, but presumably it is so by doing more than putting food into the mouth and brushing the teeth. If we consider the mouth as the organ of speaking and the hand the organ of writing, then the instrumentality is understandable. The attempt to compose in writing, to place thoughts down on paper, is not simply a matter of expressing already clear thoughts. On the contrary, writing is what gives the mouth the thoughts that will be spoken aloud. The attempt to express thoughts is what brings the thoughts forth. Writing does not merely set down what is already on the lips; on the contrary, it is writing that puts words into the mouth. To be sure, this does not apply to the hackneyed thoughts and platitudes which constitute the vast majority of our discourse; but it does apply to original thinking, to any thinking that is not mere repetition of hearsay and that requires a struggle. Such thoughts come forth only through the effort to express them, especially in writing. The effort to write teaches me my own thought. I think by writing. *Cogito scribendo.*
  Speaking—at least the speaking which amounts to more than prattle—does not merely put into words already constituted clear thoughts; that is a common phenomenological tenet. According to Husserl, "It is surely not the case that we

first form thoughts and then seek the fitting words. Thinking takes place from the very outset as something linguistic."[4] According to Merleau-Ponty, language itself speaks: the effort to express oneself in words "may surprise even myself, for it teaches me my own thought."[5] For Heidegger, language is a middle-voiced phenomenon in the Greek sense, that is, not a mere reflexive but an operation of *benefit* to the one engaging in it: "Words disclose something, not simply to the outside but *for the benefit of* (middle voice) the very one who is using the words" (*SZ*, p. 32). Thoughts become thoughts through the effort at expression, through being put down in writing, and that is what makes the word the essential realm of the hand. And that is how the hand is instrumental to the mouth; the hand that writes provides matter to the mouth that speaks.

In an analogous way, the heart is instrumental to the head. In the brief speech just quoted, Claudius touches on all three modes of Dasein's disclosedness: the heart corresponds to moods, the head to understanding, and the mouth to discourse. The relation of the heart to the head is that of a more fundamental mode of disclosedness (moods) to one that merely raises that disclosedness to the level of concepts (rationality). In a sense then, the heart does feed the head, just as the hand feeds the mouth: heart and hand provide matter to talk about and to conceptualize.

Reflection on the hand, motivated by examining the COVID-19 slogan, thereby leads to philosophizing, since Being and writing form an "original essential nexus":

> Writing, from its originating essence, is hand-writing. We call the disclosive taking up and perceiving of the written word "reading" or "lection," that is, col-lection, gathering (gleaning), in Greek λέγειν-λόγος; and this latter word, for the primordial Greek thinkers, is the name for Being itself. Being, word, gathering, writing: these denote an original essential nexus, to which the hand intrinsically belongs.[6]

The relation of the writing hand to the word is so intimate that any breach of that relation leads to destruction of the word. That is why Heidegger deprecates the typewriter:

> It is not accidental that moderns write "with" the typewriter and "dictate" [*diktiert*] (the same word as "poetize" [*dichten*]) "into" a machine. This "history" of the kinds of writing is one of the main reasons for the increasing destruction of the word. The latter no longer comes and goes by means of the writing hand, the properly acting hand, but by means of the mechanical forces it releases. The typewriter tears writing from the essential realm of the hand, the realm of the word. The word itself turns into something "stereotyped." Where typewriting is only a transcription and serves to preserve the writing, there it has a proper,

though limited, significance. In the time of the first dominance of the typewriter, a letter written on this machine still stood for a breach of good manners. Today a hand-written letter is an antiquated and undesired thing; it disturbs speed reading. Mechanical writing deprives the hand of its rank in the realm of the written word and degrades the word to a means of communication.[7]

The word as a mere means of communication is a degradation, for the word has a higher vocation, namely, to teach us our own thoughts and not simply package them so they can be shared. If the typewriter degrades, we can only wonder how appalling Heidegger would find the word processor and email. Even a typed letter on paper is now antiquated and slows down communication. And word processors allow for so many shortcuts and even predictive typing that the hand has less and less of a role to play. Word processing is not even mechanical writing; it is becoming semiautomatic writing. Accordingly, the COVID-19 slogan about washing hands and keeping them away from the face and mouth might lead us to contemplate the philosophical significance of the circumstance that, in one respect, today there is less and less need to wash the hands: no one has ink stains on the fingers anymore.

MASK UP!

Heidegger's jaundiced view of factical life is evident one more time—in the category of larvance. Factical life as a whole is larvant. That does not mean people in general "wear the mask" in the sense of being inscrutable, concealed to others. On the contrary, factical life is masked to *itself*.

The references to the larvance or masking involved in factical life all concern the hyperbolic dispersion of life into ever new attractions. Life finds only a disguise of itself in these diversions:

> In being transported by the meaningful things of the world, in the hyperbolic development of new possibilities of experiencing and caring for the world, factical life constantly eludes itself as such. . . . In its constant looking away toward new things, life is always seeking itself and does encounter itself precisely where it does not suppose—in its masking (larvance) [*Maskierung (Larvanz)*] of itself. (*PI*, pp. 106–7/80)

The looking toward constantly new possibilities amounts to life looking away from itself inasmuch as life is transported by things, carried off by things, ones to be experienced and cared for. Yet, life is still pursuing its own interest in such care, and so life finds itself in the things that transport it. But what life finds involved there in things is a mask of itself—it finds itself only as an inauthentic, calculating being.

Calculative problems are infinite in number and variety. Consequently, the self-masking of factical life can take the form of this infinity, inexhaustibility, of possible things to be busied with in order to feel assured thereby of its own significance. "This infinity is the mask factical life places upon and holds before itself or its world" (*PI*, pp. 107–8/80). Infinity itself is the mask in the sense that factical life has no motive to change its calculative attitude. There is a superabundance of problems, sufficient to last a lifetime. There will always be more calculative problems to solve, and the "primal decisions" of life can stay hidden behind them.

Factical life seeks to make things easy for itself. This is true even when boldly facing up to challenging calculative problems. Factical life goes willingly toward them and not only toward amusements in the usual sense. Difficult calculative problems are themselves amusements: "Mundane difficulties are also actually ways to take our ease" (*PI*, p. 108/81).

Factical life is confident that even the most difficult calculative problems will yield to human ingenuity. Science will always eventually solve any calculative problem. To engage with such problems is doubly assuring: it provides the assurance of accomplishing something significant and also the assurance of the mastery, in principle, of any technical problem. Yet, this assurance is a mask; factical life sees only a specter (Latin: *larva*) of itself in calculative thinking.

Heidegger concludes his discussion of larvance as follows: "making things easy; care in self-concern; delusion, masking, in the claim that 'life is difficult'!" (*PI*, p. 110/82). So factical life is delusional, masked to itself, in two respects: first, in its preoccupation with busy-work and, second, in claiming that that is difficult work.

Examining the slogan about masking in the light of Heidegger's category of larvance thereby ends in a question: Which is more difficult, calculative thinking or contemplation? Which is the easy way, which is the retreat to an ivory tower, a fleeing from the real problems of life, and which is the difficult confrontation with those genuine problems? In other words, where does the genuine masking lie? Is contemplation a mask, mere fanciful busy-work? Or is calculation the retreat, a preoccupation with mundane tasks so as not to face up to the primal decision?

It is obvious how Heidegger would answer. Yet he is of course not dismissing calculative thought as unimportant; as we saw, in *Gelassenheit* he even says that high-tech things call us to ever greater achievements. For the rest of us, each person has to answer in his or her own way. The point I would make is that inasmuch as the COVID-19 pandemic provides an occasion to raise the issue, the current plight is again a distinct opportunity for philosophizing.

At stake in the command to mask up is a decision about contemplation, philosophy, versus calculative thinking. Which is the genuine masking, the fleeing from the real problems? Where does philosophy stand with regard to what really matters? Inasmuch as the slogan about masking leads to these questions, it provokes contemplation in the form of philosophizing about philosophizing. The difference between philosophical contemplation and calculative thinking corresponds to the difference between Being and beings. Thus, philosophizing about philosophy, motivated by the slogan to mask up, is a prime way to ask the question of Being.

POETRY AND PHILOSOPHY ENTWINED

As mentioned, I was motivated to examine what is in the air today, besides the deadly corona virus, by pondering a poem about the "unexamined slogans" of the current pandemic. I wish to tarry with this poem a little while, inasmuch as I find it thoughtful poetry, the dearth of which Heidegger often laments. Instead of a poetry that amounts to mere "ink-slinging in verse"[8] and "pen-pushing,"[9] and instead of a thinking that amounts to "research,"[10] Heidegger is hoping for "a poetizing and thinking entwined in each other."[11] Such poetry would be an equal partner with philosophy in the task of contemplation.

I find in the following poem not only contemplative thought but also themes from Heidegger's own thinking. Whether or not these themes were placed there intentionally by the poet makes no matter, for an author cannot claim to be privileged in the interpretation of his or her own work. The reader may legitimately extract from the poem meaning that was not intended by the author. A thoughtful poem is called so, in part, by virtue of its capacity to *provoke* thought.

The poem in its entirety:

Four Viral Ounces of Truth

by Rita Malikonytė Mockus[12]

Into seclusion, please!
An Event of venomous atmos is
being sphered across the worldhood's jaunty tune of ethos
twenty first. Centuria
already toxicosed by affluence
of effluence and smear influence
of unexamined slogans

Observe social distance!
This will be Observance
Season measured in feet and lonely mouths
Pollinating our breath hives with the Other's
Coronated presence —
The spring of mutual appropriation

Outside civility
All Gestures furled
Unshaken hands
Rasping themselves pale
In unholy waters
Ousted Faces sealed to their own
infinite freedom   masked

Absence
lodged deep in Zoom
happy hours darning
forlorn life to screen flesh-
mislaying joystick
Technologia gods only
touch can save us now.

But the essence! Yes!
The essence is busy being
absent   longing
wears a mask too
of provisional truths
Coronial is a baby
received by the Eyes without a face
nursing for Tomorrow's fresh-
named -desire surviving the
alluvium of Covid days.

Time closes its gate before
Yesterday's measure is divulged.
What if we are always just
Seconds away from being
Pinched by grace in its
absconding dialect?

I begin with the term "event." Is the current pandemic an event (*Ereignis*) in Heidegger's sense? The word belongs—as the very center—to Heidegger's later thought, his turning from the first philosophical step to a mythological way of speaking (chapter 1). An event is an initiative on the part of the gods in relation to mortals, Being in relation to Dasein. An event is a self-showing of Being to us, a disclosure of what it means to be in general, whereby we are motivated to comport ourselves to beings in a certain way. For Heidegger, there have been only two events in history; that is, the history of Being consists of only two epochs. The original (pre-Socratic) event was a relatively wholehearted self-showing of Being, motivating the ancient epoch of respect for nature. The later epoch (from Socrates to the present) is marked by a greater and greater absconding of the gods, withdrawal of Being. With a defective idea of what it means to be in general, we are motivated to look on nature disrespectfully, as a mere storehouse of disposable resources. The ancients saw themselves as stewards; we see ourselves as masters.

Is the pandemic a new event? Of course, the pandemic *itself* is not; Being does not send plagues. But Being could be speaking through the pandemic, motivating a new way of looking at nature, perhaps a return to the earlier, respectful way. Certainly, in the midst of the pandemic, we no longer see ourselves as masters over a disposable nature. On the contrary, we view ourselves as the disposables and natural forces as masters over us. Nevertheless, this reversal in the direction of the mastery is not evidence of a new event as long as the *essence* of the modern attitude, the thinking in terms of mastery, remains in force.

An event of Being can also be called a happening of truth. The goddess Truth, Alétheia, is a guise for Being itself. How we understand what it means to be depends on how completely this goddess reveals herself to us. Thus, the word "truth" in the title of the poem indicates the overall theme: Is the pandemic an event? Is a new sense of truth dawning?

The poem will examine four phenomena connected to the pandemic ("four viral ounces") and will wonder whether they betoken an event occurring or about to occur. The four are the four slogans. By calling them "ounces," their weight is called into question. If not weighty truths, then they are flimsy and may easily turn into falsehoods. They are "viral" inasmuch as they concern the virus and also inasmuch as they have "gone viral," as is said of anything, such as a posting on the Web, that is rapidly disseminated. Only what is superficial, bearing merely an ounce of truth, can spread in that way.

The first stanza speaks of seclusion, called by Heidegger "sequestration." What does the poem see as isolated from what? Venomous air is sphered (speared?) through a jaunty world-hood. If we take this last term as referring not to the world in the sense of neighborhood but rather to "worldhood" in Heidegger's sense, then the corona virus has brought about a disruption in the cosmos, the beautiful and happy arrangement of the whole. We know that two sorts of relations constitute worldhood: the relation of things among themselves and the relation of the whole cosmos to Dasein. Breakdowns in the former relations are troubling and are feared. Breakdowns in the order of the for-the-sake-of-which constitute anxiety and motivate authenticity. Is the pandemic merely provoking fear? That is, do we merely see ruptures, isolations, in the order of worldly things? Or on the contrary is the pandemic making us question our own relation to these things? If we see ourselves as isolated, then that would be anxiety and would concern not the mere continuance of factical life but the possibility of an authentically chosen relation to life. Such sequestration, taking distance from the everyday life of busy-work, would portend an event.

The poem speaks of centuries of the toxic effluence of affluence. The toxins (and perhaps the viruses) in the atmosphere have derived from a prolonged ravaging of nature by the rich nations. Toxicity is not a breakdown in the relations among things; we call things toxic insofar as they are harmful precisely to us. Toxic things, however, are not meaningless. On the contrary, we sense ourselves totally connected to them, except that we find them threatening. Toxins are things we fear, not things we are anxious about.

Yet, the poem also speaks of the "smear influence" of the pandemic. If the viral disease has *smeared* our relation to the world, defamed it, then that would imply a calling into question of the meaningfulness of worldly things. So the poem sees in the pandemic both fear and at least also the possibility of anxiety and authenticity.

The second stanza begins a poetizing on the phenomenon of distance. If social distance is "measured in feet," then the pandemic is remaining at the level of inauthenticity. The distances brought to awareness by the pandemic would be those of calculative thinking.

Mouths are "lonely." Alone, isolated, from what?—Presumably not merely from other mouths, since the poem goes on to speak of our breath as pollinated by the presence of other people. From a Heideggerian perspective, the essential loneliness of the mouth would be that of its isolation from the hand, the hand that writes and that through struggle discloses something original to say. Instead, according to the poem, our mouth is a hive pollinated by the breath of others. Rather than the writing hand giving us words to say, other people are putting words in our mouth. Speaking is inauthentic, a repetition of hearsay, of the droning on and on of the they like the buzzing in a hive.

Nevertheless, the poem immediately refers to "the spring of mutual appropriation." In Heidegger's philosophy, mutual appropriation refers to the relation between the self-disclosure of Being and our response, our attitude toward beings. Our thinking is *called* thinking, summoned by a claim stemming from beyond us. Our thinking is the appropriation of a summons that has appropriated *us*. The spring, the font, of this mutuality lies on the side of Being or truth. To recognize this font is to change one's attitude: from discloser by way of one's own powers to shepherd and steward of what is entrusted to us from "something higher" (chapter 5). Therefore, the poem once again sees inauthenticity, lonely mouths, but is also holding open the possibility of the pandemic motivating authenticity, the possibility of an event.

The poem repeats the command to *observe* distance; that is, the word "observe" is used twice. A play on words is announced, for "observe" can mean both "practice" and "look upon." Taking "observe" in the latter sense, the poem is suggesting that the pandemic is motivating a disinterested spectating directed at distances. To take distance from the world and from other people is to contemplate, to sever the everyday attachment to the world and to the they. Accordingly, the slogan to observe distance is ambiguous; it may motivate inauthentic, calculative thinking, or it may portend the distance that is proper to anxiety and authenticity. The poem is again holding open at least the possibility of an event.

Wash your hands! "Outside civility," that is, beyond the bounds of courtesy, we do not shake hands today but instead scrub them as with a rasp. That should make the hands red, but it is making them pale since their life has been drained from them. The waters are "unholy," because instead of blessing the hands to their proper work, these waters simply sterilize them. But hands are not meant to be clean; their proper work involves them becoming dirty, especially with the stains of ink.

Don't touch your face! The mouth has been "ousted," dispossessed, of the hand. If, as the poem states, the mouth is sealed to its own, that means the hand, writing, is not feeding it; the mouth seems to be "infinite in freedom" to say whatever it wants. Without the instrumentality of the hand, however, the speaking of the mouth is mere prattle, repetition of hearsay. This infinity, like the infinity of diversions in factical life for Heidegger, is a "mask" since there is always new hearsay to repeat and no motive for quiet contemplation on the inauthenticity of this sort of talk.

Thus, the poem is here stressing the negative, the impossibility of authenticity, and the next stanza continues along the same lines. Zoom, screens, joysticks, technologia (high-tech devices) all attempt to "darn" the lacunae, the absences, of "forlorn" life, that is, a life lorn of touch, the hand. Heidegger famously claimed, "Only another god can save us."[13] The poem is identifying this other god: the god of touch.

Touch is the proper domain of the hand, and so is writing. If the god of touch is Eros, then what will save us is erotic handwriting. That means a writing which fully caresses the writing materials, namely, paper, pen, and ink, and does not merely unleash a mechanical writing by way of mere taps of the fingertips on a keyboard. One could perhaps speak of the fingers caressing the keys of a typewriter. But the keyboard attached to a word processor is so sensitive and offers such little resistance that the fingers do not caress; they barely even touch. Furthermore, they need to touch for the briefest of moments, or else the letters (and not just x) will repeat. Keyboarding is practically disembodied and keeps the hands clean; handwriting is dirty and messy. A page of handwriting is covered with crossings out and smudges. A word processing screen is "flesh-mislaying," that is, as clean and neat as pure spirit.

Erotic handwriting, a name that obviously might be taken in a wrong sense, is nothing other than contemplative thinking. A messy handwritten page is *the* locus of the struggle to be original and authentic. A word processing screen is *the* locus of calculative thought: everything as clear and unambiguous as are the propositions of mathematics.

So the poem is at least advancing the possibility of a saving god in the form of the god of touch. That would indeed portend an event. The technological age is an age of Apollo, an age of purity, spirituality, calculation, moderation, perfection. What the world needs is a messy touch!

Mask up! According to the poem, "the essence" is absent and masked in "provisional truths." The essence of what? For Heidegger, "essence" is another name for Being. The essence of things is their Being. Yet, Heidegger does not take essence in the traditional sense of the common, that in which all beings participate, that which is abstracted out from beings. On the contrary, the essence is the source which bestows[14] presence on beings, not the common attribute extracted from already present beings.

The poem is affirming this source with a Yes! and then at once goes on to speak of coronials. That is the colloquial designation for babies born in the time of the corona virus pandemic. Such a baby is surrounded by "eyes without a face," that is, eyes with the rest of the face masked. The eyes by themselves can expresses only anger or disapproval. The eyes do not smile. It is the mouth that expresses warmth and joy. A face with only the eyes showing is one that says No! Jean-Paul Sartre encountered the critique that existentialism stresses the negative and has "forgotten the smile of the child."[15] But what could be more negative than a world in which the child has forgotten the smile of the adult?

Inasmuch as a coronial is nursing for tomorrow to come, for surviving the alluvium, the outwash, of COVID days, then the poem is not only negative but also pessimistic. Desire is for the pandemic to run its course and let the survivors return to the old normal or the new normal. In any case, the pandemic will not have been an occasion for contemplation and will not prove to have been an event. The pessimism is that the pandemic will be entirely negative and its truths superficial.

There is a final stanza to the poem, however. The theme is time. In his analysis of factical life, Heidegger distinguishes the time that we possess and the time that possesses us. The time that we possess in the bustle of factical life is distinctive inasmuch as we actually have no time, no free time to do anything but attend to everyday calculative affairs, even if these are leisure-time activities. We feel bound to go on vacation, because we need to keep up with the Joneses, who send us postcards from all over the world. The other time, the time that possesses us, is called by Heidegger kairological time (καιρός: "the appointed time"). Heidegger characterizes such time: "To sit still, to bide the time, to be able to wait" (_PI_, p. 139/103).

According to the poem, time closes its gate before yesterday's measure is divulged. If time can close its own gate, open itself to us or not, then we do not dispose of time at will. The proper time, kairological time, free time, the time not filled up by our frenzied activity, would be a gift. Such a gift would divulge how our yesterdays have been measured, namely, in terms of our constant bustling about over trivialities. Is it too late? Is the gate already closed?

The poem ends by asking such a question, formulated with respect to grace. Indeed, grace absconds, the gods are fleeing, Being is concealing itself more and more. But there is a possibility of feeling the pinch of a grace which may be imminent, just seconds away. To feel the pinch, however, we would have to find the free time for it, the time to sit still and contemplate. The grace in question would precisely be the gift of the time to feel the _pinch_ of grace, the gentle goad awakening us from our slumbers in inauthenticity. To await grace would require the grace of the capacity to await.

Will this grace be bestowed on us, provided we are ready to accept it? Will the appointed time come to possess us, provided we are disposed toward it? Will the pandemic prove to be an event, provided we are ready to be the steward of an event? The poem leaves these questions open, but inasmuch as it provokes them, it is entwined with Heidegger's philosophy in the task of contemplation. That task is to bide the time while remaining watchful. Thereby, thoughtful poetry and poetic philosophy might prepare[16] for a return of the goddess Truth—should she be willing again to show herself more than "provisionally," by more than "four ounces" of superficial truth gone "viral."

Conclusion

Platonic-Heideggerian Intimations of Mortality

WORDSWORTHIAN INTIMATIONS OF MORTALITY

I conclude this disquisition on mortality with a poem about immortality. The poem is William Wordsworth's "Great Ode." I will interpret the Ode from the viewpoint of the Platonic-Heideggerian understanding of being-toward-death as that understanding has been worked out in the course of the preceding chapters. My intention is to show Wordsworth poetizing authentic dying as philosophizing.

The title of the Great Ode speaks of intimations of immortality from recollections of early childhood. The recollections "of" early childhood are the ones *carried out* by the child. This is a subjective genitive. Wordsworth is not poetizing his recollections aimed at early childhood; the Ode is about the incomparable power of the child to recollect.

Indeed, the poet does look back to his childhood, but that is not recollection in the proper sense, recollection that offers an intimation of immortality. According to the poem, only the child, the young child of six, is capable of such genuine recollection. Thereby the immortality intimated by the recollection is not the poet's own deathlessness, not human immortality, but is the eternity of that which is recollected, namely, the "immortal sea which brought us hither," the hyper-heavenly realm of the soul's preexistence according to the Platonic doctrine of recollection, the realm of the Ideas. With regard to the poet himself, this poem is about mortality, not immortality, and names the proper response to the approach of death, not grief but a cultivation of the philosophic mind. Thus, the Ode poetizes intimations of human *mor*tality, not *im*mortality, and identifies recollection—that is, Platonic recollection, philosophizing—as the authentic human way of being-toward-death.

The Great Ode is a lengthy one, comprising more than 200 verses. That length makes it impractical to reproduce here in its entirety. I will offer only the epigraph and the first stanza and will then summarize the course of thought of the remainder. This poem is not a mere *song* in Heidegger's sense (chapter 5). It is a *thoughtful* poem, and the course of thought can be abstracted out. This abstraction, however, is by no means offered with even the slightest suggestion that it substitutes for reading the poem itself.

Wordsworth must have been at least extrinsically familiar with Plato's theory of recollection as presented mythically in the *Phaedrus* (246A–249D). We have already encountered this myth in chapter 1 as a supposed explanation of the human soul's possession of a light by which beings can be recognized as beings or, in terms of Wordsworth's Ode, the "master-light of all our seeing." The Platonic myth tells of the origin of the soul and of its embodiment. All souls, in their primordial existence, join in procession in heaven and nourish themselves when they banquet by gazing out on the hyper-heavenly place, a vast expanse of truth, a veritable sea of glory, where the changeless and deathless Ideas dwell. Divine souls gaze fully at the Ideas; souls destined for human embodiment are afforded a mere glimpse, but indeed a definite glimpse. Upon falling to earth, these souls forget—but do not entirely forget—the earlier visions at the divine banquet; they retain enough memory of the Ideas to be able to recollect—that is, unforget—them.[1]

The Ideas are lustrous, and something of their luster shines through visible things on earth, especially beautiful things, making possible the recollection. Recollection is the seeing of the Ideas wrapping earthly things in a celestial light. Without this light, visible things will seem common and everyday; they will lack luster and will not provoke recollection.

The preceding is the general Platonic background visible in Wordsworth's Great Ode. The poem is written in the first person, and the speaker is presumably the poet himself. It begins as follows:

Ode: Intimations of Immortality
From Recollections of Early Childhood
by William Wordsworth

The child is father of the man;
And I could wish my days to be
Bound each to each by natural piety.

There was a time when meadow, grove, and stream,
The earth, and every common sight,
To me did seem
Apparelled in celestial light,

The glory and the freshness of a dream.
It is not now as it hath been of yore;—
Turn whereso'er I may,
By night or day.
The things which I have seen I now can see no more.[2]

I now offer an account of the subsequent course of thought. I have placed in italics words taken directly from the poem.

There was a time, when I was a child, that *every common sight* seemed *apparelled in celestial light*. Things had a *glory* about them; I could see the heavenly Ideas shining through them. Now that I am a man, *I know, where'er I go*, that *a glory has past away*; every common sight is now just plain common. In relation to what the soul previously experienced in a heavenly life, *our birth is but a sleep and a forgetting*. Yet we do not come into this earthly world in *entire forgetfulness*; on the contrary, we are born *trailing clouds of glory. We come from God*, whose home *is our home. Heaven lies about us in our infancy*; in early childhood the world we just left behind is still fresh before us, open to recollection. As the child grows, *shades of the prison-house begin to close upon* him. *Yearnings* and *pleasures* form a dark prison cell confining the soul, keeping it from the *celestial light*. The *growing boy* becomes a *youth* and *must travel* ever *farther from the east*, the sun, the Ideas. Nevertheless, *the vision splendid* is still available to the youth; he is indeed *attended* by it, but its strength weakens. *At length the man perceives* the divine light *die away and fade into the light of common day*. Things lose their luster, by which they reflect the Ideas, and now seem dull and commonplace. *Earth*, everydayness, is the jailer, and her *inmate* the grown *man*. Everyday concerns make the man *forget the glories he hath known* and the *imperial palace*, the hyper-heavenly realm, the divine procession, *whence he came*. But a child of *six years*, though *of a pygmy size*, has an *immensity* of *soul*. He is the *best philosopher*, he retains his *heritage*, he keeps his *eye* among us adults, who are *blind*. The child can see the *eternal deep* and is *haunted* by *the eternal mind*. This child is *mighty prophet* and *seer blest*. On him *those truths do rest* which we adults *are toiling all our lives to find*, though we are lost in *darkness*. Alas, *little child, the years* will *bring the inevitable yoke. Full soon* your *soul* will bear an *earthly freight*, namely, *custom*, everydayness, which will *lie upon thee with a weight heavy as frost*. Your *recollections* will become more and more *shadowy*. Yet it is impossible that *custom* could *utterly abolish or destroy* them. Your *recollections* will be to us a *perpetual benediction*, the *fountain-light of all our day*. Our adult *souls* still *have sight of that immortal sea which brought us hither*, still can glimpse that vast hyper-heavenly expanse of the deathless Ideas. Although nothing can restore *the radiance which was once so bright*, and nothing can bring back *the hour of splendour* of childhood, yet *we will grieve not*, will not be preoccupied with dying. *Clouds* begin to *gather round the setting sun*, but my *eye, that hath kept watch o'er man's mortality*, gives those clouds a *sober*, temperate *colouring* and not one which provokes grief. Although I recognize the recollective fading that portends my death, I *find strength* in the fact that *years*, old age, can *bring the philosophic mind*. Accordingly, when I now see the even most common things, such as the landscape or *the meanest flower*, I can think *thoughts* so *deep* that I have no *tears* for my approaching death.

PLATONIC INTIMATIONS OF MORTALITY

The Platonic background of the Ode is unmistakable. Wordsworth's theme is the intimation of the immortal sea, the hyper-heavenly expanse of the deathless Ideas, the eternal truths. This intimation is made possible by Platonic recollection. In Wordsworth's version of the doctrine of recollection, advancing age, that is, greater and greater distance from the soul's origin in heaven, makes the recollections more and more shadowy. That is an intimation of human mortality, over which (viz., mortality and not immortality) the poet has kept watch. The proper response is not to grieve, or to brood over death, but to cultivate a philosophic mind, to think thoughts so deep that fear of death is vanquished. But there is only one such thought, the meaning of Being itself. Thus the Ode expresses what could be called, in view of the Platonic background, a *Platonic* intimation of human mortality. The Ode also identifies the authentic response, the one exemplified by Socrates, namely, preoccupation with Being.

To be sure, Wordsworth has put his own construction on the Platonic myth. It is to all appearances a most questionable construction. According to the Ode, priority of recollective powers is accorded to early childhood, indeed to the child of six. The reasoning is that the young child is nearest in time to the prenatal heavenly procession; the child still trails clouds of glory, heaven is still lying about the child, truth still rests on the child. That is an utterly un-Platonic notion. In the dialogues, what makes a person close or distant in relation to the Ideas is not age, distance in time from the divine banquet. Recollective powers are a matter of casting off custom, everydayness, hearsay, and separating the soul to its own autonomous existence. In the dialogues, the best philosopher is the *old* Socrates. He most sees the Ideas, he is most proficient in recollection, he is most authentic, and he acts as a midwife helping the *young* men who surround him to un-un-remember the Ideas. These young men are closer in time to the original experience of the heavenly realm, but their memory is duller than that of Socrates.

With respect to this priority accorded the child, the Great Ode does not make Platonic sense. But it does make phenomenological sense. As mentioned in a discussion of the primitive mentality in chapter 2, the child is closest to the phenomena—not in time, but in attitude. What separates the adult from the phenomena is custom and hearsay, and these are constituted for the most part today by the scientific outlook. The child is close by reason of being innocent of the attitude of science,[3] the current Western adult attitude which covers the phenomena with debris. That attitude is what makes for distance. The child is still in touch with phenomena as they are lived. Therefore, the child is indeed the best phenomenologist.

HEIDEGGERIAN INTIMATIONS OF MORTALITY

To show the Ode as expressing a Heideggerian intimation of mortality, that is, a Heideggerian understanding of authentic dying, we need to consider the epigraph. There we find a temporal complexity that calls to mind the Being of Dasein: child, father, man, day bound to day, natural piety.

The child is father of the man. Only a dolt would understand that in the literal, generational sense. Gerard Manley Hopkins, in a tongue-in-cheek composition, pokes fun at anyone so sluggish as not to grasp the poetic sense.

[Untitled Triolet]

by Gerard Manley Hopkins

"The child is father to the man."
How can he be? The words are wild.
Suck any sense from that who can:
"The child is father to the man."
No; what the poet did write ran,
"The man is father to the child."
"The child is father to the man!"
How can he be? The words are wild![4]

Hopkins slightly misquotes the Great Ode and does not actually identify the poet, but the repeated statement that the "words are wild" is obviously an allusion to Wordsworth. By raising the question of the proper sense of the epigraph, Hopkins may be indicating that there is more at issue here than a doltish obliviousness to the conventional understanding. Indeed it is difficult to believe anyone could be so literal-minded; the figurative understanding is even proverbial. We say that as the twig is bent, so grows the tree. Hopkins is asking whether we can be so sure this proverb has grasped the proper sense of Wordsworth's Ode. Have we, like babies, merely sucked what has been fed to us? Are we as far from understanding how the child is parent of the adult as is anyone who takes it literally?

The proverb about the twig and the tree reverts at least as far back as Alexander Pope. Almost a century prior to Wordsworth's Great Ode, Pope writes this couplet in *Epistles to Several Persons*, 1734:

'Tis education forms the common mind;
Just as the twig is bent, the tree's inclined.[5]

Pope is speaking of the twig being bent by the adult who planted it. The adult who educates a child inclines him or her to a certain way of thinking. Thus, the way adults bend the twig has an effect on development. Early education (Pope's theme) sets the child on a certain path that will be followed up in adulthood. In this sense, however, the adult is still the parent of the child, since the adult is the one who plants the twig, who educates the child. On this understanding, the child actually is not the parent but instead is a twig bent by the parent. Accordingly, this sense is not in play in the Great Ode.

In general, the conventional understanding of the child as parent of the adult is that early inclinations prefigure future dispositions. But this understanding is also not appropriate to the poem. Indeed the poem is saying the opposite, namely: early inclinations fade away and die. The recollections of early childhood are no longer possible in adulthood. The poem is saying that the child dies in the adult; the child is no longer visible at all in the adult. The early inclinations are not carried on into adulthood. A more appropriate epigraph would have been: The child is parent of the adult but leaves the adult an orphan.

I believe the most pertinent sense of parenthood in this context is the one suggested in Aristotle's *Physics*. The Stagirite is discussing the "efficient cause" (Heidegger[6] points out that this term and the concept of causality behind it are in fact utterly foreign to Aristotle) and offers two sets of examples (*Physics*, 194b, 195a). In both sets, the primary instance of the "efficient cause" is not the maker, the sculptor, as the term "efficient cause" would lead us to expect, but is the counselor. According to Aristotle, counseling is the prime example of this sort of causality, and he specifies: "such as a parent counsels the child" (*Physics*, 194b30). Accordingly, Aristotle is thinking of parenthood not just as begetting an offspring but as nurturing that offspring all the way to maturity. Such nurturing is a matter of counseling, supporting, encouraging, setting a good example. I believe it is in this sense of parenthood as counseling and setting a good example that the child is parent of the adult in the Ode on immortality. The adult takes heart from the child, takes the recollection of the child as an example to emulate. The child bestows a "perpetual benediction" on the adult, keeping open the possibility of recollection in old age. That is how the child is parent of the adult, namely, in Aristotle's sense, as counselor.

Indeed the adult, the poet of the Great Ode, does follow the counsel. He cultivates the philosophic mind. He is able to think deep thoughts even about the meanest things. The poet is practicing exactly what Heidegger described as contemplative thinking. Heidegger stipulated that such thinking does not have to be about things that are "lofty" (*hochhinaus*); any common thing lying close by will do (*G*, 16/47). The point is to think about it in the correct way, that is, to contemplate rather than calculate. There is only one thought so deep as to stanch the tears for death, and that is the thought of Being, the Idea of Being. So the old poet is able to emulate the child and recollect the Ideas after all.

There still remains the task of understanding the reference to natural piety. Wordsworth seems to be describing a most unnatural piety. The young are supposed to be pious toward the old, defer to them and take them as an example, not vice versa. The old are supposed to bestow benediction on the young, not vice versa. But if the adult is emulating the child, then the piety and deference have been inverted. Furthermore, how are day and day to be bound by natural piety? Presumably the newest day is to feel piety toward the old. What sort of natural piety is that? What could it mean? What sense can we suck from it?

Husserl does prefer the example of a melody for the sake of illustrating the passive synthesis of time. But all temporal experience is structured by the same synthesis. The future and the past constitute a horizon for all experience. The future is already present to some extent, and the past is still present to some extent. A day is lived within the horizon of the next day and the previous day. The present day is respectful of these horizons. That is to say, the present day appears as setting in motion a certain, perhaps vaguely outlined, future and as resulting from a certain past. Any instant of time is beginning and end—the impetus toward a future and the final result of the past. It may take reflection to make these relations explicit; after the fact, I can see that the future which actually eventuated was prepared in the present, and I can see that the present was foreshadowed in the past and is the logical outcome of the past. But at least some sense of the present as prefiguring a future and culminating a past is always part of lived experience. Reflection merely makes this implicit sense explicit.

Day is bound to day by these complex temporal relations. The present day is, as it were, *deferential* toward the future and past. The present day recognizes the rights of the future and past and allows itself to be influenced by future and past. That is why the present day seems like both a beginning and an outcome. The present pays respect to the future and the past. In other words, the present day shows piety toward the future and past.

It is a natural piety at least inasmuch as this temporal complexity is natural to Dasein. It is indeed the very meaning of the Being of Dasein. Therefore, in these terms, that is, in terms of the Being of Dasein, it makes sense to say the child is parent of the adult, just as the adult is parent of the child. The child shows piety toward the parent by taking direction from the parent; the parent is pious toward the child in the exact same way, by taking direction from the child. This complexity perfectly characterizes parenthood in the sense of counseling. The parent indeed counsels the child and gives direction to the child. The parent calls up the child to some sort of action. But the counseling must be appropriate. There is no universal counseling. Therefore, the counselor must take direction from the counseled. The counseled calls up the counseling as much as the counseling calls up the counseled. But to take direction is to show piety. Accordingly, the relations of child to parent and day to day are indeed ruled by piety.

Inasmuch as the Great Ode poetizes these complex temporal relations, it amounts to a Heideggerian intimation of mortality. Days are joined each to each; that includes even the last day. To recognize the child as parent of the adult is to recognize days as so intertwined that we are neither too old for our victories nor too young for our defeats. Death is not entirely outstanding.

HEIDEGGER, PLATO, PHILOSOPHY, DEATH

Wordsworth's Great Ode expresses not merely a Platonic-Heideggerian *intimation* of mortality but also exemplifies the Platonic-Heideggerian response. The poet acknowledges human mortality and indeed has kept close watch over it. Yet he does not grieve; instead, he seeks the philosophic mind. The poet is seeking the Idea of Being while recognizing that death looms. The poet lives in an atmosphere of mortality and says "Yes" to death. And he also says "No" by preoccupying himself with common things in an attitude of philosophizing, Platonic recollection, Socratic love, Heideggerian anticipation, detachment, contemplation. The poet is carrying out authentic being-toward-death.

FINAL WORD: PROOF OF IMMORTALITY?

After a long discourse on mortality, let us take up, as does Socrates at the very end, the theme of immortality. If the way to live one's mortality is to philosophize, to commune with the immortal Ideas, then is there not a connaturality of the soul with the deathless Ideas? And would that not suggest the soul is immortal as well? Indeed Socrates does use this connection to demonstrate immortality.

In the *Phaedo*, on Socrates' last day of earthly existence, he discourses in a comedic vein about philosophy and death, as we have seen. The conversation ultimately turns to the question of immortality. His friends are afraid that the soul after death is simply dissipated like smoke. Socrates offers various proofs of immortality, such as the one just mentioned based on the connaturality of the Ideas and the soul. Then Socrates proceeds to assure his friends they can put aside any fear that the soul after death will be dissipated like smoke, "especially if a person dies on a windy day and not in calm weather" (*Phaedo*, 77D).

Notes

CHAPTER 1

1. Heidegger, *Sein und Zeit* (hereafter *SZ*), p. 39.
2. Dionysius of Halicarnassus, "On literary composition," pp. 224 and 226.
3. Dionysius of Halicarnassus, p. 224.
4. Diogenes Laertius, *Lives of Eminent Philosophers*, Vol. I, p. 312.
5. For a fully elaborated and compelling interpretation of the opening of the Republic as Socrates' descent into Hades, see John Sallis, *Being and Logos: Reading the Platonic Dialogues*, entire Chapter V, especially pp. 313–323.
6. *Being and Time* as a stand-alone book is actually an offprint (*Sonderdruck*) from Volume 8 of the *Jahrbuch für Philosophie und phänomenologische Forschung*, a periodical founded and edited by Husserl. "Mathematische Existenz" by Oskar Becker constituted the second half of that large (809 pages) Volume 8.

Heidegger contributed again to Husserl's *Jahrbuch*. Heidegger's "Vom Wesen des Grundes" formed part of the supplement to Volume 10, a Festschrift for Husserl on his 70th birthday. Heidegger himself was the editor of this Festschrift, published in 1929.

7. Heidegger, *Kant und das Problem der Metaphysik*, p. 239. English translation, p. 233.
8. On Thrasymachus as Cerberus, see John Sallis, *Being and Logos*, p. 334. For a comprehensive view of Socrates as Heracles, see Eva Brann, *The Music of the Republic: Essays on Socrates' Conversations and Plato's Writings*, pp. 119–22.
9. Heidegger, "Aus einem Gespräch von der Sprache zwischen einem Japaner und einem Fragenden," in *Unterwegs zur Sprache*, p. 131. English translation, p. 36.
10. "Dialectic," from the Greek δια-, "in opposed directions," "asunder," and λέγειν, "gather," fundamentally means "oppositional gathering." Thus "dialectic" is itself a dialectical term.
11. Husserl's term is *Einklammerung*, "placing in clamps." It could refer to either bracketing or parenthesizing, and various translators of Husserl render it one way or

the other. "Bracketing" is definitely superior, as hinting at the mathematical sense, but the best American translation would be: "placing in slashes."

12. Scholarly debate abounds concerning whether the *Timaeus* does follow immediately after Socrates' recollection as recorded in the *Republic*. The grounds for doubt center primarily on the circumstance that in the *Timaeus* Socrates' summary of his speech of the preceding day is so lacunary. He must be referring to some other, unrecorded account of his founding of a city in thought. The way I am about to explain the deficient summary, however, makes more certain rather than more questionable that Socrates is indeed referring to the *Republic*. The other reason for doubt concerns the date of the Lesser Panathenaea. The *Timaeus* takes place on this festival of Athena, and Socrates visits the Piraeus to participate in the festival of Bendis. Proclus, in his commentary on the *Timaeus*, fixes the date of the Lesser Panathenaea as the 21st of the month of Thargelion (*Procli Diadochi in Platonis Timaeum commentaria*, p. 85, lines 29–30), and so exactly two days after the festival of Bendis, 19 Thargelion. Thus the dramatic dates confirm the *Timaeus* following the day after Socrates' recollection in the *Republic*, which follows the day after his visit to the Piraeus. Proclus, called Diadochus ("Successor," namely, to the head of the Platonic Academy in Athens), should be reliable, yet his dating of the Lesser Panathenaea is now in dispute. For careful arguments that the *Timaeus* does not occur immediately after the *Republic*, see Brann, *The Music of the Republic*, p. 138.

13. Indeed Socrates left Athens on military service. But that must have occurred when Socrates was somewhat younger (his last battle, at age 47, was Amphipolis, 422 BC), since he describes himself in the *Phaedrus* (327C) as "elderly." Phaedrus certainly does not greet him as a long-absent friend returning from war, and Phaedrus explicitly refers to Socrates' already established reputation for not leaving Athens, calling this Socratic practice "something to be wondered at as most extraordinary" (230C–D). Phaedrus could scarcely speak that way to someone who was just then coming from Amphipolis. Furthermore, Amphipolis lies to the north of Athens, whereas Phaedrus says in detail that he has been "visiting Epicrates, whose house, which used to belong to Morychus, is near the Olympieum" (*Phaedrus*, 227B). Thus, the house was near the temple of Olympian Zeus on the southeast side of Athens. Phaedrus was eager to "meander on country lanes rather than tread the public streets" (*Phaedrus*, 227A), and so he would hardly walk all the way through the city to exit at a northern gate. For further evidence that Socrates meets Phaedrus the morning after the events of the *Republic*, see my "The festive and the workaday in Plato's *Phaedrus*," pp. 215–19.

14. Socrates gets himself all "fancied up" (*Timaeus*, 20C). He is described as attired the same way at a notable dinner party (*Symposium*, 174A). It is the attire of a comedian. When Socrates is dressed out of character, we can suspect he is about to poke fun at someone.

15. The phrase by Dionysius of Halicarnassus, πάντα τρόπον ἀναπλέχων, is ambiguous. The braiding could apply to each individual dialogue or to them all together. Indeed both senses hold good. The well-braided dialogues are themselves braided together.

16. As expressed in Heidegger's concept of *Jemeinigkeit* (*SZ*, pp. 41–2), Dasein is always "mine to some person or other." There is always a respective (*je-*) person who can

say, "This Dasein is mine (*-mein-*)." Dasein is always some person's "mine." Although Dasein is not the person as such, there is no Dasein that is not mine to some person. Heidegger therefore says explicitly in *Being and Time* that a *personal* pronoun (*das* Personal*pronomen*) should be used when referring to Dasein (*SZ*, p. 42). German, unlike English, is a gender language, and pronouns must agree with the gender of the noun they modify, not, as in English, with the sex of the antecedent. Therefore, the rules of German grammar make it impossible to refer back to Dasein, a neuter noun, with pronouns meaning "he or she." I will at times make use of that locution to capture the sense of what Heidegger means by a personal pronoun in reference to Dasein, although it does not, and could not, literally correspond to the pronouns used by Heidegger.

17. Heidegger is presumably referring to *Thus Spoke Zarathustra*, Part I, section 21.

18. For a full account of this comedy and for the evidence that it is a comedy and precisely not a tragedy portraying Socrates as utterly mired in carnality, see my "Platonic love: Dasein's urge toward Being." I account there also for the claim made above that in the *Phaedrus*, the beautiful lad, Phaedrus himself, surrenders to Socrates' seduction.

19. For an exemplarily careful and deeply insightful reading of the *Phaedo*, see John Sallis, *The Figure of Nature: On Greek Origins*, Chapter 6, "Earthbound. The return of nature." I am indebted to Sallis for much of what I say here about the comedic elements of the Socratic discourse on philosophy and death.

20. *Zeit* in German and *tempus* in Latin both mean "time." So *Zeitlichkeit* and *Temporalität* could both be translated as "temporality," and the distinction would have to be brought out by a convention, such as using a capital for the latter or calling it "primal time" or "time proper." Or else a different time-word could be employed for one or the other, such as "chronicity."

21. In Heidegger's *Beiträge zur Philosophie (Vom Ereignis)*, this characterization of Dasein as steward or preserver occurs at least sixty times.

22. Heidegger, *Platon: Sophistes*, pp. 12–13. English translation, pp. 8–9.

CHAPTER 2

1. Heidegger, *SZ*, p. 37. Other terms Heidegger employs here for the same distinction: phenomenological-prephenomenological, existential-existentiell, ontological-ontic.

2. This paragraph and the next draw on my discussion of Heidegger's concept of world in "Anxiety, melancholy, shrapnel: Contribution to a phenomenology of desire," p. 144.

3. Husserl, *Logische Untersuchungen. 2. Bd. Untersuchungen zur Phänomenologie und Theorie der Erkenntnis*, p. 24. English translation, pp. 169–70. For an attempt at a vigorous defense of Husserl's theory of signs against the influential critique of Jacques Derrida in *La voix et le phénomène: Introduction au problème du signe dans la phénoménologie de Husserl*, see my "Husserl versus Derrida."

4. Since for Husserl, a genetic investigation concerns childhood experience, he explicitly relates the genetic and the psychological, for instance, in *Ding und Raum Vorlesungen 1907* Husserliana XVI, pp. 178 and 369. English translation, pp. 149 and 334.

5. Science is actually making a concession to lived experience by claiming these images are *flat*. Since the retina of the eye is the sensitive surface of a *sphere*, the images should all be convex. Everything we see would look like the surface of a ball if we did see strictly in accord with anatomy and optics.

6. Heidegger, *Phänomenologische Interpretationen zu Aristoteles: Einführung in die phänomenologische Forschung*, p. 91. English translation, p. 69.

7. Mockus is a contemporary Lithuanian-American poet. She was born in 1970 in Kaunas and now resides in Pittsburgh. She writes in English, her third language, after Lithuanian and Russian. Her poetry has been published in *World Literature Today* and other literary magazines. I have engaged with her work already in my "Out of the experience of poetry." In Chapter 6, on COVID-19 and mortality, I will again appeal to one of her poems. Mockus is at work on a large poetry project, to be called "She-Riffs," which will include the full text of "Sans soleil."

8. Thomas Aquinas does say something similar in the *respondeo* section of the question about truth cited by Heidegger (*SZ*, p. 14, n. 2)

9. "Compliance" could very well translate a Heideggerian term for Being: *der Fug*. The general idea is "fitting closely together," "seamlessly dovetailing." Being is featureless, indeterminate, contourless, impossible to be denominated. On the other hand, beings are *unfügsam*, "intractable." They do not seamlessly dovetail but instead take on definite contours, are not compliant, and therefore can be tied to price tags. Heidegger's most extensive discussion of beings as differentiated from Being in these terms occurs in his lecture course on Anaximander, *Der Anfang der abendländischen Philosophie: Auslegung des Anaximander und Parmenides,* pp. 10–15. English translation, pp. 9–13.

10. Hölderlin, *Übersetzungen,* vol. 5, p. 242. Translation of Sophocles' *Antigone*, Strophe A, v. 926.

CHAPTER 3

1. Aristotle, *Metaphysics*, Book I, 982b. Socrates expresses the same: "There is no other beginning of philosophy than wonder" (*Theaetetus*, 155D).

2. I will examine the justification of this conclusion a few pages below, in discussing the "obstinacy" of the nothing and nowhere.

3. I owe this way of understanding Kant's reasoning to John Sallis, *Kant and the Spirit of Critique*, pp. 29–30.

4. Heidegger, *Parmenides*, p. 77. English translation, pp. 52–53.

5. Throughout *Being and Time*, Heidegger uses the term "moment" (*das Moment*, not the purely temporal *der Moment*) in the sense worked out by Husserl in the theory of parts and wholes in the third of the *Logical Investigations*. Husserl distinguishes two kinds of parts: relatively independent parts are "pieces" (e.g., a petal of a rose)

and relatively non-independent parts are "moments" (e.g., the color of the rose). By using the term "moment" in this sense of inseparable constituent, Heidegger is emphasizing that the parts of a structure always function in unison, even if each part does make its own specific contribution to the whole.

6. Kant, *Critique of Pure Reason*, Introduction, A5/B8.

7. "An object appears to be attractive or repulsive before it appears to be black or blue, circular or square." Maurice Merleau-Ponty, *Phénoménologie de la perception*, p. 32. Merleau-Ponty is quoting the Gestalt psychologist Kurt Koffka.

8. I am here contradicting a conclusion I had drawn earlier in "Anxiety, melancholy, shrapnel," p. 148.

9. "*Philosophiam e coelo devocavit et in urbibus collocavit.*" Cicero, *Tusculanae disputationes*, p. 434.

10. Diogenes Laertius, p. 170.

11. *Phénoménologie*, p. viii. Merleau-Ponty is approving the term used by Husserl's assistant Eugen Fink.

12. Sonnet written in 1818; published posthumously in 1848. *The Complete Poetical Works and Letters*, p. 39.

CHAPTER 4

1. In another place, however, Heidegger does credit Hegel with "experiencing something of the essence of negativity, even though the negative occurs in Hegel's dialectic only to disappear and keep the movement of co-opting in play" (Heidegger, *Beiträge*, p. 264. English translation, p. 208).

2. Grimm, and Grimm, *Deutsches Wörterbuch*.

3. Heidegger, *Platon: Sophistes*, p. 55. English translation, p. 39.

4. I had earlier proposed "discernment" but was thinking along the same lines as those leading to phronesis. See my "Corrigenda to the Macquarrie-Robinson translation of *Being and Time*," pp. 232–33.

5. I have discussed this voice more fully in my "Corrigenda," pp. 220–21.

6. Jacques Derrida has called attention to this voice in "Heidegger's ear: Philopolemology (Geschlect IV)." Derrida takes Heidegger literally and questions who this friendly Dasein could be. Indeed Heidegger uses very little figurative language in *Being and Time*, and so Derrida's approach to the passage is a motivated one. Yet, I believe that, inasmuch as it takes the voice of the friend in an ontic rather than ontological sense, it misses the point.

CHAPTER 5

1. Heidegger, *Gelassenheit*. Hereafter *G* with German page number followed after a slash by the page number of the translation.

2. The violin is mentioned eight times in *Ideas II*, for example. E. Husserl, *Ideen zu einer reinen Phänomenologie und phänomenologischen Philosophie. Zweites*

Buch: Phänomenologische Untersuchungen zur Konstitution, pp. 22, 149, 186–87. English translation, pp. 24, 156, 196–97.

3. The "Discussion of Gelassenheit" did indeed precede the commemorative address. In the German publication, however, notice of that fact is hidden away in the back of the book. The discussion was taken from conversations in the years 1944–1945. The commemoration of Conradin Kreutzer took place on October 30, 1955, a few days prior to his actual 175th birthday.

4. The exact title is "Toward a Discussion of Detachment." There is a subtitle: "Out of a field-path conversation about thinking." The published English translation omits the main title.

5. Heidegger, *Parmenides*, pp. 172–73. English translation, p. 115.

6. Heidegger, *Beiträge*, p. 295. English translation, p. 233.

7. Heidegger, *Überlegungen VII–XI (Schwarze Hefte 1938/39)*, p. 150. English translation, pp. 115–16.

8. Heidegger, "Die Frage nach der Technik," p. 36. English translation, p. 35.

9. Merleau-Ponty, *Phénoménologie de la perception*, p. 260.

10. Merleau-Ponty, *Phénoménologie*, p. 256.

11. Merleau-Ponty, *Phénoménologie*, p. 256.

12. Merleau-Ponty, *L'Oeil et l'Esprit*, p. 14. English translation, p. 161.

13. Husserl, *Ideen zu einer reinen Phänomenologie und phänomenologischen Philosophie. Erstes Buch: Allgemeine Einführung in die reine Phänomenologie*, p. 132. English translation, p. 160.

CHAPTER 6

1. Heidegger, *Phänomenologische Interpretationen zu Aristoteles*. Hereafter *PI*, with German page number followed by that of the published translation.

2. Robert W. Service, *The Spell of the Yukon and Other Verses*, p. 56.

3. Heidegger, *Parmenides*, pp. 118–19. English translation, p. 80.

4. Husserl, *Formale und transzendentale Logik*, p. 359.

5. Merleau-Ponty, "Sur la phénoménologie du langage," p. 111.

6. Heidegger, *Parmenides*, p. 125. English translation, p. 85.

7. Heidegger, *Parmenides*, p. 119. English translation, pp. 80–81.

8. Heidegger, *Überlegungen VII-XI (Schwarze Hefte 1938–1939)*, p. 182. English translation, p. 142.

9. Heidegger, *Überlegungen XII-XV (Schwarze Hefte 1939–1941)*, p. 195. English translation, p. 154.

10. Heidegger, *Überlegungen II-VI (Schwarze Hefte 1931–1938)*, p. 214. English translation, p. 157.

11. Heidegger, *Überlegungen II-VI*, p. 65. English translation, p. 50.

12. See chapter 2, note 7.

13. Heidegger, "Nur noch ein Gott kann uns retten," p. 209.

14. It is with respect to the essence of technology that Heidegger first redetermines the sense of essence from what is common to what bestows. See "Die Frage nach der Technik," p. 32.

15. Sartre, *L'Existentialisme est un humanisme*, p. 10.

16. "The only possibility remaining for us is to prepare a readiness for the advent or absconding of the saving god (an absconding that might draw us to itself) and to do so in thinking and poetizing." Heidegger, "Nur noch ein Gott kann uns retten," p. 209.

CONCLUSION

1. Plato's term translated as "recollection" is ἀνάμνησις, *anámnesis*, "un-forgetting." The Greek term contains a double alpha-privative and literally means "un-un-remembering."

2. *The Complete Poetical Works of William Wordsworth*, pp. 353–56. The three lines forming the epigraph are from Wordsworth's "My heart leaps up," p. 277. The Great Ode was composed in 1804, "My heart leaps up" in 1802.

3. The scientific attitude has the same roots as the aesthetic one. They both ultimately derive from metaphysics, which, as we saw in Chapter 5, is the Platonic attitude versus the pre-Platonic one. Indeed science and aesthetics are the same, the same subjectivistic attitude (Dasein as discloser rather than shepherd) applied respectively to nature and art.

4. *Poems of Gerard Manley Hopkins*, p. 87.

5. Alexander Pope, lines 149–50 from "Moral Essays, Epistle I, To Sir Richard Temple, Lord Cobham," in *The Complete Poetical Works of Pope*, p. 159.

6. Heidegger, "Die Frage nach der Technik," p. 11; English translation, p. 8. I have fully worked out Heidegger's understanding of Aristotle's four causes in my *The Gods and Technology: A Reading of Heidegger*, pp. 15–66.

Bibliography

Aristotle. *De anima*. Loeb Classical Library, 288. Cambridge: Harvard University Press, 1957.

———. *Metaphysics*. Loeb Classical Library, 271, 287. Cambridge: Harvard University Press, 1933.

———. *Physics*. Loeb Classical Library, 228, 255. Cambridge: Harvard University Press, 1957.

Brann, Eva. *The Music of the* Republic*: Essays on Socrates' Conversations and Plato's Writings*. Philadelphia: Paul Dry, 2004.

Cicero, Marcus Tullius. *Tusculanae disputationes*. Loeb Classical Library, 141. Cambridge: Harvard University Press, 1927.

Derrida, Jacques. "Heidegger's ear: Philopolemology (Geschlecht IV)." In *Reading Heidegger: Commemorations*, edited by J. Sallis. Bloomington: Indiana University Press, 1993.

———. *La voix et le phénomène: Introduction au problème du signe dans la phénoménologie de Husserl*. Paris: PUF, 1967.

Diogenes Laertius, *Lives of Eminent Philosophers*, Vol, I. Loeb Classical Library, 184. Cambridge: Harvard University Press, 1925.

Dionysius of Halicarnassus, "On literary composition." In *Critical Essays* II. Loeb Classical Library, 446. Cambridge: Harvard University Press, 1985.

Grimm, Jacob, and Grimm, Wilhelm. *Deutsches Wörterbuch*. Leipzig: Hirzel, 1854.

Heidegger, Martin. *Beiträge zur Philosophie (Vom Ereignis)*. Frankfurt: Klostermann, 3. ed., 2003. Translated by R. Rojcewicz and D. Vallega–Neu, *Contributions to Philosophy (Of the Event)*. Bloomington: Indiana University Press, 2012.

———. *Der Anfang der abendländischen Philosophie, Auslegung des Anaximander und Parmenides*. Frankfurt: Klostermann, 2012. Translated by R. Rojcewicz, *The Beginning of Western Philosophy: Interpretation of Anaximander and Parmenides*. Bloomington: Indiana University Press, 2015.

———. "Die Frage nach der Technik." In *Vorträge und Aufsätze*. Frankfurt: Klostermann, 2000. Translated by W. Lovitt, "The question concerning technology."

In *The Question Concerning Technology and Other Essays*. New York: Harper, 1977.

———. *Gelassenheit*. Pfullingen: Neske, 1959. Translated by J. Anderson and E. Freund, *Discourse on Thinking*. New York: Harper, 1966.

———. *Kant und das Problem der Metaphysik*. Frankfurt: Klostermann, 2. ed., 2010. Translated by R. Taft, *Kant and the Problem of Metaphysics*. Bloomington: Indiana University Press, 1990.

———. "Nur noch ein Gott kann uns retten." In *Der Spiegel* 23 (1976): 193–219. Translated by W. Richardson, "Only a god can save us." In *Heidegger: The Man and the Thinker*, edited by T. Sheehan. Chicago: Precedent Publishing, 1981.

———. *Parmenides*. Frankfurt: Klostermann, 1982. Translated by A. Schuwer and R. Rojcewicz, *Parmenides*. Bloomington: Indiana University Press, 1992.

———. *Phänomenologische Interpretationen zu Aristoteles: Einführung in die phänomenologische Forschung*. Frankfurt: Klostermann, 1985. Translated by R. Rojcewicz, *Phenomenological Interpretations of Aristotle: Initiation into Phenomenological Research*. Bloomington: Indiana University Press, 2001.

———. *Platon: Sophistes*. Frankfurt: Klostermann, 2. ed., 2018. Translated by R. Rojcewicz and A. Schuwer, *Plato's Sophist*. Bloomington: Indiana University Press, 1996.

———. *Sein und Zeit*. Tübingen: Max Niemeyer Verlag, 1927-. The pagination of the Niemeyer editions is indicated in the margins of the Gesamtausgabe edition (Frankfurt: Klostermann, GA2, 1977) and in the margins of the two published English translations: *Being and Time*, translated by J. Macquarrie and E. Robinson (NY: Harper & Row, 1962) and *Being and Time*, translated by J. Stambaugh, revised by D. Schmidt (Albany: SUNY Press, 2010).

———. *Überlegungen II–VI (Schwarze Hefte 1931–1938)*. Frankfurt: Klostermann, 2014. Translated by R. Rojcewicz, *Ponderings II–VI: Black Notebooks 1931–1938*. Bloomington, Indiana University Press, 2016.

———. *Überlegungen VII–XI (Schwarze Hefte 1938–1939)*. Frankfurt: Klostermann, 2014. Translated by R. Rojcewicz, *Ponderings VII–XI: Black Notebooks 1938–1939*. Bloomington, Indiana University Press, 2017.

———. *Überlegungen XII–XV (Schwarze Hefte 1939–1941)*. Frankfurt: Klostermann, 2014. Translated by R. Rojcewicz, *Ponderings XII–XV: Black Notebooks 1939–1941*. Bloomington, Indiana University Press, 2017.

———. *Unterwegs zur Sprache*. Pfullingen: Neske, 1959. Translated by P. Hertz, *On the Way to Language*. New York: Harper, 1971.

Hölderlin, Friedrich. *Übersetzungen*. Stuttgart: Kohlhammer, 1952.

Hopkins, Gerard Manley. *Poems of Gerard Manley Hopkins*. Edited by R. Bridges. London: Humphrey Milford, 1918.

Husserl, Edmund. *Ding und Raum Vorlesungen 1907*. Haag: Nijhoff, 1973. Translated by R. Rojcewicz, *Thing and Space: Lectures of 1907*. Dordrecht: Kluwer Academic Publishers, 1997.

———. *Formale und transzendentale Logik*. Haag: Nijhoff, 1927.

———. *Ideen zu einer reinen Phänomenologie und phänomenologischen Philosophie. Erstes Buch: Allgemeine Einführung in die reine Phänomenologie*. Haag: M.

Nijhoff. Translated by F. Kersten, *Ideas Pertaining to a Pure Phenomenology and to a Phenomenological Philosophy. First book: General Introduction to Pure Phenomenology*. Dordrecht: Kluwer, 1982.

———. *Ideen zu einer reinen Phänomenologie und phänomenologischen Philosophie. Zweites Buch: Phänomenologische Untersuchungen zur Konstitution.* Haag: M. Nijhoff, 1952. Translated by R. Rojcewicz and A. Schuwer, *Ideas pertaining to a Pure Phenomenology and to a Phenomenological Philosophy. Second Book: Studies in the Phenomenology of Constitution.* Dordrecht: Kluwer, 1988.

———. *Logische Untersuchungen. 1. Bd. Prolegomena zur reinen Logik. 2. Bd. Untersuchungen zur Phänomenologie und Theorie der Erkenntnis.* Tübingen: Max Niemeyer, 2nd ed., 1913. Translated by J. Findlay, *Logical Investigations. Vol. One, Prolegomena and Investigations I-II. Vol. Two, Investigations III-VI.* New York: Humanities Press, 1970.

Jahrbuch für Philosophie und phänomenologische Forschung, Edited by E. Husserl. Tübingen: Max Niemeyer, 10 vols., 1913–30.

Kant, Immanuel. *Kritik der reinen Vernunft*, Studienausgabe. Hamburg: Meiner, 1998; originally published 1781. Translated by N. Smith, *Critique of Pure Reason.* London: Macmillan, 1958.

Keats, John. *The Complete Poetical Works and Letters of John Keats.* Boston: Houghton, Mifflin, 1899.

Merleau-Ponty, Maurice. *L'Oeil et l'Esprit.* Paris: Gallimard, 1964. Translated by C. Dallery, "Eye and Mind." In *The Primacy of Perception and Other Essays on Phenomenological Psychology, the Philosophy of Art, History and Politics.* Evanston: Northwestern University Press, 1964.

———. *Phénoménologie de la perception.* Paris: Gallimard, 1945.

———. "Sur la phénoménologie du langage." In *Signes.* Paris: Gallimard, 1960. Translated by R. McCleary, "On the phenomenology of language." In *Signs.* Evanston: Northwestern University Press, 1964.

Plato. *Phaedo.* Loeb Classical Library, 36. Cambridge: Harvard University Press, 1990.

———. *Phaedrus.* Loeb Classical Library, 36. Cambridge: Harvard University Press, 1990.

———. *Republic.* Loeb Classical Library, 237, 276. Cambridge: Harvard University Press, 2013.

———. *Socrates' Apology.* Loeb Classical Library, 36. Cambridge: Harvard University Press, 1990.

———. *Sophist.* Loeb Classical Library, 123. Cambridge: Harvard University Press, 1987.

———. *Symposium.* Loeb Classical Library, 166. Cambridge: Harvard University Press, 1987.

———. *Theaetetus.* Loeb Classical Library, 123. Cambridge: Harvard University Press, 1987.

———. *Timaeus.* Loeb Classical Library, 234. Cambridge: Harvard University Press, 1929.

Pope, Alexander. "Moral Essays, Epistle I, To Sir Richard Temple, Lord Cobham." In *The Complete Poetical Works of Pope*, edited by H. Boynton. Boston: Houghton, Mifflin, 1931.

Proclus Lycius, surnamed Diodochus. *Procli Diadochi in Platonis Timaeum commentaria*. Edited by E. Diehl. Leipzig: Teubner, 1903.

Rojcewicz, Richard. "Anxiety, melancholy, shrapnel: Contribution to a phenomenology of desire." In *Somatic Desire: Recovering Corporeality in Contemporary Thought,* edited by S. Horton et al., 143–61. Lanham: Lexington Books, 2019.

———. "Corrigenda to the Macquarrie–Robinson translation of *Being and Time*." *Journal of Phenomenological Psychology* 45 (2014): 209–44.

———. "The Festive and the Workaday in Plato's *Phaedrus*." In *Essais de psychologie phénoménologique–existentielle*, edited by C. Thiboutot, 213–36. Montreal: CIRP, 2006.

———. *The Gods and Technology: A Reading of Heidegger*. New York: SUNY Press, 2006.

———. "Husserl versus Derrida." In *The Redirection of Psychology: Essays in Honor of Amedeo P. Giorgi*, edited by T. Cloonan, 217–31. Montreal: CIRP, 2010.

———. "Platonic love: Dasein's urge toward Being." *Research in Phenomenology* 27 (1997): 103–20.

Sallis, John. *Being and Logos: Reading the Platonic Dialogues*. Bloomington: Indiana University Press, Collected Writings Edition, 2019.

———. *The Figure of Nature: On Greek Origins*. Bloomington: Indiana University Press, 2016.

———. *Kant and the Spirit of Critique*. Bloomington: Indiana University Press, 2020.

Sartre, Jean-Paul. *L'Existentialisme est un humanisme*. Paris: Nagel, 1964.

Service, Robert W. *The Spell of the Yukon and Other Verses*. New York: Barse & Hopkins, 1907.

Shakespeare, William. *The Complete Works of William Shakespeare*. Edited by W. Craig. Oxford: Oxford University Press, 1919.

Wordsworth, William. *The Complete Poetical Works of William Wordsworth*. Edited by A. George. Boston: Houghton, Mifflin, 1904.

Index

aesthetics, *versus* Heidegger's philosophy of art, 124–26
Agathon, 117
Alétheia, goddess, 29, 152
Amphipolis, Battle of, 9n13
Anaximander, 50n9
anticipation: as authentic dying, ix, 19–20, 60–61; as contemplative thinking, 122–23; as detachment, 121; joined to phronesis, 113–14
anxiety: as being-in, 71; as break in the connection of the world to Dasein, 54–56; as constant, 77–79; as essentially being-toward-death, 53; as gift, 80; its about-which as the Being of Dasein, 68; its before-which as nothing, 56–57; its before-which as the Being of Dasein, 65; motives of, 74–77; as phenomenal evidence of the unity of being-in-the-world, 72; and wonder, 53
Aphrodite, 23
Apollo, 22, 136, 155
Aristophanes, 77–78
Aristotle, 1, 34, 54, 75, 109, 141, 162–63
asthéneia, "lethargy," 10
asylum ignorantiae, "recourse out of ignorance (exasperation)," 28
Athens, ix, 2–3, 9, 9n13, 78

atmosphere, x, xii, 15, 17, 19, 33, 49–50, 115, 123, 137, 145, 153, 164
Aufhebung, Hegelian dialectical "co-opting," 6, 8
authenticity, "self-effectuation": authentic being-toward-death, 18–20; as condition of anxiety, 73; conscience as urge to authenticity, 84–91, 98; as exceptional, not constant, 61; as individuation, motivated by anxiety, 68; as more original than inauthenticity, 64; possible by following a hero, but not as hero-worship, 5–7; as possibly constant, 77; as primal decision, 142; as radical break with the past, 5; as telos of Dasein, 76; as a taking over of one's existential guilt, 100
ἀγχιβασίη, "dunning," theme of Heidegger's trialogue, 134–35

barcodes, 43–45, 48–50
beauty: as loved by the philosopher, 21; as the most lustrous Idea, 12, 78; as recollected in Socratic love, 112
Becker, Oskar, 3n6
being-in: anxiety as affect a primordial phenomenon of, 71–74; and COVID–19 slogans, 144–45; as disclosive activity, one of the three

179

storytelling: as concrete answer
to question of Being, 28; in
mythological sense, 26; in Stranger's
sense, 4, 10–11
Stranger (in the dialogues), 3–4, 8–11,
14, 20, 28–29, 73
suicide, 19, 22–23

technology, 99, 111, 120–22, 126,
154–55
temporality: of Being, *Temporalität*,
28, 28n20; and COVID–19 slogans,
145; of Dasein, *Zeitlichkeit*, xii, 27,
75; of guilt, 103; as intertwining
of moments, xii, 27, 117; as the
meaning of the Being of Dasein, xi,
27, 75, 145; of music, xii, 131, 135;
as temporalizing out of the future,
back to the past, and into the present,
97–98
Theodorus, 13–14
theology, 99
the they, defined in contrast to
authenticity, 5
thief, guilt of, 95
Thomas Aquinas, 50n8
Thrasymachus, 5
thrownness, 90–98
transcendental reduction, Husserl's, 8,
79, 130
treatise, *Being and Time* as Aristotelian,
1–2
typewriter, 44, 146–48, 155
tyrant, as hero, 6

uncanniness, defined, 62
unconcealment, significance of as
Heideggerian passive and negative
name for truth, 29, 32, 102, 124
unsurpassability of death, 17
Urania, 136

use-objects (tools, gear, equipment),
defined, in relation to the hand, as on
hand, at hand, or in hand, 15

violin, 118, 118n2
virtue: for Aristotle, difficult because
of many more ways leading to vice,
141; for Socrates, self-sameness, 112
voice: of art, 126; of Being, 113, 128–
29, 135; of conscience, 84, 88–91,
106; of COVID–19 slogans, 137;
of the friend, 113, 113n6; of music,
123; of the they, 84–85, 114–15. *See
also* middle voice

wash your hands, as COVID–19
command, 137–38, 145, 154
wholeness, of Dasein: attested
phenomenally by anxiety, 72; and
authentic being-toward death, 25; not
precluded by future death, x, 13, 18;
synchronic and diachronic, 114
wonder: as anxiety, 53, 57, 60, 76; as
the beginning of philosophy, 54;
provoked by art, 140–43; provoked
by myth, 12; as the transcendental
reduction, 79, 79n11. *See also* leisure
word processor, 148, 155
Wordsworth, William, 157–64
worldhood of the world: as correlate of
a mood, 48; as essential moment of
the Being of Dasein, 43; as obtrusive
in anxiety, 57, 59–60, 68, 152–53;
sense of things fitting together prior
to experience of any individual
things fitting together, 33, 43; *versus*
the world in the dark, 74

Xanthippe, young wife of Socrates, 23

Zen, 132–33

About the Author

Richard Rojcewicz is either author, editor, or translator of seventeen previous books in Continental philosophy.

www.ingramcontent.com/pod-product-compliance
Lightning Source LLC
Chambersburg PA
CBHW022315280326
41932CB00010B/1113